THE
MULTINATIONAL
CORPORATION

INTERNATIONAL RELATIONS INFORMATION GUIDE SERIES

Series Editor: Garold W. Thumm, Professor of Government and Chairman of the
Department, Bates College, Lewiston, Maine

Also in this series:

ARMS CONTROL AND MILITARY POLICY—*Edited by Donald F. Bletz**

EASTERN EUROPE—*Edited by Robin Remington**

ECONOMICS AND FOREIGN POLICY—*Edited by Mark A. Amstutz*

THE EUROPEAN COMMUNITY—*Edited by J. Bryan Collester**

INTELLIGENCE, ESPIONAGE, COUNTERESPIONAGE, AND COVERT
OPERATIONS—*Edited by Paul W. Blackstock and Frank Schaf, Jr.**

INTERNATIONAL AND REGIONAL POLITICS IN THE MIDDLE EAST
AND NORTH AFRICA—*Edited by Ann Schulz*

INTERNATIONAL ORGANIZATIONS—*Edited by Alexine Atherton*

LATIN AMERICA—*Edited by John J. Finan**

POLITICAL DEVELOPMENT—*Edited by Arpad von Lazar and Bruce Magid**

SOUTH ASIA—*Edited by Richard J. Kozicki**

SOUTHEAST ASIA—*Edited by Richard Butwell**

THE STUDY OF INTERNATIONAL RELATIONS—*Edited by Robert L. Pfaltzgraff, Jr.*

SUB-SAHARAN AFRICA—*Edited by W.A.E. Skurnik*

U.S.S.R.—*Edited by David Williams and Karen Williams**

U.S. INVOLVEMENT IN VIETNAM—*Edited by Allan W. Cameron**

*in preparation

The above series is part of the
GALE INFORMATION GUIDE LIBRARY

The Library consists of a number of separate series of guides covering
major areas in the social sciences, humanities, and current affairs.

General Editor: Paul Wasserman, Professor and former Dean, School of
Library and Information Services, University of Maryland

Managing Editor: Dedria Bryfonski, Gale Research Company

THE
MULTINATIONAL
CORPORATION

A GUIDE TO INFORMATION SOURCES

Volume 4 in the International Relations Series

Helga Hernes

First Lecturer in Comparative Politics
University of Bergen, Norway

Gale Research Company
Book Tower, Detroit, Michigan 48226

Library of Congress Cataloging in Publication Data

Hernes, Helga.
   The multinational corporation.

   (International relations information guide series : v. 4)
(Gale information guide library)
      1. International business enterprises--Social aspects.
I. Title.
HD2755.5.H47   338.8'8   73-17509
ISBN 0-8103-1327-8

VITA

Helga Hernes is currently First Lecturer in Comparative Politics at the University of Bergen, Norway. She received her B.A. from Mount Holyoke College and her M.A. and Ph.D. from the Johns Hopkins University. She spent the year 1974-75 as a postdoctoral fellow in the NIMH (National Instititute of Mental Health) Training Program in Organizational Research at Stanford University.

CONTENTS

Contents

ACKNOWLEDGMENTS

This bibliography was compiled while the author was a postdoctoral fellow in the NIMH (National Institute of Mental Health) Training Program in Organizational Research at Stanford University. I would like to thank the staff of the Stanford libraries for help in locating materials, and the Meltzer Fund of the University of Bergen, Norway, for the travel grant awarded me during the summer of 1973. Thanks are also due to Jonathan Aronson of the Political Science Department at Stanford who kindly let me use his own bibliography. Special thanks and gratitude go to Mary Ann Knight who gave invaluable research assistance in the final phases of this project. She also typed the manuscript and gave editorial assistance.

Stanford, California

Introduction

THE ROLE OF THE MULTINATIONAL CORPORATION (MNC) IN INTERNATIONAL POLITICS

The volume of direct private foreign investments has increased greatly over the past two decades. Descriptive terms for the organizational vehicle of this form of investment have likewise proliferated. Among those used most frequently are multinational enterprise (MNE) or corporation (MNC), and international business firm. As a group, they are often called simply "the multinationals." These firms are large commercial organizations which operate--produce, extract, or provide services--in several countries, although their ownership, management, and control are usually centralized in the one country which confers upon the parent firm or headquarters its nationality.

Multinational corporations are powerful organizations by virtue of their integrated management, their control over large resources, their influence on the market, their role as employer, their role in the transfer of technology, their role as employer, their role in the transfer of technology, and their role as agents of development. Because they control and distribute large resources, the power of these firms is both economic and political. MNCs are political in a narrower sense as well since they depend for their successful operation on legislation and policies which allow the movement of capital, goods, services, and personnel across national borders. To achieve their goals, they will act as pressure and interest groups both in national and international forums.

This bibliography is intended to facilitate study of the role of multinational corporations in international politics and relations. Given the division of our universities and professions into a variety of disciplines, the influence one upon another of those activities we label political, economic, commercial, social, and cultural has in the past often been neglected. Marxist scholars have never accepted these boundaries, and in the recent past they have been joined by a great many scholars who share their interests and concerns if not their ideology.

MNCs engage only in direct foreign investment; the two other forms of international economic activity--international trade and international monetary policy-- are not directly affected by MNCs. MNCs have been the object of intense academic study mainly within the field of international business administration. In international economics they are but one indicator and aspect of the increasing institutionalization of international economic activity. This institutionalization calls into question classical theory since the market is no longer regarded as the major allocator.

In the field of international politics the MNC has been designated a new trans-national actor or organization since the vast majority of MNCs are national organizations which operate across national borders. Strictly speaking, then, they are not international organizations.

Because they are among the major allocators of resources and values on a global level, MNC activities are of increasing interest to a variety of social scientists: economists, political scientists, sociologists, and industrial relations specialists. Furthermore, MNCs have contributed greatly to calling into question the con-ceptual division between domestic and international politics and economics, as well as the state-centric view of international politics. To students of politics it becomes quickly apparent that the study of multinational corporations cuts across the boundaries of national, comparative, and international politics, and that a choice of perspective is both necessary and limiting to an understanding of the subject.

Since MNCs present a relatively new field of interest for social scientists--if one excludes somewhat arbitrarily specialists in international business administra-tion--the literature includes more expressions of enthusiasm and suggestions for "what needs to be done" than theoretical innovation or empirical analysis. The combined skills which are required to analyze the role of MNCs in international politics--knowledge of organization theory, international business management, international economics and politics, and industrial relations--are very rarely found among social scientists. Yet a second phase of research is already dis-cernible: data-based case studies as well as theoretical frameworks and approaches which include MNCs in theories of public policy, political development, and international political economy are now being compiled.

The books included in this bibliography fall into two major categories: those written by specialists in international business administration for students and practitioners of that field, and those written by social scientists for a more general audience in order to examine the phenomenon from a perspective hither-to largely ignored. A particular item is included here only if it does indeed contribute to our understanding of the role of multinational corporations--either by serving as a source of information or by providing analysis. Many of the books written by business administration specialists are listed in this bibliography as source books, in that they provide information about the operations of these firms which can be translated into basic "data" for the social scientist. The second category consists of books and articles written by social scientists ana-lyzing MNCs from the perspective of their own disciplines.

Part I of the bibliography is intended mainly to satisfy the need for basic infor-mation about MNCs as organizations. The majority of the items listed fall under the first category mentioned above. Part II deals with the interaction between single countries and regions and the corporations. In addition to items concern-ing the interactions of MNCs with governments, this part includes subsections on such issues as the impact on labor, the impact on local business, and the transfer of technology. In other words, part II concentrates on the activities of MNCs within countries and their effect on certain sectors of that country. Part III presents the more purely international aspects of MNCs and includes items which define their legal, political, financial, and industrial dimensions. Part III, then, concerns the effect of MNCs on relations among states and other international actors.

Books and longer articles are annotated; short articles are listed without annotation. Because the field is relatively new, a large number of articles have been included because they contain important theoretical statements or basic data.

THE MNC AS A LARGE ORGANIZATION

Although general interest in the activities of MNCs is of relatively recent origin, the phenomenon itself is not. The two comprehensive volumes by Wilkins (THE EMERGENCE OF MULTINATIONAL ENTERPRISE, 1970, and THE MATURING OF MULTINATIONAL ENTERPRISE, 1974) which trace U.S. foreign investment to the colonial era, as well as the works by Franko (THE OTHER MULTINATIONALS, 1973) and Dunning (STUDIES IN INTERNATIONAL INVESTMENT, 1970) give ample evidence of its historical roots. The issues raised by these and other authors, notably Hymer (THE INTERNATIONAL OPERATIONS OF NATIONAL FIRMS, 1960) and Kindleberger (AMERICAN BUSINESS ABROAD, 1969) turn on two questions: the first is whether the MNC as we know it today is the same as the original form of direct investment usually dated to the mid-nineteenth century in America and a century earlier in England, or whether the recent quantitative increase has brought about a qualitative change. Wilkins clearly takes the former view, considering the MNC as the foreseeable, cumulative product of "a process developing over time out of the requirements of the innovative business enterprise" (THE MATURING OF MULTINATIONAL ENTERPRISE, p. 414). Overseas expansion is historically related to the growth of the firm, its increasing complexity, and external factors which influence that growth. The book value of U.S. investments has remained stable at 7 or 8 percent of the annual gross national product (GNP) from 1914 to 1970.

The argument for the essential "newness" of the phenomenon is made by a host of writers who claim that only modern means of information processing and communication make possible the centralization, autonomy, and control which mark the modern MNC. These authors contend that the combined effects of increased magnitude and managerial control have led to a restructuring of the international economic system. MNCs are said to severely limit the traditional market mechanisms of international competition and augur a new era in world capitalism.

The second issue around which these comprehensive historical studies are organized is related to the history of corporate expansion and the motives for direct foreign investment, a question which is not only of historical interest but which is also a cornerstone of modern theories of direct foreign investment, and thus dominates much of the literature listed in chapters 2 and 4. Wilkins, following Chandler (STRATEGY AND STRUCTURE, 1962), sees international expansion as an integral part of the growth of the firm, its final stage of evolution, and she outlines a three-stage model from export to overseas production to global consolidation. A more detailed but related theory is the so-called product cycle theory of Vernon and the Harvard Multinational Enterprise Project group which outlines a sequence of six steps from home production and innovation, to exposure by foreigners, leading to increased demand, export, direct foreign investment, and finally reimport to the home market from overseas facilities.

Another group of theorists argues that direct foreign investment can best be explained on the basis of firms' advantage with respect to their own national currency (Aliber in Kindleberger, THE INTERNATIONAL CORPORATION, 1970), their superior technology (Johnson and Vernon in Kindleberger, THE INTERNATIONAL CORPORATION, 1970), or their location in industries which are marked by a high degree of concentration (Hymer, THE INTERNATIONAL OPERATIONS OF NATIONAL FIRMS, 1960). The difference between Wilkins and these last groups is largely one of emphasis, although environmental factors do play a greater role in their theories than in hers. Wilkins seems to disregard defensive investments, that is, investments which rest on the "perception of threat to established markets" (Vernon, SOVEREIGNTY AT BAY, 1971, and Knickerbocker, OLIGOPOLISTIC REACTION AND MULTINATIONAL ENTERPRISE, 1973). Dunning argues along similar lines that a firm will invest either to secure its source of raw materials or will attempt to buy up its competitors, aiming at specialization among its subsidiaries and securing its markets. This theory accounts for the movement toward vertical integration within one industry on a global level, a phenomenon especially apparent in the raw materials industry.

Expansion as a result of competitive motivation and behavior is also stressed by Marxist theories which consider direct investment abroad as a strategy based on overproduction and thus necessary for survival. Yet another group supports the view of U.S. labor unions that firms move in order to utilize cheap foreign labor and thus export jobs from the industrialized countries, notably the United States. Both the evolutionists such as Wilkins and those that stress the importance of the "environment"--factors such as tariff differentials, availability of foreign capital, the desire to maintain a market share, or access to a low-risk climate--agree that competition and the international movement of capital, management, and technology lead to greater global efficiency. Economic efficiency is regarded as good. Critics claim that such greater economic efficiency and the subsequent specialization across national borders lead to monopolies, domination, and exploitation of less developed economies, as well as general loss of decision-making control in any host country. Still others add that such interpenetration of capital is inefficient since it preempts the indigenous development of local economies (Hymer, "The Efficiency [Contradictions] of Multinational Corporations," 1970, and Hirschman, A BIAS FOR HOPE, 1972).

The various strategies of expansion have important consequences for the organizational structures and ownership preferences of multinational corporations (Stopford and Wells, MANAGING THE MULTINATIONAL ENTERPRISES, 1972, p. 171). There is general agreement that MNCs come into being with the goal of making and selling goods more effectively and profitably across several borders. They are mechanisms, directed by the parent companies, for integrating commercial and industrial activities across these borders. How they organize in order to achieve that end, and which aspects of their operations determine the organizational form of individual companies, form one of the more interesting questions in the business literature. From the political point of view, this question is seen in terms of the power of MNCs: "Whether the multinational enterprise really uses [its] potential to frustrate the policies of various governments depends a great deal on how the enterprise is organized" (Wells, INTERNATIONAL ORGANIZATION, 1971). This potentially fruitful line of research--explaining variation in political behavior in terms of organizational structure--has not been pursued by political scientists. However, some participants in the Harvard Project (Wells, Fouraker, Stopford, and Franko) as well as Brooke and Remmers in Britain, have developed classification systems of organizations which relate differences in organizational pattern to stage of historical development, size, industry, product line, and degree of ownership. There seems to be agreement that the financial relationship is usually the most centralized in each corporation, while other aspects such as management, employment, or even technology may be less so.

The countless ways of organizing for multinational business have usually been classified in the literature into four major categories: (1) An international division, set up under one senior executive responsible for all foreign operations, has often been the first step in the internationalization process. (2) The second step, that of setting up foreign operations under several senior executives, leads either to an area organization, partitioning responsibilities geographically, or (3) to a product organization. (4) In recent years a fourth form, the grid structure, has been developed by some firms; it combines aspects of the third and fourth types by establishing several reporting channels (Wells and Fouraker, Brooke and Remmers).

The choice of organizational structure is initially a function of the company's strategy concerning its product(s), markets, and resources. The structure in turn will influence a firm's policy concerning ownership and control of its subsidiaries, both of which have important consequences for the host country. There is general agreement that the degree of ownership is positively related to control over a firm's subsidiaries and negatively related to a subsidiary's independence. The actual degree of control, the strategies of firms, and the power relationship within firms are often mentioned as crucial topics in the literature. Yet empirical evidence is very sparse, since such information can only be gathered in a series of case studies and social scientists, in their persistent search for generalizations, tend to prefer quantitative surveys over case studies which, as Vernon points out, "can be costly in execution and unrepresentative in results" (Vernon in Bergsten, THE FUTURE OF THE INTERNATIONAL ECONOMIC ORDER, 1973, p. 108). Yet these are the risks which need be taken if one wants to answer questions about the relationship between the MNCs' organizational structures and their behavior with respect to important policy issues such as investments, trade, balance of payments, and the locus of control. At present the understanding of their behavior is so limited that governments would have a very difficult time establishing regulations and policies to effect the desired results. As Robock and Simmonds write: "The practice of international business has clearly run ahead of the development of a theoretical framework for explaining and predicting international business patterns" (INTERNATIONAL BUSINESS AND MULTINATIONAL ENTERPRISES, 1973, p. 32).

Judging from the literature, most firms seem to be moving towards greater centralization by aiming at complete ownership. Governments, on the other hand,
are generally more in favor of joint ventures in order to maintain the locus of
decision-making within their boundaries and therefore under their legal control.
Structural innovation and reorganization are thus much slower in joint-venture
type organizations; moreover, that kind of diversification often leads initially
to greater decentralization.

It seems, then, that the public policy implications of these large organizations
is a large area of interest still to be investigated. Firms are usually treated as
unitary actors which follow a rational strategy of expansion, based on their product, from which the organizational structure logically follows (Vernon in Bergsten,
THE FUTURE OF THE INTERNATIONAL ECONOMIC ORDER, 1973, p. 106).
This is probably not consonant with the facts. First, structures, once developed,
tend to guide strategy; second, large complex organizations do not necessarily
behave rationally (Aharoni, THE FOREIGN INVESTMENT DECISION PROCESS,
1966); third, the "environment"--that is nation states and their policies--impose
constraints, often unforeseen, on planned behavior. Yet, the tendencies towards monopolies, oligopolies, and various forms of restrictive business practices
have obvious public policy implications. The political character and implications
of the organizational structure and behavior of MNCs, therefore, form a research
lacunae at this time. The language and theories employed in the books and
articles in part I of this bibliography are those of management, business administration, and economic theory. They still await translation into those concepts
which form the tools of political analysis. We turn now to the literature in
part II which describes and analyzes the interactions of MNCs with governments
and other political actors.

THE MNC AND THE NATION STATE

The two attributes which political scientists ascribe to states are control over a
given territory and its population and an independent government. These ele-
ments--internal control and external independence--have legal and political
implications which are important both in fact and in fiction. Governments are
expected to act in the public interest, and domestic as well as foreign policies
are usually justified in those terms. It is becoming increasingly clear, however,
that governments share their political power with large interest organizations and
groups, especially industrial, commercial, and financial firms. The intricacies
of their relations are analyzed in many of the works listed in part II. The
phenomenon of legitimate control over the national economy is usually viewed
as an "environmental constraint" by theorists and practitioners of large enterprises and subsumed in their books under the general heading of "nationalism."
The major consequence of these political "constraints" is their interference with
the firm's efficiency, which is seen as the essence of its service to national
and international society.

Jack N. Behrman, one of the principal analysts of the relations between MNCs
and nation states, points out:

> Concern over the multinational enterprise would not be so great if national governments had not been asked to assume expanding responsibilities of national security, personal protection, judicial system, education and maintenance of competition; the responsibilities of governments have ballooned greatly and are continuing to expand. This new nationalism is not a return to simple mercantilism but an increasing imposition on governments of the responsibility for economic growth and social welfare of citizens.
>
> (Behrman in Wallace, INTERNATIONAL CONTROL OF INVESTMENTS, 1974, p. 182)

This expansion of governmental concerns is undoubtedly an important part of the picture--especially in the United States where the role of the state has only recently become more active. But the acceleration of the internationalization of business has also been a contributing factor in destablizing the nation state system. In other words, the causal direction is by no means clear. Existing legislation, or the lack of it, certainly facilitated the growth of multinational enterprises, especially in Western Europe. Among the consequences of that growth are at least as many unintended and unanticipated ones as expected ones. Social scientists, however, are most interested in the largely unintended side effects of the growth and spread of corporate giants, particularly those unanticipated by national governments. The intended and explicit consequences, of course, are themselves the subject of heated debate among the critics of MNCs, but even those positively inclined toward direct foreign investment are often concerned about the political, economic, and social consequences for which no adequate control mechanism exists.

The general interest in and concern with the impact of the MNC on the nation state arose within the debate in the 1960s about the balance-of-payments effects of foreign investments and the various solutions suggested to achieve a more favorable balance. Some suggested restrictions on the export of capital; some proposed new rules for the repatriation of capital; and labor unions began to voice concern with "run-away" industry. However, the debate quickly broadened into more general discussions concerning the loss of national sovereignty and assessments of conflicts of interest between MNCs and national governments.

The literature dealing with the nation state-MNC relationship is concerned with several technical and policy issues as well as a lively ideological debate. We will account for each of these concerns.

Countries of origin--mainly the United States, the European states, and Japan--have been particularly concerned with the balance-of-payments issue, although the legislation passed in connection with this issue has been relaxed considerably and is only loosely enforced. The major outcome of these concerns (in addition to the impetus provided by the ITT-Chile debacle) has been massive governmental, United Nations, and OECD (Organization for Economic and Cultural Development) investigations and documentation of MNCs' activities (see U.S. Government publications, the Reddaway report in Britain, and the Gray and Watkins reports in Canada). In addition to the balance-of-payments question, they have been concerned with tax-revenue losses brought on by the MNCs' ability to distort prices through transfer pricing, the market behavior of the firm (that is, its export-import behavior), its preferential treatment of its own subsidiaries and other restrictive business practices, and its general tendency toward global profit maximization, all of which serve to undermine domestic policy controls and discriminate against domestic business firms.

There are several arguments against routine MNC behavior: one concerns the issues listed here, all of which imply that MNCs circumvent and emasculate national policy in most countries since they centralize decision-making and remove it from the purview of governmental control. Global MNC strategy has a tendency to invalidate domestic political and economic strategy.

Another argument related to the removal of decision centers is that the power balance between trade unions and management has shifted further in favor of the latter. Unions in developed countries fear the export of jobs to countries with lower wages, less troublesome unions, and more favorable tax laws. In addition, there are grave organizational problems to be solved. The predominantly national organizations of the labor movement have had to realign their strategies towards more international cooperation and the establishment of international organizational structures (Guenter, TRANSNATIONAL INDUSTRIAL RELATIONS, 1972).

In developing countries, unions and governments face two issues: one is the loss of jobs due to the import of technology-intensive rather than labor-intensive industries; the other is the development of a "labor aristocracy" of highly paid workers which presses for separate interests that frequently do not coincide with those of the labor force at large.

The labor issue is raised as an organizational and a welfare problem by trade unions and as a national and regional development issue by governments. MNCs, as is to be expected, deny that any "export of jobs" has occurred and point to their contribution to development, employment, and training. Labor unions are deeply integrated with the national structure; as a result, they face great obstacles in meeting the internationalization of business. Unions across the globe are divided along political lines; their structures differ; their recruitment policies differ, as do their bargaining procedures, and the subject matters covered by the bargaining process. All these factors stand in the way of the professed ideal of international solidarity (Weinberg in Said and Simmons, THE NEW SOVEREIGNS, 1975). In addition it cannot be ignored that workers in developed and developing countries often compete with each other--some say even exploit each other. Thus the goals of an incipient international labor movement are by no means clearly defined. In addition, there are the practical problems of information gathering, exchange, and consultation which require funds not as readily available to the labor movement as to MNCs.

A third argument is centered around the transfer of technology, skills, and management know-how. MNCs are often described as the most efficient vehicles for the transfer of these factors, yet critics claim that it is precisely the completeness of these transfers--precluding the development of indigenous domestic sources of technology--which is the problem. The appropriateness of highly capital-intensive technology, typical for MNCs, in countries marked by underemployment is also questionable.

Host countries, especially developing ones, are especially concerned with the royalties paid for the use of imported technology; the possibility of acquiring only limited inputs rather than having to buy whole "packages" in order to control more effectively the wider non-economic objectives of national development, the most important of which is the training of local personnel for all levels of the hierachy; and the development of local technological capabilities.

Countries of origin have attempted to direct the outflow of highly advanced technology to any potential enemy, either directly or through third countries. For the United States there exists a list of "prohibited destinations" as well as categories of prohibited technologies such as aerospace, aircraft, and computers. For both destination and technology special licenses are required and both have always been susceptible to extensive bargaining. Export of advanced technologies, however, was strongly supported by the government in the case of Japanese and European reconstruction after the war.

A fourth set of arguments is concerned with the more diffuse subject of economic interpenetration and is of concern to governments as well as domestic business elites. While governments will be concerned primarily with the control over natural resources and sensitive defense-related industries, business leaders argue against the larger size of foreign firms, which affects the competitive nature of the market, and also against the general tendency towards industrial concentration dominated by foreign firms. Other critics claim that the traditional consumption patterns and life styles are disrupted by the increasing "Americanization" of many societies. In other words, it is not always clear whether it is the foreignness of the corporations or their size and influence which is perceived as the major problem.

We have outlined four areas of concern to government and certain organized interests: the issue of control over national policy, the impact on labor, the transfer of technology, and economic interpenetration. Each of these areas has important policy implications, and the activities of MNCs, therefore, have given rise to an extended ideological debate which pervades the literature. There are two reasons for giving a short account of this debate (see also Lall, "Less-Developed Countries and Private Foreign Direct Investment," 1974). One is that it divides the literature into meaningful categories, although (with one exception in Chapter 9) it is not the basis of the classification system employed in this bibliography. The second is that the ideological stances have important policy as well as research implications.

There are two basic attitudes toward the phenomenon of the MNC--one of acceptance and one of opposition. Within these two major groupings, there are differences based in part on different opinions concerning policies towards the MNC.

The most uncritical approach to the field is found in the literature emanating from business schools, especially among those authors whose major concern is a risk-free investment climate and a friendly political environment. As is to be expected, their concerns are efficiency and organizational effectiveness, bolstered by a strong belief in the free enterprise system. Even among these authors, however, there are some (notably Vernon and Behrman) who would welcome some international controls and regulations in order to maintain some political control and ease communications among states.

The second group consists of neoclassical economists who state that free movement of the factors of production ought to be maximized because it will eventually lead to an equalization of those factors across the globe and so to increased global welfare. Their theoretical assumptions lead them quite logically to the proposition that MNCs accelerate the rate of growth and economic development on the basis of superior technology, management techniques, and access to world markets. Reuber, Kindleberger, Balassa, and Dunning are among the most prominent proponents of these views; yet, among them, too, one will find support for international regulation of direct foreign investment, albeit mostly with the intent of facilitating the international flow of capital and other factors of production.

Those who oppose the MNC may be separated into three groups, each characterized by a distinct approach: those concerned mainly with maintaining national political control of host country economies, those of the dependency school, which originated in South America, and those employing Marxist analysis.

The first group is inspired in part by corporativist concerns with bigness, technological primacy, and economic concentration (Galbraith, Barber, Bannock, Calleo, and Rowland) and resultant monopolistic tendencies. In the case of developed countries like Canada (from which much of this literature comes) or the European states, it is feared that the largely American foreign investments destroy the balance between political and economic interest groups and have negatively affected the whole political infrastructure. This implies mainly that the development toward more centrally directed welfare economies has been halted in favor of a resurgent free enterprise system and its accompanying ideology. This group, for the most part, would opt for increased national controls over the import of capital and the expansion of existing MNCs in the respective countries. They are usually wary of weak, ineffective international controls or regulations.

In the case of developing countries, the arguments are similar; yet, there is even more skepticism as to the appropriateness of the technologies and techniques imported by MNCs and the ability of governments to bargain for acceptable terms. It is argued that, for these countries, unlike for developed countries, no resilient infrastructure exists, and that the already existing unfavorable class divisions are accentuated by the foreign presence.

The dependency school views the MNC as the newest arrival in a long line of foreign invaders which has resulted in the underdevelopment of large parts of the respective economies and rendered them dependent on the major economic powers who dominate the international system. Dos Santos, Sunkel, and Hymer are among the exponents of this school of thought. "Dependency" and "development" are both technical terms which include the whole spectrum of social, economic, political, and cultural aspects of national society into one integrated framework. They are fully committed to social change in Latin American and African countries, yet the major unit of action remains the national society.

The Marxist school analyzes the MNC within the framework of agressive capitalist expansion and describes it as the new agent of imperialist exploitation. Marxists stress the "need by monopolistic type firms to control raw material sources and markets in order to protect their dominant position and to secure their investments" (Magdoff, THE AGE OF IMPERIALISM, 1970, p. 19). The large MNCs, not the state or the market, are the major institutions of the international capitalist system, and it is the competition among them, not among nation states, which determines the course of that system (Barratt-Brown, THE ECONOMICS OF IMPERIALISM, 1974, pp. 207, 225). The relationship among MNCs within and among developed states is one of competition (Mandel, EUROPE VS AMERICA, 1970) while the relations with the LDCs (Less-Developed Countries) are marked by neoimperialist exploitation from which they cannot extricate themselves. The policy recommendations, therefore, aim at complete rejection of foreign investment and at social revolution in the case of LDCs and the destruction of the capitalist system through revolution in the developed countries.

The literature collected in part II of this bibliography, then, presents the effect of an international actor--the MNC--on many of the issues which have become central to political science in general; the relations between big business and the government; the growing interface between the two; and the effects of this development on the distribution of power within societies as it affects important interests such as labor and local business elites and their respective political parties. The technology issue affects the future of research and development and science policy in general. The fact that the impulse for these changes and developments comes from the outside adds additional dimensions to the problems. The permeability of the nation state seems exemplified by the impact of the multinational corporation upon it. Part III gives a short review of the literature which takes the international system rather than the nation state as its point of departure.

THE ROLE OF THE MNC IN THE INTERNATIONAL SYSTEM

"The men who run modern international corporations are the first in history with the organization, the technology, the money, and the ideology to make a credible try at managing the world as an integrated unit" (Barnet and Mueller, GLOBAL REACH, 1974, p. 13). Thus opens the first text in international politics to concentrate exclusively on the power of MNCs within the international system. Authors differ, however, as to the role assigned the MNC in the present and future international system. Nye outlines three roles of the MNC: (1) direct involvement, albeit illegitimate, as in the ITT case in Chile; (2) governmental tool in the competition among states; and (3) creator of new issues to which the governments of the world must react and find solutions ("Multinational Corporations in World Politics," 1974).

The centrality of the MNC as a new actor in world politics is a debated issue. As we pointed out in the beginning, the state-centric view of international politics has been challenged by those who opt for a model of international interdependence in which transnational actors operate increasingly across national boundaries (Keohane and Nye, TRANSNATIONAL RELATIONS AND WORLD POLITICS, 1972). The relative weight of the MNC among these actors is judged differently by different authors. There are those like Ball and H. G. Johnson who consider the MNC the harbinger of international peace to which outmoded political institutions must adjust. Vernon and Kindleberger foresee a similar trend in which comparative advantage and factor equalization of labor, capital, and management will lead toward a global economy which calls for global political controls.

Then there are the critics who agree with that description of the facts but describe the MNC as instrumental in creating a malevolent world which is based on an international division of labor and resources across a North-South axis (Hymer, "The Multinational Corporation and the Law of Uneven Development," 1972; Galtung, "A Structural Theory of Imperialism," 1971; Hveem, "The Global Dominance System," 1973; Barrat-Brown, THE ECONOMICS OF IMPERIALISM, 1974; Barnet and Mueller, GLOBAL REACH, 1974; Fann and Hodges, READINGS IN U.S. IMPERIALISM, 1971). Hymer (1972) has outlined a model of the international division of labor among the regions of the world which coincides with the structure of vertically integrated MNCs. It is a model which divides MNCs into three hierarchical levels of (1) control, planning, and research; (2) coordination and management at intermediary national levels; and (3) the level of production and extraction. This corresponds to the division of labor and unequal division of rewards among the center (United States, United Kingdom, Japan), the relatively highly developed host countries which serve as intermediaries and regional centers, and the poor countries in the periphery who provide the cheap labor and resources. It is a class analysis applied to organizations and countries. The "transnationalism" of one group is the conceptual equivalent of "neo-imperialism" of the second (Gilpin, "Three Models of the Future," WORLD POLITICS, 1975).

There is, however, a persuasive argument to be made that the theory of interdependence is not consonant with the factual developments (Waltz, "The Myth of National Interdependence," in Kindleberger, 1970; Huntington, "Transnational Organizations in World Politics," 1973; Gilpin, "The Politics of Transnational Economic Relations," in Keohane and Nye, 1972; Heilbroner, "None of Your Business," 1975). Nation states are viewed as increasing their control over their own territories as well as over their economic affairs, including the operations of MNCs. It is clear, however, that the entry of powerful MNCs into a political system will strengthen those groups and forces who are in their favor; the immediate impact might therefore be conservative. Some radical scholars, then, while agreeing with the facts, will consider the results unfavorable (Calleo and Rowland, 1973).

This conceptual triangle--the MNC, the state, and the international system--is central to the new models of international politics; and theorists will differ about the assignment of relative power and influence to each. Until recently, power in international politics has been associated with military capability and force and, in that kind of model, the United States, the Soviet Union, and China remain the supreme actors. However, economic power has become a strong conceptual and empirical rival; in this respect, the United States, and Europe, and Japan dominate. The foreign policy agenda of major powers has thus been influenced by this major shift (Keohane and Nye "World Politics and the International Economic System," in Bergsten, 1973).

What then are the issues raised by the new international economic system, and what role does the MNC play? According to Bergsten, Keohane and Nye ("International Politics and International Economics: A Framework for Analysis," 1975), the most prolific and influential of the scholars addressing these questions, the major issues today are no longer connected to the problem of unemployment. Now, questions of access to supplies (and not markets alone) and of global inflation determine domestic demands and, therefore, foreign policy. The activities of MNCs are thus of extreme importance both to the external behavior of states and the development of the international system.

As noted above, access to supplies, resources, and markets leading to a vertical integration of industries and firms is also one of the major motivations of investment on the part of MNCs. Control of the balance of payments and of international currencies is of major policy interest to states as well as to MNCs. Hence, the interests of the industrialized dominant powers and of MNCs coincide to a large degree. They will, therefore, shape policies concerning inflation and access to resources. The policies, in turn, will greatly affect the status of individual powers within the international system. Bargaining will take place in international fora, such as GATT (General Agreement on Tariff and Trade) and UNCTAD (United Nations Conference on Trade and Development) meetings, about agreements concerning monetary issues, trade, and direct investment.

The original power balance has thus been shifted to include states which control major resources, such as the OPEC (Organization of Petroleum Exporting Countries), and those that can affect monetary stability, such as Japan. As the recent United Nations report (1974) points out, there exist no international regulations to deal with these two new issue areas and international institutions comparable to the GATT or UNCTAD. So there is the possibility that countries will attempt to control each other's resources through their own MNCs and seek to export their own inflation through the same agencies.

In order to arrive at international regulations, there must be some agreement on the part of signatories concerning the desirable shape of the international economic order. It seems quite clear that the "global welfare" so freely referred to in the literature on MNCs will be perceived very differently by the MNCs, by LDCs and developed countries, or by countries aiming at economic autonomy and those desiring a liberal policy extended to all international transactions.

Firms may aim at efficiency and growth, states with high rates of inflation at price stability, developed countries at economic security, and developing countries at full employment and income redistribution; finally, increasing pressure for improving the quality of life will have a negative effect on growth. Most of these criteria aimed at increasing "global welfare" are in conflict with each other (Bergsten, Keohane and Nye, "International Politics and International Economics: A Framework for Analysis," 1975).

Most regulatory efforts have been bilateral and have concentrated on investment guarantees and other incentive programs. However, the possibility of international action has been the subject of a United Nations report (1974), several OECD meetings, conferences in the Andean group, and at an international conference in 1973 at Dusseldorf (Wallace, INTERNATIONAL CONTROL OF INVESTMENTS, 1974).

The United Nations panel which compiled the 1974 report states that the Economic and Social Council (ECOSOC), aided by a special commission, would be the appropriate institution to develop internationally acceptable "rules of the game." The long-term objective would be to arrive at a general agreement on MNCs which would have the force of an international treaty and would contain provisions for machinery and sanctions. The program of work outlined for the commission and ECOSOC covers eight issue areas in which international regulation is deemed necessary: a code of conduct for MNCs; information and reporting procedures; technology; employment; consumer protection; competition and market structure; transfer pricing; and taxation.

The OECD has concentrated on antitrust issues and restrictive business practices, as well as the issue of technology, which is probably the most sensitive one to the highly developed members of the OECD. In addition, there are the problems of capital movements and exchange rates which have troubled the Atlantic community for a decade. Yet, the Dusseldorf conference, called expressly to investigate the feasibility and desirability of a GATT for international investment, based on the model first proposed in the Goldberg-Kindleberger article on a General Agreement for the International Corporation (GAIC), came to the conclusion that at present GAIC was neither desirable nor feasible--at least in institutionalized form (Rubin in Wallace, INTERNATIONAL CONTROL OF INVESTMENTS, 1974).

There are, then, political, economic, and legal pressures toward dealing with the "emerging global industrial system" (Perlmutter, "A View of the Future" in Said and Simmons, 1975). However, at this point it is quite unclear whether liberal internationalism (as in the United States), or defensive regionalism (as in the Andean Group), or protective nationalism (as in Canada) will form the ideological base for any new international agreements. The competitive strength of international organizations, governments, unions, and the MNCs themselves will determine final policy outcomes. In addition, it would seem that future developments will be at least as much influenced by the actual global distribution of the MNCs as by the theoretical constructs we find in the literature.

The actual scope of international business activity, political attitudes notwithstanding, is steadily expanding. The movement of goods, services, capital, personnel, and technology continues and expands into new areas. Although raw materials ventures and manufacturing continue to play the major role in terms of investment and sales, other sectors have seen tremendous growth in the past decade (Wilkins, THE MATURING OF MULTINATIONAL ENTERPRISE: AMERICAN BUSINESS ABROAD FROM 1914 TO 1970, 1974, chapter 14). There has been great increase in foreign participation in such service industries as the hotel business, construction, retailing, and business consulting. Banking--especially commercial and investment banking and securities and insurance banking--is undergoing rapid internationalization, as are air and ocean transport and the communications industries such as telegraph and telephone, news services, publishing, and the film industry. In terms of sheer volume, the sales of United States-controlled firms abroad have long surpassed the volume of sales through export, and the trend is likely to continue. Advances in technology, uniqueness of product, superior marketing techniques, and management know-how continue to be the forces which propel the expansion of American investments.

As in the past, most investments occur in the developed part of the world, although the share that goes to the developing countries has been steadily increasing. However, even among those, the five largest and most advanced economies attract the majority of investors (Reuber, PRIVATE FOREIGN INVESTMENT IN DEVELOPMENT, 1973, Appendix A). In general, market-oriented investments have risen more sharply than supply-oriented investments, although foreign stakes in the oil industry have increased despite recent policies of national assertion in the Mideast (OPEC), Norway, and Great Britain.

In summary, we can say that MNCs increasingly control production, technology, finance capital, and marketing on a global level. Industry conforms less and less to territorial division into nation states. Yet, knowledge about the restructuring of international economic and commercial activities does not automatically translate into knowledge of their effects on the political behavior and structure of the international system. There is as yet little testing of the theories and hypotheses contained in the literature in chapters 14, 15, and 16 of this bibliography on the basis of the information presented in chapter 17. The political economy of the international system in general, and the effect of the MNC on that system in particular, raise unanswered questions for the student of international relations.

Part I

THE MULTINATIONAL
CORPORATION AS A LARGE ORGANIZATION

Chapter 1

HISTORICAL EVOLUTION

Cairncross, Alexander K. HOME AND FOREIGN INVESTMENT, 1870-1913:
STUDIES IN CAPITAL ACCUMULATION. Cambridge: At the University Press,
1953. 267 p.

> Concentrates on foreign investment in Britain and British investments
> overseas, as well as domestic British savings and investment behavior.

Cameron, Rondo E. FRANCE AND THE ECONOMIC DEVELOPMENT OF EUROPE,
1880-1914: CONSEQUENCES OF PEACE AND SEEDS OF WAR. Princeton:
Princeton University Press, 1961. 604 p.

> Contains an account of French foreign direct investments in a num-
> ber of European countries, especially Russia, and the complications
> arising from them.

Chandler, Alfred D., Jr. STRATEGY AND STRUCTURE: CHAPTERS IN THE
HISTORY OF THE INDUSTRIAL ENTERPRISE. Cambridge, Mass.: MIT Press,
1962. 477 p.

> Analyzes the historical development of American business organiza-
> tion in response to the challenges presented by growing market size
> and diversity of products. The study outlines three basic phases.
> Several analysts of the development of multinationals have expanded
> upon Chandler's basic theme and argument in depicting the expan-
> sion of American business abroad (see Hymer, THE INTERNATIONAL
> OPERATIONS OF NATIONAL FIRMS: A STUDY OF DIRECT IN-
> VESTMENT, 1960, and Kindleberger, AMERICAN BUSINESS ABROAD:
> SIX LECTURES OF DIRECT INVESTMENT, 1969).

Dunning, John H., ed. STUDIES IN INTERNATIONAL INVESTMENT. London:
George Allen and Unwin, 1970. 400 p.

> Most of the material in this book appeared elsewhere from 1962-69.
> The following topics are treated: the role of capital movements in
> the twentieth century; British investments in the United States from
> 1860-1913; the impact of American and British investments on Euro-
> pean economic growth; the effects of American investment on British

technological development; and inter-firm efficiency comparisons of American and British firms operating in the United Kingdom. Contributors are MacDougall, Nurske, Penrose, Vernon, Caves, Dunning, Johnson, and Streeten.

Feis, Herbert. EUROPE, THE WORLD'S BANKER 1870-1914. New Haven: Yale University Press, 1931. Reprint. New York: Norton, 1964. 469 p.

An account of European financial investments and the connection of world finance with diplomacy before World War I.

Franko, Lawrence G. "Origins of Multinational Manufacturing by Continental European Firms." BUSINESS HISTORY REVIEW (special issue on the multinational enterprise) 48 (Autumn 1974): 277-302.

European MNCs followed a different path of development from that pursued by U.S. firms, and their spread began earlier than in America. The article presents data and analysis concerning the evolution of direct foreign investment by Western European manufacturers.

_____. THE OTHER MULTINATIONALS: THE INTERNATIONAL FIRMS OF CONTINENTAL EUROPE, 1870-1970. Geneva: Center for Education in International Management, 1973. 99 p.

A historical growth study of European MNCs, their position in their national industrial structure, and their competition with U.S. MNCs.

Gillette, Philip S. "American Capital in the Contest for Soviet Oil 1920-23." SOVIET STUDIES 24 (April 1973): 477-90.

Hou, Chi-ming. FOREIGN INVESTMENT AND ECONOMIC DEVELOPMENT IN CHINA, 1840-1937. Cambridge, Mass.: Harvard University Press, 1965. 306 p.

The book outlines the contributions to Chinese economic development made by a small number of foreign investors. The author regards the Chinese Communist critique of these investments as unfounded.

Kindleberger, Charles P. "Origins of United States Direct Investment in France" BUSINESS HISTORY REVIEW (special issue on the multinational enterprise) 48 (Autumn 1974): 382-413.

The article concentrates on the pre-1950 developments in the areas of finance, insurance, marketing, services, and manufacturing.

McKay, John P. "Foreign Enterprise in Russian and Soviet Industry: A Long-Term Perspective." BUSINESS HISTORY REVIEW (special issue on the multinational enterprise) 48 (Autumn 1974): 336-56.

Covers the period from 1632 to the present. Tsarist and Soviet governments have succeeded in acquiring advanced industrial technology while maintaining control of their own economic affairs.

MacKenzie, Fayette A. THE AMERICAN INVADERS. London: Grant Richards, 1902. 244 p.

An early study which warns of U.S. domination of British industry.

Phelps, Clyde W. THE FOREIGN EXPANSION OF AMERICAN BANKS: AMERICAN BRANCH BANKING ABROAD. New York: Ronald, 1927. 217 p.

Examines the motives for moving abroad, the legal status of banks, the question of reciprocal arrangements.

Simon, Matthew. "New British Investments in Canada, 1865-1914." CANADIAN JOURNAL OF ECONOMICS 3 (May 1970): 238-54.

An excellent collection of data about the type of investments made by British interests in Canada.

Southard, Frank A., Jr. AMERICAN INDUSTRY IN EUROPE. Boston: Houghton Mifflin, 1931. 264 p.

An important standard work which contains a comprehensive bibliography dealing with U.S. corporations in Europe and with industrial trusts in Europe.

Stead, William T. THE AMERICANIZATION OF THE WORLD, OR THE TREND OF THE TWENTIETH CENTURY. London: The "Review of Reviews" Office, 1902. 182 p.

An early predecessor of THE AMERICAN CHALLENGE (see Servan-Schreiber, chapter 7) which warns of domination of international business by the United States.

Stopford, John M. "Origins of British-Based Manufacturing Enterprises." BUSINESS HISTORY REVIEW (special issue on the multinational enterprise) 48 (Autumn 1974): 303-35.

Explains the patterns of British direct investment in overseas manufacturing in the nineteenth and twentieth centuries. Victorian entrepreneurship, the opportunities and problems presented by the Empire and later the Commonwealth are emphasized.

Watstein, Joseph. "Soviet Economic Concessions: The Agony and the Promise." ACES [ASSOCIATION OF COMPARATIVE ECONOMIC STUDIES] BULLETIN 16 (Spring 1974): 17-31.

Concessions offered in the 1920s to induce foreign capital and entrepreneurs to help restore Russia's war-ruined productive forces.

Wilkins, Mira. THE EMERGENCE OF MULTINATIONAL ENTERPRISE. Cambridge, Mass.: Harvard University Press, 1970. 310 p.

Covers the period from colonial times until 1914. Establishes that United States foreign policy and corporate growth are not related historically. Shows that the United States has always been a significant country of origin for foreign investments and that leading key industries have always been involved in foreign operations. Contains an extensive bibliography.

_____. THE MATURING OF MULTINATIONAL ENTERPRISE: AMERICAN BUSINESS ABROAD FROM 1914 TO 1970. Cambridge, Mass.: Harvard University Press, 1974. 590 p.

Certain to become the standard work in the field. Wilkins defines three phases in the evolution of MNCs: (1) the monocentric phase with single foreign ventures, (2) the polycentric phase which is marked by decentralization, and (3) a centralization phase toward one single conglomerate structure with a global strategy. Contains an extensive bibliography.

_____. "Multinational Oil Companies in South America in the 1920's." BUSINESS HISTORY REVIEW (special issue on the multinational enterprise) 48 (Autumn 1974): 414-46.

Examines marketing, refining, production, exploration, and transportation in seven countries in South America. The author throws light on the development of business-government relations.

Wilson, Joan Hoff. AMERICAN BUSINESS AND FOREIGN POLICY, 1920-1933. Lexington: University of Kentucky Press, 1971. 339 p.

Shows that American business opinions toward U.S. foreign policy were by no means unanimous, and that various sectors had conflicting goals. Concentrates on conflicts between banking and commercial interests. Shows how the issues of disarmament and war debts affected the "closed door policy" in Latin America and the "open door policy" in Asia.

Winkler, Max. INVESTMENTS OF U.S. CAPITAL IN LATIN AMERICA. Boston: World Peace Foundation, 1928. 297 p.

Yoshino, M.Y. "The Multinational Spread of Japanese Manufacturing Investment since World War II." BUSINESS HISTORY REVIEW (special issue on the multinational enterprise) 48 (Autumn 1974): 357-81.

Explores the evolution of direct investment in overseas manufacturing by Japanese enterprises in the postwar era. A considerable increase in Japanese investments abroad is foreseen for the future.

Chapter 2

DISTRIBUTION, GROWTH,
AND BUSINESS ENVIRONMENT

DATA SOURCES ABOUT SIZE AND DISTRIBUTION

Angel, Juvenal L. DIRECTORY OF AMERICAN FIRMS OPERATING IN FOR-
EIGN COUNTRIES. 7th ed. New York: Simon and Schuster, 1969. 1006 p.

> Contains information on about 3,200 American corporations. Di-
> vided into three sections: Section I is an alphabetical index of
> firms including firms' U.S. addresses, names of corporate officers
> in charge of foreign operations, principal products or services, and
> foreign countries in which they operate; Section II, arranged geo-
> graphically by host country, gives addresses in host country and
> country of origin; Section III classifies firms by principal product
> or service offered.

Belli, David R., and Maley, Leo C., Jr. "Sales by Majority-Owned Foreign
Affiliates of U.S. Companies, 1966-72." SURVEY OF CURRENT BUSINESS 54
(August 1974): 25-40.

Diamond, Marcus. "Trends in the Flow of International Private Capital, 1957-
1965." INTERNATIONAL MONETARY FUND STAFF PAPERS 14 (March 1967):
1-42.

> Examines short- and long-term capital flows of seventy-four coun-
> tries.

Dunning, John H., and Pearce, R. D. "The World's Largest Enterprises: A
Statistical Profile." BUSINESS RATIOS 3 (1969): 4-30.

> A detailed analysis of the geographical distribution of MNCs ac-
> cording to industries. Based on the FORTUNE lists of the 500 largest
> U.S. and 200 largest foreign firms.

Freidlin, Julius N., and Lupo, Leonard A. "U. S. Direct Investment in 1973."
SURVEY OF CURRENT BUSINESS 54 (August 1974): 10-24ff.

_____. "U. S. Direct Investments Abroad in 1971." SURVEY OF CURRENT BUSINESS 52 (November 1972): 21-34.

Lupo, Leonard A. "Worldwide Sales by U. S. Multinational Companies." SURVEY OF CURRENT BUSINESS 53 (January 1973): 33-39.

Michael, Walther P. MEASURING INTERNATIONAL CAPITAL MOVEMENTS. National Bureau of Economic Research, Occasional Papers, no. 114. New York: Columbia University Press, 1971. 148 p.

> The author uses mainly data published by the IMF (International
> Monetary Fund) to attempt an accurate account of international capital
> flows, including those between individual countries. He develops four
> categories of countries depending on their degree of development.
> Includes an interesting discussion of the difficulties of data-gather-
> ing with regard to MNCs.

Polk, Judd. "The New International Production." WORLD DEVELOPMENT 1 (May 1973): 15-20.

Roach, John M. "The Mini-multinationals: Operating Overseas, 50 Smaller Companies Report Their Experience." CONFERENCE BOARD RECORD 11 (February 1974): 27-31.

Rowthorn, Robert, and Hymer, Stephen. INTERNATIONAL BIG BUSINESS, 1957-1967: A STUDY OF COMPARATIVE GROWTH. Cambridge: At the University Press, 1971. 108 p.

> An economic analysis of growth rates and international differences
> in growth rates. Shows that growth is not related to size and that
> smaller firms grew faster. American firms are not the fastest growers.

Vaupel, James W., and Curhan, Joan P. THE MAKING OF MULTINATIONAL ENTERPRISE: A SOURCEBOOK OF TABLES BASED ON A STUDY OF 187 MA-JOR U.S. MANUFACTURING CORPORATIONS. Boston: Harvard University Press, 1969. 511 p.

> Presents selected data on the growth and characteristics of more
> than 10,000 foreign subsidiaries of 187 major U.S. manufacturing
> corporations since 1900. The data were collected under the auspices
> of the MNE (Multinational Enterprise) study at the Harvard Business
> School. Data are organized under four headings: (1) the interna-
> tional expansion of the 187 parent systems, (2) the expansion of
> the foreign subsidiaries, (3) the mode of subsidiary acquisition and
> establishment, and (4) percentage of ownership held by the parent
> system.

_____. THE WORLD'S MULTINATIONAL ENTERPRISES: A SOURCEBOOK OF TABLES. Boston: Division of Research, Harvard Business School, 1973;

Geneva: Centre d'Etudes Industrielle (CEI), 1974. 605 p.

This volume does on a global basis what the 1969 volume by the same authors did on the basis of U.S. firms.

GENERAL OVERVIEW

Aharoni, Yair. "On the Definition of a Multinational Corporation." QUARTERLY REVIEW OF ECONOMICS AND BUSINESS 11 (Autumn 1971): 27-37.

A classification of definitions used to determine the "multinationality" of a firm based on structure, performance (sales), and behavior.

Bain, Joe S. INDUSTRIAL ORGANIZATION. 2d ed. New York: Wiley, 1968. 678 p.

The standard introductory text on the subject. Does not deal with international aspects, but lays the conceptual groundwork for any analysis of largescale industrial organization.

Bannock, Graham. THE JUGGERNAUTS: THE AGE OF THE BIG CORPORATION. New York: Bobbs Merrill, 1971. 363 p.

A popular study on concentration which warns against the danger of bigness at home and abroad.

Barber, Richard J. THE AMERICAN CORPORATION: ITS POWER, ITS MONEY, ITS POLITICS. New York: E. P. Dutton, 1970. 309 p.

The book, which is a popularization of Polk's data (in Polk, Judd, et al., U.S. PRODUCTION ABROAD AND THE BALANCE OF PAYMENTS, cited in chapter 8) on concentration, claims that, by the year 1980, 300 corporations will control 75 percent of the world's manufacturing assets. Barber describes U.S. companies as the chief colonizers of this century. Part V, entitled "The Internationalization of Business," is especially relevant.

Behrman, Jack N. SOME PATTERNS IN THE RISE OF THE MULTINATIONAL ENTERPRISE. Chapel Hill: University of North Carolina Press, 1969. 180 p.

The book is based on a series of interviews with American and European governmental officials and business executives. Behrman explains the reasons for the increasing centralization of multinational corporations and why companies opt increasingly for a greater degree of integration and full ownership control. The author considers internationalization of management personnel and heightened sensitivity to local laws and customs as the only viable antidotes to this development.

Bertin, Gilles Y. LA CROISSANCE DE LA GRANDE FIRME MULTINATIONALE. Paris: Centre National de la Recherche Scientifique, 1973. 614 p.

> Proceedings of a conference held in Rennes in 1972. Twenty-five papers in English and French cover the growth of MNCs and theories of investment and their consequences. The English papers are by Adam, Adelman, Dunning, Hirsch, Hymer, Behrman, Franko, Kindleberger, Bertin, Penrose, and Arndt.

Brown, Courtney C., ed. WORLD BUSINESS: PROMISE AND PROBLEMS. New York: Macmillan, 1970. 339 p.

> A collection of articles, most of which were published previously in the COLUMBIA JOURNAL OF WORLD BUSINESS. The twenty-four authors are scholars as well as prominent business leaders. Topics covered range from the emergence and growth of MNCs to their conflicts with aspects of nationalism in countries other than the United States. The conclusion points to the "need for global legislative jurisdiction." Quality of the entries is very uneven.

Colebrook, Philip. GOING INTERNATIONAL: A HANDBOOK OF BRITISH DIRECT INVESTMENT. London: McGraw-Hill, 1972. 210 p.

> An informative uncritical introduction to the subject. Part I gives an introduction to the history of British direct investment and suggests major problem areas. Part II is an overview of practical problems facing the investor abroad. Part III, entitled "Toward One Business World," resembles George Ball's Cosmocorp-vision of the world (see the second item by Ball in chapter 14).

Dunning, John H. "Multinational Enterprises, Market Structure, Economic Power and Industrial Policy." JOURNAL OF WORLD TRADE LAW 8 (November-December 1974): 575-613.

> A conference paper concerning interaction between MNCs, or their affiliates, and the market structures in which they operate, and sources of tension between governments and corporations. Illustrated with cases of U.S. affiliates in Great Britain.

_____ , ed. THE MULTINATIONAL ENTERPRISE. London: George Allen and Unwin, 1971. 368 p.

> The stated purpose of this collection of essays is to throw light on the impact of multinational enterprises, on the transfer of goods and factor inputs across national boundaries, and on the impact of nation states or sectors of nation states. The volume provides a good introduction to most aspects of the multinational enterprise. Included are articles by Dunning on the background of the MNC, Aliber on multiple currencies, Pavitt on the technology transfer, Gennard and Steuer and Lea on the labor issue, Robertson on trade flows, Penrose on the MNC in LDCs, Robin Murray on the internationalization of capital, Behrman on alternative policies and international controls, and Whitehead on Agfa-Gevaert.

Farmer, Richard N., et al. READINGS IN INTERNATIONAL BUSINESS. Encino, Calif.: Dickenson Publishing Co., 1972. 521 p.

A collection of well-known articles to be used as a textbook in courses on international business.

Gabriel, Peter P. "Adaptation: The Name of the MNC's Game." COLUMBIA JOURNAL OF WORLD BUSINESS 7 (November-December 1972): 7-14.

Discusses the institutional adaptations necessary for continued spread and growth of MNCs. The "adaptation" required will be reduced ownership and the willingness to sell separate functions such as managerial skills and technology.

Gray, H. Peter. THE ECONOMICS OF BUSINESS INVESTMENT ABROAD. London: Macmillan, 1972. 249 p.

A general introductory text which discusses the costs and benefits of foreign investment for governments. Gray's premise is that benefits will outrun costs.

Hawrylyshyn, Bohdan. "The Internationalization of Firms." JOURNAL OF WORLD TRADE LAW 5 (1971): 72-82.

Describes the historical evolution of MNCs, their motives for investments abroad, and the reasons for America's dominance.

Hymer, Stephen. "The International Operations of National Firms: A Study of Direct Investment." Ph.D. Dissertation, Massachusetts Institute of Technology, 1960.

This unpublished but often quoted dissertation represents a major advance in the theory of direct foreign investment: Hymer here developed the oligopoly model on the basis of industrial organization theory.

Kapoor, Ashok, and Grub, Phillip D., eds. THE MULTINATIONAL ENTERPRISE IN TRANSITION: SELECTED READINGS AND ESSAYS. Princeton: Darwin Press, 1972. 505 p.

A textbook designed for the student and the practictioner. Contains thirty-four articles about the operations of multinationals. Part III deals with the political aspects of the subject with essays by Johnson, Fayerweather, Vernon, Behrman, Hymer, and Richard D. Robinson.

Kindleberger, Charles P., ed. THE INTERNATIONAL CORPORATION: A SYMPOSIUM. Cambridge, Mass.: MIT Press, 1970. 415 p.

A comprehensive presentation of the most important issues and topics relevant to MNCs. Among the contributors on economic aspects are Harry G. Johnson, Robert Aliber, Stephen Hymer and Robert Rowthorn, David Wiley, Eli Shapiro and Francis Deastlov,

---

and John Dunning. Contributors on political topics are Seymour Rubin, Kenneth Waltz, M. A. Adelman, J. W. Sundelson, J. P. Koszul, Donald Brash, Raymond Vernon, Diaz-Alejandro, and Yoshino.

Kolde, Endel J. INTERNATIONAL BUSINESS ENTERPRISE. Englewood Cliffs, N.J.: Prentice-Hall, 1968. 679 p.

A general text. Includes chapters on general concepts, international integration, developing countries, and the motivation of managers.

_____. THE MULTINATIONAL COMPANY: BEHAVIOR AND MANAGERIAL ANALYSIS. Lexington, Mass.: D.C. Heath, 1974. 285 p.

The author aims at an "in-depth interdisciplinary treatment" of the MNC. The topics covered are definition of the MNC, transnational linkages, motives for investment, organizational structure, the international executive, and interaction with society.

Penrose, Edith T. THE GROWTH OF FIRMS, MIDDLE EAST OIL AND OTHER ESSAYS. London: Frank Cass, 1971. 336 p.

Entitled "Growth of Firms and Private Foreign Investment," Section I contains seven of the author's articles on problems created for host countries by multinational corporations. Among those covered are reinvestment of retained earnings as it affects the host country's balance of payments, transfer pricing, monopoly, self-financing, equity participation for local investors, foreign economic control in cases where the interests of the host country and the country of origin conflict, and the threat posed to the economic functions of the host government by the administrative apparatus of the MNCs.

Perlmutter, Howard V. "The Tortuous Evolution of the Multinational Corporation." COLUMBIA JOURNAL OF WORLD BUSINESS 4 (January-February 1969): 9-18.

This basic article presents the author's system of classification of multinational corporations as ethnocentric, polycentric, and geocentric according to their system of values, their basic orientation, their personnel policies, and their response to home or host country needs. Few if any firms appear at the geocentric end of the scale.

Phatak, Arvind V. MANAGING MULTINATIONAL CORPORATIONS. New York: Praeger, 1974. 358 p.

The legal, fiscal, political, and cultural environment of a multinational company and its planning framework.

Robinson, Richard D. INTERNATIONAL BUSINESS POLICY. New York: Holt, Rinehart and Winston, 1964. 224 p.

The author presents a systematic overview of the history and present conduct of business abroad and speculations on the geographical and functional horizons of future international business. Robinson's thesis is that multinational corporations will transform the present warlike state system into a peaceful international order.

Robock, Stefan H., and Simmonds, Kenneth. INTERNATIONAL BUSINESS AND MULTINATIONAL ENTERPRISES. Homewood, Ill.: Richard D. Irwin, 1973. 652 p.

A general text which contains sections on interactions with the international environment and the nation state, as well as a lucidly written account of present theories of direct investment. Cases and problems in international business.

Rolfe, Sidney E. THE MULTINATIONAL CORPORATION. New York: Foreign Policy Association, 1970. 62 p.

The paper begins with general aspects of the rise and distribution of MNCs and then assesses their impact on world economy. Rolfe identifies three factors: the MNC as a good vehicle for the transfer of technology, the stimulation of new capital markets, and the stimulation of international economic integration.

Schoellhammer, Hans. "Strategies and Methodologies in International Business and Comparative Management Research." MANAGEMENT INTERNATIONAL REVIEW (Wiesbaden) 13 (1973): 17-41.

A systematic review of research on international business and comparative management research trends and future research needs.

Sethi, S. Prakash, and Sheth, Jagdish N. MULTINATIONAL BUSINESS OPERATIONS. Vol. I: ENVIRONMENTAL ASPECTS OF OPERATING ABROAD. Vol. II: LONG-RANGE PLANNING, ORGANIZATION, AND MANAGEMENT. Pacific Palisades, Calif.: Goodyear Publishing Co., 1973. 246 p.

The first volume, containing many valuable items, is arranged under three subheadings: (1) Economic and Monetary Environment, (2) Business and Government Interface, and (3) Multinational Corporations and Transfer Technology. The second volume contains articles related more directly to questions of organizational structure and planning and is also arranged under three subheadings: (1) Long-Range Planning, (2) Conceptual Models and Methodological Approaches to Cross-Cultural Comparisons, and (3) Organization and Management. Both volumes contain selected, annotated bibliographies.

Vernon, Raymond. THE ECONOMIC ENVIRONMENT OF INTERNATIONAL BUSINESS. Englewood Cliffs, N.J.: Prentice-Hall, 1972. 245 p.

A basic and comprehensive introduction to the global environment of the MNC. See especially chapter 10 which discusses the link between strategy and ownership preference.

Wriston, Walter B. "The World Corporation--New Weight in an Old Balance." SLOAN MANAGEMENT REVIEW 15 (Winter 1974): 25-33.

Chapter 3

ORGANIZATIONAL STRUCTURE

Bodinat, Henri. "Multinational Decentralization: Doomed if You Do, Doomed if You Don't." EUROPEAN BUSINESS 41 (Summer 1974): 64-70.

Discusses the paradoxical needs of decentralization for the purposes of production control and centralization for management controls.

Brooke, Michael Z., and Remmers, H. Lee. THE STRATEGY OF MULTINATIONAL ENTERPRISE: ORGANIZATION AND FINANCE. London: Longmans, 1970. 389 p.

A thorough study of motivational aspects of the external and internal financing practices and policies of multinationals and of the variety of organizational patterns of such firms. The authors sampled more than eighty manufacturing concerns and thirty banking businesses in the United States and seven European countries between 1964 and 1969. An excellent analysis of the strong trends toward centralization and the streamlining of production across borders.

_____, eds. THE MULTINATIONAL COMPANY IN EUROPE: SOME KEY PROBLEMS. Ann Arbor: University of Michigan Press, 1974. 194 p.

Papers on various aspects of management, organization and administration of multinationals, and the role of the executive in them. Contributors are Barto Roig on the role of the executive, Lawrence Franko on joint ventures, John Stopford on organizational structures, Michael Brooke on decision-making, Theodore Weinshall on cultural differences among managers, and David Frogatt on resource allocation.

Duerr, Michael G., and Roach, John M. ORGANIZATION AND CONTROL OF INTERNATIONAL OPERATIONS. Report no. 597. New York: Conference Board, 1973. 151 p.

Trends and developments in multinational companies since the mid-1960s; based on interviews with executives of North American, West European, and Japanese companies.

Organizational Structure

Dymsza, William Alexander. MULTINATIONAL BUSINESS STRATEGY. New York: McGraw-Hill, 1972. 253 p.

> A textbook for managers at the international headquarters level. Covers organization, planning, control.

Fouraker, Lawrence E., and Stopford, John M. "Organizational Structure and Multinational Strategy. ADMINISTRATIVE SCIENCE QUARTERLY 13 (June 1968): 47-64.

> A basic and important article in which the authors present types of organizational structures of American multinational corporations and their relative success in dealing with their overseas subsidiaries.

Franko, Lawrence G. "International Joint Ventures in Developing Countries: Mystique and Reality." LAW AND POLICY IN INTERNATIONAL BUSINESS 6 (Spring 1974): 315-36.

> The author argues that the joint venture debate has distracted attention from income distribution and antitrust, the "real issues."

_____. JOINT VENTURE SURVIVAL IN MULTINATIONAL CORPORATIONS. New York: Praeger, 1971. 217 p.

> A study of joint venture instability, in which that term is defined by significant changes in shares of ownership. Explores the relationship between both instability and particular business policies and instability, growth, and development of multinational corporate strategy and organization.

Friedmann, Wolfgang G., and Kalmanoff, George. JOINT INTERNATIONAL BUSINESS VENTURES. New York: Columbia University Press, 1961. 558 p.

> A general analysis of the existence, types, and operations of joint international business ventures, and the legal, managerial, and governmental problems they face both in developed and developing countries. The second half of the book presents case studies of joint ventures in Latin America, the Far East, and the Middle East, along with studies of selected investment companies.

Goggin, William C. "How the Multidimensional Organizational Structure Works at Dow Corning." HARVARD BUSINESS REVIEW 52 (January-February 1974): 54-65.

> Describes the "multidimensional organization" developed by Dow Corning which is a matrix organizational structure with dual reporting channels. This structure is found to be well suited for highly diversified international firms.

Hildebrandt, H. W. "Communication Barriers between German Subsidiaries and Parent American Companies." MICHIGAN BUSINESS REVIEW 25 (July 1973): 6-14.

Mazzolini, Renato. "Creating Europe's Multinationals: The International Merger Route." JOURNAL OF BUSINESS 48 (January 1975): 39-51.

Phatak, Arvind V. EVOLUTION OF WORLD ENTERPRISES. New York: American Management Association, 1971. 213 p.

> A book about the evolution from multinational to "world" enterprises, their institutional predecessors, and the factors that help and hinder such development. Useful for its description of the organizational pattern of enterprises.

Rutenberg, David P. "Organizational Archetypes of a Multi-National Company." MANAGEMENT SCIENCE (APPLICATION) 16 (February 1970): B337-49.

> Argues that decisions should be formulated with a view to the organization that will implement them. Four types of relationships between headquarters and subsidiaries are described.

Stopford, John M., and Wells, Louis T., Jr. MANAGING THE MULTINATIONAL ENTERPRISES: ORGANIZATION OF THE FIRM AND OWNERSHIP OF THE SUBSIDIARIES. Harvard Multinational Enterprise Series. New York: Basic Books, 1972. 223 p.

> Two aspects of the organizational structure and policies of multinational enterprises form the basis of this study: development of the structure and decision-making system of MNCs to achieve effective coordination, and strategies and policies regarding the satisfaction of host country interests. The book consists of three parts: multinational structure and strategy, ownership policies, and prospects for the future. Part I is especially valuable.

Tomlinson, James W. C. THE JOINT VENTURE PROCESS IN INTERNATIONAL BUSINESS: INDIA AND PAKISTAN. Cambridge, Mass.: MIT Press, 1970. 227 p.

> Based on a survey of fifty British firms, the book accounts for the most important variables in international corporate decision making in joint ventures. Political dimensions are not included.

Waite, Donald C. III. "The Transnational Corporation, Corporate Form for the Future." EUROPEAN BUSINESS, Summer 1974, pp. 40-49.

Wells, Louis T., Jr. THE EVOLUTION OF CONCESSION AGREEMENTS. Economic Developments Reports, no. 117. Cambridge, Mass.: Harvard Development Advisory Service, 1969. 90 p.

> States that joint ventures with local partners are only possible if the host government itself is in a very strong bargaining position.

Organizational Structure

_____ . "Joint Ventures--Successful Handshake or Painful Headache?" EURO-PEAN BUSINESS, Summer 1973, pp. 73-79.

Based on a survey of American multinational firms, the paper shows how the choice of joint venturing is matched to the particular needs and skills of the parent company.

Chapter 4
THEORIES AND DETERMINANTS
OF DIRECT FOREIGN INVESTMENT

Adler, F. Michael, and Stevens, Guy V. G. "The Trade Effects of Direct Investment." JOURNAL OF FINANCE 29 (May 1974): 655-76.

> Presents model of a global-profit-maximizing multinational produc-
> ing nonidentical products. Empirical test on U. S. foreign sub-
> sidiaries in the chemical and electrical engineering industries in
> Germany, Canada, and Japan.

Aharoni, Yair. THE FOREIGN INVESTMENT DECISION PROCESS. Boston:
Division of Research, Harvard Business School, 1966. 362 p.

> A well-known study of the foreign investment behavior of American
> firms which concentrates on developing countries. The author traces
> the effect of the decision process on governmental policies and sug-
> gests methods for achieving better understanding between govern-
> ments and firms. An organizational study which tests concepts of
> economic "rationality" and finds it an unrealistic assumption.

Ahlburg, D. A., and Parry, Thomas G. DETERMINANTS OF U. S. INVEST-
MENT IN AUSTRALIAN MANUFACTURING INDUSTRY. Discussion Papers in
International Investment and Business Studies, no. 2. Reading, Pa.: University
of Reading, 1973. 20 p.

> The time periods covered are 1951-52 and 1966-67 in this econo-
> metric analysis of the motives of U. S. investment in Australia.
> Market size is found to be the most important determinant, but
> trade barriers and technological advantage are also important.

Bandera, V. N., and White, J. T. "U. S. Direct Investments and Domestic
Markets in Europe." ECONOMICA INTERNAZIONALE, 1968, pp. 117-33.

> The authors find on the basis of data from 1953-62 that market
> size was the most important determinant of investments in Europe.

Basi, Raghbir S. DETERMINANTS OF UNITED STATES DIRECT INVESTMENT IN
FOREIGN COUNTRIES. Kent, Ohio: Kent State University Press, 1966. 34 p.

Direct Foreign Investment

The determinants considered are market size, political stability, and host government policies. All are found to be significant factors in the investment decision process.

Caves, Richard E. "Causes of Direct Investment: Foreign Firms' Shares in Canadian and United Kingdom Manufacturing Industries." REVIEW OF ECONOMICS AND STATISTICS 56 (August 1974): 279-93.

Confirms in part the MNC's advantage in overcoming entry barriers. Stocks of intangible assets due to advertising and research expenditures are the major explanatory factors.

_____. "International Corporations: The Industrial Economics of Foreign Investment." ECONOMICA 38 (February 1971): 1-27.

One of the basic articles on investment patterns and their causes. Analyzes the importance of market structure and oligopolies and the factor-equalization theorem.

Dunning, John H. "The Determinants of International Production." OXFORD ECONOMIC PAPERS 25 (November 1973): 289-336.

A comprehensive review of theories of foreign investment and production. Dunning thinks that a synthesis of location theory and industrial organization theory yields the best results.

Fayerweather, John. INTERNATIONAL BUSINESS MANAGEMENT: A CONCEPTUAL FRAMEWORK. New York: McGraw-Hill, 1969. 220 p.

Contains some important articles, especially the essay "International Transmission of Resources" which is important for its explanation of the investment process and the international investment pattern. The book represents a reasonably comprehensive and integrated discussion of behavioral theories of firms, economic theories, and investment theories. Valuable for those who need insight into management from the business perspective.

Green, Robert T. POLITICAL INSTABILITY AS A DETERMINANT OF U. S. FOREIGN INVESTMENT. Studies in Marketing, no. 17. Austin: Bureau of Business Research, Graduate School of Business, University of Texas, 1972. 122 p.

The purpose of the study is to investigate the relationship between political instability and U. S. foreign direct marketing investment. The author finds that political instability is not a factor. He tests five hypotheses and finds some variations in different regions of the world.

Green, Robert T., and Korth, Cristopher M. "Political Instability and the Foreign Investor." CALIFORNIA MANAGEMENT REVIEW 17 (Fall 1974): 23-31.

Greene, James, and Duerr, Michael G. INTERCOMPANY TRANSACTIONS IN THE MULTINATIONAL FIRM. New York: National Industrial Conference Board, 1970. 55 p.

A survey of 130 firms which indicates that overall profit maximization and return in U. S. dollars is the primary concern of firms.

Hirsch, Seev. LOCATION OF INDUSTRY AND INTERNATIONAL COMPETITIVENESS. Oxford: At the University Press, 1967. 133 p.

Uses the product life cycle theory to determine which firms will be competitive in the international market.

Iversen, Carl. ASPECTS OF THE THEORY OF INTERNATIONAL CAPITAL MOVEMENTS. 1936. Reprint. New York: Kelley, 1967.

A skillful blend of theoretical and historical discussion on the nature, causes, and effects of international capital movements. Still regarded as one of the most comprehensive treatments of the subject.

Keegan, Warren J. "A Conceptual Framework for Multinational Marketing." COLUMBIA JOURNAL OF WORLD BUSINESS 7 (November-December 1972): 67-76.

_____. "Multinational Marketing Control." JOURNAL OF INTERNATIONAL BUSINESS STUDIES 3 (Fall 1972): 33-47.

Practices of large United States multinational companies.

_____. "Multinational Scanning: A Study of the Information Sources Utilized by Headquarters Executives in Multinational Companies." ADMINISTRATIVE SCIENCE QUARTERLY 19 (September 1974): 411-21.

Kitching, John. "Winning and Losing with European Acquisitions." HARVARD BUSINESS REVIEW 52 (March-April 1974): 124-36.

An account of various strategies and tactics.

Knickerbocker, Fredrick T. OLIGOPOLISTIC REACTION AND MULTINATIONAL ENTERPRISE. Boston: Basic Books, 1973. 424 p.

A study of defensive direct investment which gives a lucid introduction to the theory of direct investment as well as being a study on international oligopolies. Deals with entry barriers, concentration, and economies of scale as explanations of investment motives.

Kreinin, Mordechai E. "Freedom of Trade and Capital Movement: Some Empirical Evidence." ECONOMIC JOURNAL 75 (December 1965): 748-58.

On the basis of a survey of 169 firms, the author finds that freedom of trade can lead both to expansion and contraction of foreign investment.

Lindenberg, Marc. "Multinational Corporations and Reinvestment Rates: The Case of the Pioneer Industry Program in Malaysia." INTERNATIONAL STUDIES QUARTERLY 19 (March 1975): 3-15.

Lloyd, Bruce. "The Identification and Assessment of Political Risk in the International Environment." LONG RANGE PLANNING 7 (December 1974): 24-32.

Mauer, Laurence J. "The Emerging Theory of Direct Foreign Investment." ECONOMIE (Netherlands) 38 (October 1973): 41-49.

Nehrt, Lee Charles. THE POLITICAL CLIMATE FOR PRIVATE FOREIGN INVESTMENT: WITH SPECIAL REFERENCE TO NORTH AFRICA. New York: Praeger, 1970. 424 p.

> The author attempts to develop and test a model by which the political climate for private investment of a newly independent underdeveloped country can be evaluated. Based on policy statements, government actions, and the historical context of the country. Case studies of Algeria, Morocco, Tunisia.

Otterbeck, Lars. "Multinational Companies and International Site Selection." SKANDINAVISKA ENSKILDA BANKEN QUARTERLY REVIEW 54, no. 3 (1973): 86-94.

> Presents several theories that have been used to analyze the selection of sites for production investment in an international perspective.

Parry, Thomas G. "Some Aspects of Asset Creation by the International Firm." JOURNAL OF BUSINESS POLICY 3 (Autumn 1972): 37-47.

> Analyzes why firms move abroad and why they stay there.

Priel, Victor Z. "Some Management Aspects of Multinational Companies." MANAGEMENT INTERNATIONAL REVIEW 14 (1974): 45-68.

> A detailed description of the management system and flow of information system in an MNC.

Ragazzi, Giorgio. "Theories of the Determinants of Direct Foreign Investment." INTERNATIONAL MONETARY FUND STAFF PAPERS 20 (July 1973): 471-98.

> Discusses the economic advantages of various forms of investment such as portfolio and direct investment. Variations are explained on the basis of imperfections in the competitive environment.

Robinson, Richard D. INTERNATIONAL BUSINESS MANAGEMENT: A GUIDE TO DECISION MAKING. New York: Holt, Rinehart and Winston, 1973. 686 p.

Presents a long list of factors which firms consider in the decision to invest abroad, showing how factors and variables influence the decision outcomes in the corporations.

Sachdev, J. C. "Disinvestment: A New Challenge to Multinationals and a New Threat to Developing Countries." MULTINATIONAL BUSINESS 3 (September 1974): 23-30.

Disinvestment by British multinationals engaged in manufacturing industries abroad.

Scaperlanda, Anthony E., and Mauer, Laurence J. "Determinants of U. S. Direct Investment in the EEC." AMERICAN ECONOMIC REVIEW 59 (September 1969): 558-68; (June 1971): 509-10.

The determinants discussed are size of markets, economic growth, and tariff discrimination, only the first of which is found to be statistically significant. See also the September 1972 issue of AMERICAN ECONOMIC REVIEW for comments by M. A. Goldberg and a reply by Scaperlanda and Mauer (pages 692-704).

Sethi, S. Prakash, and Hogle, John K. "A Conceptual and Operational Framework for Developing the Long-Range Planning Process." JOURNAL OF INTERNATIONAL BUSINESS STUDIES 4 (Fall 1973): 31-50.

The authors analyze how greater uncertainty, sociopolitical conditions, and market conditions enter into the international planning process.

Skinner, Wickham. AMERICAN INDUSTRY IN DEVELOPING ECONOMIES: THE MANAGEMENT OF INTERNATIONAL MANUFACTURING. New York: Wiley, 1968. 278 p.

The book investigates the manufacturing operations of thirteen American corporations in several developing countries and considers a variety of problems connected with management, including investment, labor, technology, etc. Written for managers.

Spitaller, Erich. "A Survey of Recent Quantitative Studies of Long-Term Capital Movements." INTERNATIONAL MONETARY FUND STAFF PAPERS 18 (March 1971): 189-220.

Reviews recent empirical studies and finds that size of market is the most important determinant, but that financial limitations affect the flow as well.

Tornedon, Roger L., and Boddewyn, Jean J. "Foreign Divestments: Too Many Mistakes." COLUMBIA JOURNAL OF WORLD BUSINESS 9 (Fall 1974): 87-94.

Wells, Louis T., Jr., ed. THE PRODUCT LIFE CYCLE AND INTERNATIONAL TRADE. Boston: Division of Research, Graduate School of Business Administration, Harvard University, 1972. 259 p.

Although highly technical, the subject is important from a broader theoretical and political point of view, since most of the Harvard Project authors employ the product life cycle theory to explain the course of international investment.

Chapter 5

FINANCE

Arpan, Jeffrey S. INTERNATIONAL INTRACORPORATE PRICING: NON-AMERICAN SYSTEMS AND VIEWS. New York: Praeger, 1972. 126 p.

A study in financial decision-making, based on a sample of sixty firms.

_____. "Multinational Firm Pricing in International Markets." SLOAN MANAGEMENT REVIEW 14 (Winter 1972-73): 1-9.

Deals with internal sales.

Bates, Thomas H., and Baker, James C. "Finance Function in a Multinational Corporation." FOREIGN TRADE REVIEW 8 (October-December 1973): 260-74.

Describes the finance function of MNCs and its degree of centralization and internationalization.

Burge, Marianne. "Current Trends in the Taxation of Multinational Enterprises." TAXES 52 (December 1974): 746-55.

Bursk, Edward Collins, et al. FINANCIAL CONTROL OF MULTINATIONAL OPERATIONS. New York: Financial Executives Research Foundation, 1971. 229 p.

Business International Corporation. FINANCING FOREIGN OPERATIONS. New York, 1966--.

A looseleaf publication which is revised monthly. Gives case histories of firms which have obtained foreign financing as well as information on the investment policies of foreign countries. Information is obtained from the firms as well as from governmental sources in foreign countries. Useful data source for case studies.

Casey, William J. "Foreign Investment and Free Capital Markets." DEPARTMENT OF STATE BULLETIN 70 (February 18, 1974): 170-75.

Statement before the Subcommittee on International Finance, Committee on Banking, Housing and Urban Affairs, U. S. Senate, January 23, 1974.

Dunning, John H. "Multinational Enterprises and Domestic Capital Formation." MANCHESTER SCHOOL 41 (September 1973): 283-310.

An analysis of the determinants of capital formation by MNCs and their subsidiaries, and governmental policies regulating capital formation and its macroeconomic implications.

Eiteman, David K., and Stonehill, Arthur I. MULTINATIONAL BUSINESS FINANCE. Reading, Mass.: Addison-Wesley, 1973. 399 p.

A textbook which presents environmental and institutional aspects in the first part and managerial aspects in the second.

Fleck, Florian H., and Mahfouz, Rashwan. "The Multinational Corporation: Tax Avoidance and Profit Manipulation via Subsidiaries and Tax Havens." SCHWEIZERISCHE ZEITSCHRIFT FUER VOLKSWIRTSCHAFT UND STATISTIK 110 (June 1974): 145-59.

Lall, Sanjaya. "Transfer Pricing by Multinational Manufacturing Firms." OXFORD BULLETIN OF ECONOMICS AND STATISTICS 35 (August 1973): 173-95.

Determinants, inducements, and limits of the use of transfer prices. Evidence in American and British surveys of intra-firm trade and transfer pricing.

Leftwich, Robert B. "U. S. Multinational Companies: Profitability, Financial Leverage and Effective Income Tax Rates." SURVEY OF CURRENT BUSINESS 54 (May 1974): 27-36.

Manser, William A. P. THE FINANCIAL ROLE OF MULTI-NATIONAL ENTERPRISES. New York: Halsted Press, 1973. 176 p.

Deals with the financial operations of MNCs and their effect on the balance of payments, and international capital markets. The second part of the book considers the MNC in terms of the host country's policies and regulations. The author claims that production and marketing are more primary functions than financial operations.

Mellors, John. "Multinational Corporations and Capital Market Integration." BANKERS' MAGAZINE (London) 215 (June 1973): 255-60.

Musgrave, Peggy B. "International Tax Base Division and the Multinational Corporation." PUBLIC FINANCE 27, no. 4 (1972): 394-412.

Examines one aspect of current practices which govern international tax shares in multinational corporate profit.

Ness, Walter L., Jr. "A Linear Programming Approach to Financing the Multinational Corporation." FINANCIAL MANAGEMENT 1 (Winter 1972): 88-100.

Ricks, David A., and Tischer, Larry E. "Multinational Corporate Financial Control Systems: Problems and Recommendations." AKRON BUSINESS AND ECONOMIC REVIEW 5 (Spring 1974): 20-25.

Robbins, Sidney M., and Stobaugh, Robert B. MONEY IN THE MULTINA-TIONAL ENTERPRISE: A STUDY OF FINANCIAL POLICY. New York: Basic Books, 1973. 231 p.

Describes the financial relationship between parent and subsidiaries. This book is mainly concerned with reasons for financial inefficiency and methods for correcting these. The strategic importance of transfer pricing is stressed. The book contains a simulation model by D. M. Schydlowsky.

_____. "The Profit Potential of Multinational Enterprises." COLUMBIA JOURNAL OF WORLD BUSINESS 8 (Fall 1973): 140-53.

Stanley, Marjorie T., and Stanley, John D. "The Impact of U. S. Regulation of Foreign Investment." CALIFORNIA MANAGEMENT REVIEW 15 (Winter 1972): 56-64.

Based on questionnaires sent to the financial officers of U. S. parent companies whose financing subsidiaries obtained overseas financing via bond issue in 1968.

Texas. University of. Bureau of Business Research. AN INTRODUCTION TO FINANCIAL CONTROL AND REPORTING IN MULTINATIONAL ENTERPRISES. Studies in International Business, no. 1. Austin: 1973. 89 p.

U. S. Department of Commerce. Bureau of Economic Analysis. SPECIAL SUR-VEY OF U. S. MULTINATIONAL COMPANIES, 1970. Washington, D.C.: 1972. 100 p.

Contains financial information (sales, expenses, income, employment, trade) for 298 U. S. MNCs for the period 1966-70.

U. S. Department of Commerce. Office of Foreign Direct Investments. THE FINANCIAL STRUCTURE OF THE FOREIGN AFFILIATES OF U. S. DIRECT INVESTORS. Prepared by Anthony E. Scaperlanda. Washington, D.C.: Government Printing Office, 1974. 94 p.

Based on data from the balance sheets of the foreign affiliates of
440 large U. S. firms. A highly detailed statistical analysis of
financial structures by industry and country.

Wasserman, Max J. "International Money Management of Multinational Corporations." WALL STREET REVIEW OF BOOKS 2 (December 1974): 286-95.

Wilson, J. S. G., and Scheffer, C. F., eds., in association with SUERF.
MULTINATIONAL ENTERPRISES: FINANCIAL AND MONETARY ASPECTS.
Leiden: Sijthoff, 1974. 260 p.

Based on papers from a Societe Universities Europeenne de Recherches
Financieres (SUERF) colloquium held in Nottingham in 1973. Includes
papers on general background of the multinationals by Lord O'Brien,
E. Thielemans, and G. Y. Bertin; financial management of multinationals and problems of long- and short-term capital transfers by
J. Koning, A.J.W.S. Leonard, and F. H. Brittenden; multinationals and international financial markets by W. A. P. Manser,
and S. Plasschaert; financial institutions and the growth of multinationals by J. Hendley, P. de Vallee, and D. W. Vollmer; multinationals and national monetary and financial policies by J. H.
Dunning, N. Lundgren, and S. Rometsch; general report on the
colloquium by S. E. Rolfe.

Wundisch, Karl. "Centralized Cash Management Systems for the Multinational
Enterprise." MANAGEMENT INTERNATIONAL (Wiesbaden) 13, no. 6 (1973):
43-64.

Chapter 6

THE INTERNATIONAL EXECUTIVE

Borrmann, Werner A. "The Problem of Expatriate Personnel and Their Selection in International Enterprises." MANAGEMENT INTERNATIONAL (Wiesbaden) 8, no. 45 (1968): 37-48.

> A study of American and German executives in multinational corporations.

Fayerweather, John. THE EXECUTIVE OVERSEAS. Syracuse, N.Y.: Syracuse University Press, 1969. 195 p.

> Discusses the difficulties of overseas executives within the framework of cultural differences. Based on an extensive study of Mexican management.

Franko, Laurence G. "Who Manages Multinational Enterprise? Trends in the Nationality Mix of International Staffing." COLUMBIA JOURNAL OF WORLD BUSINESS 8 (Summer 1973): 30-42.

Gonzalez, Richard F., and Neghandi, Anant R. THE UNITED STATES OVERSEAS EXECUTIVE: HIS ORIENTATIONS AND CAREER PATTERNS. East Lansing: Institute for International Business and Economic Development Studies, Division of Research, Graduate School of Business Administration, Michigan State University, 1967. 118 p.

Guvenc, Alpander G. "The Foreign MBA: Potential Managers for American International Corporations." JOURNAL OF INTERNATIONAL BUSINESS STUDIES 4 (Spring 1973): 1-13.

Haire, Mason, et al. MANAGERIAL THINKING: AN INTERNATIONAL STUDY. New York: Wiley, 1966. 298 p.

> The book emphasizes the similarities in outlook and attitude toward such subjects as leadership and motivation among 3,641 managers in fourteen countries and discusses the implications of the findings for multinational business.

Kean, Geoffrey. THE PUBLIC RELATIONS MAN ABROAD. New York: Praeger, 1968. 204 p.

> A descriptive study of the special features of international public relations written by a former practitioner. Public relations is described as an important, integral part of marketing and image manipulation.

Kuin, Pieter. "The Magic of Multinational Management." HARVARD BUSINESS REVIEW 50 (November-December 1972): 89-97.

Lovell, Enid Baird. THE CHANGING ROLE OF THE INTERNATIONAL EXECUTIVE. Studies in Business Policy, no. 119. New York: National Industrial Conference Board, 1966. 254 p.

> The study describes how the authority of the international executive fits into the overall management structure of multinational corporations.

Part II

THE MULTINATIONAL

CORPORATION AND THE NATION STATE

Chapter 7

NATIONAL POLICIES AND
CORPORATE RELATIONS WITH GOVERNMENT

Adam, Gyorgy. "Standing Up to the American Challenge." THE NEW HUN-
GARIAN QUARTERLY 9 (Autumn 1968): 111-30.

> Points out the increasing dominance of U. S. multinationals in
> Western European industry, especially in highly profitable growth
> industries like electronics, nuclear power, and telecommunications.
> Sees cooperation among Eastern Europe, the Soviet Union, and
> Western Europe as a way to pool market size and the capital avail-
> able for research and development to meet the U. S. challenge.

_____. "World Corporations: 'Dual Power' in the International Economy?"
NEW HUNGARIAN QUARTERLY 11 (Autumn 1970): 201-14.

> The dual power theory holds that political institutions such as nation
> states are being superseded by large economic organizations such as
> MNCs. Adam examines the growing conflicts between states and
> MNCs and the methods used by states and firms to cover up the
> existence of the conflict. The author suggests means of reestab-
> lishing the primacy of politics.

Ball, George W. "Multinational Corporations and Nation-States." ATLANTIC
COMMUNITY QUARTERLY 5 (Summer 1967): 247-53.

> The author considers nation states and their restrictive policies to be
> impediments to the integrative appeasement activities of the MNCs.

Bandera, V. N. FOREIGN CAPITAL AS AN INSTRUMENT OF NATIONAL
ECONOMIC POLICY: A STUDY BASED ON THE EXPERIENCE OF EAST EU-
ROPEAN COUNTRIES BETWEEN THE WORLD WARS. The Hague: Nijhoff,
1964. 169 p.

> A study of the interwar period and the negative role of foreign
> capital in six Eastern European countries.

Baum, Daniel J. "Global Corporation: An American Challenge to the Nation
State." IOWA LAW REVIEW 55 (1969-70): 410-37.

The author considers the charges and issues raised by Servan-Schreiber (THE AMERICAN CHALLENGE, below) and analyzes them partly in the more general terms of state power and partly in terms of the Canadian case. The general assumption is that MNCs organize more effectively than states and that the latter must reassess their goals.

Behrman, Jack N. "Actors and Factors in Policy Decisions on Foreign Direct Investment." WORLD DEVELOPMENT 2 (August 1974): 1-14.

_____. CONFLICTING CONSTRAINTS ON THE MULTINATIONAL ENTER-PRISE: POTENTIAL FOR RESOLUTION. New York: Council of the Americas, 1974. 109 p.

The essay outlines U. S. government policies toward international business and the potential for international controls.

_____. INTERNATIONAL BUSINESS AND GOVERNMENTS. New York: McGraw-Hill, 1971. 244 p.

The book is concerned with the interrelationship between U. S. business abroad, host governments, and the U. S. government. It describes the ways in which business communicates with its own and foreign governments as well as the impact of foreign-owned companies on host governments. It includes an interesting discussion of the ways in which foreign enterprises fail to fit into normal communication procedures.

_____. "The Multinational Enterprise: Its Initiatives and Government Reactions." THE JOURNAL OF INTERNATIONAL LAW AND ECONOMICS 6 (January 1972): 215-34.

Discusses the need for international control and contrasts this with the likelihood of national unilateral action.

_____. NATIONAL INTERESTS AND THE MULTINATIONAL ENTERPRISE, TENSIONS AMONG THE NORTH ATLANTIC COUNTRIES. Englewood Cliffs, N.J.: Prentice-Hall, 1970. 194 p.

Discusses the investment activities of American firms in Canada, Europe, and Australia and the reactions of the various host governments in three major areas: industrial dominance, technological dependence, and the disturbing effects of MNCs on national economic plans. The author investigates the ability of the U. S. government to extend its influence into host countries through affiliates of U. S. corporations by means of antitrust policies and imposing controls on investments, exports, and technology.

Benoit, Emile. "The Attack on the Multinationals." COLUMBIA JOURNAL OF WORLD BUSINESS 7 (November-December 1972): 15-22.

If U. S. multinational corporations are to survive, some obvious misconceptions on the part of their critics must be corrected.

Bergsten, C. Fred. "Coming Investment Wars?" FOREIGN AFFAIRS 53 (October 1974): 135-52.

Discusses the impact of host country policies and efforts to protect their own interests.

Bivens, Karen K., and Lambeth, Helen S. A WORLD-WIDE LOOK AT BUSINESS-GOVERNMENT RELATIONS: PRESENT PROBLEMS AND FUTURE CO-OPERATION. New York: National Industrial Conference Board, 1967. 58 p.

Written mainly for future investors, the book treats the state system as part of the "environmental constraints" of multinational operation.

Cameron, Virginia Shook, ed. PRIVATE INVESTORS ABROAD--PROBLEMS AND SOLUTIONS IN INTERNATIONAL BUSINESS IN 1970. New York: Bender, 1970. 360 p.

This book and the four entries below are based on annual symposia held by the Southwestern Legal Foundation and its International and Comparative Law Center in Dallas, Texas. The volumes cover a wide variety of legal and economic issues relating to international business and multinational corporations: country studies, taxation issues, arbitration and antitrust, and industry studies in petroleum, banking, and other industries. A variety of countries is represented by the contributors, most of whom are attorneys. The articles, which average twenty pages in length, are good sources of information on government policies and legal regulations.

_____, ed. PRIVATE INVESTORS ABROAD--PROBLEMS AND SOLUTIONS IN INTERNATIONAL BUSINESS IN 1971. New York: Bender, 1971. 350 p.

_____, ed. PRIVATE INVESTORS ABROAD--PROBLEMS AND SOLUTIONS IN INTERNATIONAL BUSINESS IN 1972. New York: Bender, 1972. 428 p.

_____, ed. PRIVATE INVESTORS ABROAD--PROBLEMS AND SOLUTIONS IN INTERNATIONAL BUSINESS IN 1973. New York: Bender, 1973. 318 p.

_____, ed. PRIVATE INVESTORS ABROAD--PROBLEMS AND SOLUTIONS IN INTERNATIONAL BUSINESS IN 1974. New York: Bender, 1974. 420 p.

The Economist Intelligence Unit. THE GROWTH AND SPREAD OF MULTINATIONAL COMPANIES. QER [Quarterly Economic Review] Special, no. 5. London: 1969. 81 p.

A general introduction to the spread of MNCs, the governmental concerns in industrialized and developing countries, the concerns of labor, and the need for regulation.

Fatouros, Arghyrios A. GOVERNMENT GUARANTEES TO FOREIGN INVESTORS.
New York: Columbia University Press, 1962. 411 p.

> The book contains both arguments for governmental guarantees to
> foreign investors as well as an analysis of existing forms of agree-
> ments between states and firms, including the regulation of export
> and industrial relations. The author also presents an analysis of
> the legal effects of governmental guarantees.

Fayerweather, John. "Elite Attitudes Toward Multinational Firms: A Study of
Britain, Canada, France." INTERNATIONAL STUDIES QUARTERLY 16 (December 1972): 472-90.

> Based on a questionnaire study of businessmen, politicians, and
> trade union officials. The attitudes, though marked by nationalism,
> are generally found to favor direct investment.

_____, ed. INTERNATIONAL BUSINESS-GOVERNMENT AFFAIRS: TOWARD
AN ERA OF ACCOMMODATION. Cambridge, Mass.: Ballinger Publishing
Co., 1973. 134 p.

> The book emphasizes the common interests of business and govern-
> ment. Contains an introduction and eight essays on the evolution
> of a new system of control of resource allocation and related eco-
> nomic decisions.

Fukuda, Haruko. BRITAIN IN EUROPE: IMPACT ON THE THIRD WORLD.
London: Macmillan, 1973. 194 p.

> A study of changes in Britain's trade and aid policies towards the
> less-developed countries effected by Britain's entry in the European
> Economic Community, and their implications for the EEC associa-
> tion system and GATT (General Agreement on Tariff and Trade).
> Relevant from the perspective of EEC and United Kingdom invest-
> ment policies.

Galbraith, John Kenneth. THE NEW INDUSTRIAL STATE. Boston: Houghton
Mifflin, 1967. 427 p.

> Although the book is not specifically concerned with multinationals,
> it contains several relevant discussions. One is an analysis of the
> reasons why corporations attempt to circumvent or control the mech-
> anisms of the domestic market; another is a discussion of the argu-
> ment for bigness, in which Galbraith emphasizes the importance of
> planning for control of inputs and demand, and easy provision of
> capital and minimization of risk, apart from economies of scale
> and possibilities for the exercise of monopoly power. Galbraith's
> book is important because it discusses the interface between eco-
> nomics and politics.

Galloway, Jonathan F. "The Military-Industrial Linkages of U. S. Based Multi-national Corporations." INTERNATIONAL STUDIES QUARTERLY 16 (December 1972): 491-510.

The author states that, because there are "symbiotic relationships" between governmental aid policy, investment policy, and military policy, the MNC-nation state conflict dimension is usually over-drawn.

Hadari, Yitzhak. "The Structure of the Private Multinational Enterprise." MICHIGAN LAW REVIEW 71 (March 1973): 731-806.

General discussion of multinationals and the legal problems they pose. Concludes that states generally have adequate power to control MNCs, but suggests that states might exercise control in areas such as transfer pricing in which they do not now have that power. Also points to possibilities of international cooperation short of rigid international control.

Hahlo, H. R., et al., eds. NATIONALISM AND THE MULTINATIONAL ENTERPRISE: LEGAL, ECONOMIC AND MANAGERIAL ASPECTS. Leiden: Sijthoff; Dobbs Ferry, N.Y.: Oceana Publications, 1973. 373 p.

Papers from a conference on the legal, economic, and business management aspects of MNCs in a variety of industrialized countries and Africa. The costs and benefits of MNCs, and problems concerning their management and legal control are the subject of nineteen chapters written by a variety of scholars in different fields. The conference was held at McGill University and many of the entries refer to Canada.

Heilbroner, Robert L. "The Multinational Corporation and the Nation-State." NEW YORK REVIEW OF BOOKS, February 11, 1971, pp. 20-25.

A review of the issues raised in some of the early accounts of multinationals and their relations to the nation state.

_____. "None of Your Business." NEW YORK REVIEW OF BOOKS, March 20, 1975, pp. 6-10.

Heilbroner discusses the lack of reliable data and information about the operations of MNCs, and the features of the so-called "new capitalism," which he considers not very new, and the changes in the balance of power among various groups brought about by the MNC.

Hernes, Helga. "The Visible Hand of the Multinational Corporation: A Review." EUROPEAN JOURNAL OF POLITICAL RESEARCH 1, no. 3 (1973): 265-92.

A review of seven books on MNCs in which Hernes outlines relevant research problems for political scientists on the basis of existing

Policies and Relations with Government

lines of conflict and cooperation between the four basic actors involved: parent companies, subsidiaries, countries of origin, and
host countries.

Kavanagh, Dennis. "Beyond Autonomy? The Politics of Corporations." GOV-
ERNMENT AND OPPOSITION 9 (Winter 1974): 42-60.

Discusses whether or not corporations, particularly multinational
corporations, pose a threat to the sovereignty of small and medium-
sized states.

Lea, Sperry, and Webley, Simon. MULTINATIONAL CORPORATIONS IN DE-
VELOPED COUNTRIES: A REVIEW OF RECENT RESEARCH AND POLICY THINK-
ING. London: British-North American Committee, 1973. 77 p.

Includes a chapter each on the United States, Canada, and Europe,
all based on recent research.

Litvak, Isaiah A., and Maule, Christopher J. "The Multinational Corporation:
Some Perspectives." CANADIAN PUBLIC ADMINISTRATION 13 (Summer 1970):
129-39.

The authors provide a good summary of the problems created by
multinationals for host countries and portray the tensions between
national sovereignty and company control by examining several
issues: the impact of direct investment on growth, financial policies, taxes and employment, the application of U.S. antitrust
laws, and the curtailment of exports. The article concludes with
an outline of several control schemes.

_____. "The Multinational Firm and Conflicting National Interests." JOUR-
NAL OF WORLD TRADE LAW 3 (1969): 309-18.

Outlines a framework for the analysis of host-home country conflict.

_____, eds. FOREIGN INVESTMENT: THE EXPERIENCE OF HOST COUN-
TRIES. New York: Praeger, 1970. 406 p.

A description of policies and attitudes of host countries as viewed
by the investor. Includes a useful introductory chapter by the
editors, as well as case studies of thirteen countries, including
Australia, Japan, South Africa, Canada, Argentina, India, Tunisia,
Spain, Norway, and Yugoslavia.

Martyn, Howe. "Resistance to the Multinational Corporation." WORLD AFFAIRS
132 (September 1969): 140-59.

The article describes the restraints which nationalism and different
religious creeds put upon the operations of multinationals in host
countries. Martyn exhorts companies to put more emphasis on the
benefits which accrue to host countries as a result of their activities.

Mason, Edward S. "The Corporation in the Post-Industrial State." CALIFORNIA MANAGEMENT REVIEW 12 (Summer 1970): 5-25.

> Discusses the fact that host countries of MNCs fear loss of control over certain economic sectors, and considers the ability of states to impose restrictions and the capacity of MNCs to circumvent them.

Mason, R. Hal. "Conflicts Between Host Countries and the Multinational Enterprise." CALIFORNIA MANAGEMENT REVIEW 17 (Fall 1974): 5-14.

Mikesell, Raymond F., ed. UNITED STATES PRIVATE AND FOREIGN INVESTMENT ABROAD. Eugene: University of Oregon Press, 1962. 599 p.

> A highly diversified collection of essays on the historical and modern forms of foreign investments by the government and by certain industries. Treats many specialized topics such as licensing of trademarks in exchange for equity interests, skill transfer, and economic effects on parent and host countries. Papers by Mikesell, several by Behrman, one by Wells.

Moore, Jack, and Weiss, Ernest G. "Corporate Marriage—European Style." PRICE WATERHOUSE REVIEW 18, no. 3 (1973): 23-35.

> A close look at the tax consequences of cross-frontier mergers and amalgamations, documented with examples—particularly those involving companies in the EEC and the United States.

Paquet, Gilles, ed. THE MULTINATIONAL FIRM AND THE NATION STATE. Don Mills, Ontario: Collier-Macmillan, Canada, 1972. 182 p.

> An introduction to the subject divided into four parts: conceptual clarification, elements for a theoretical framework, the operations of the multinational firm, and the multinational firm and the nation state, now and then. Includes Hymer's "The Efficiency (Contradictions) of MNCs," (also cited in chapter 15).

Parry, Thomas G. "The International Firm and National Economic Policy: A Survey of Some Issues." THE ECONOMIC JOURNAL 83 (December 1973): 1201-21.

> A good survey of the major economic issues in developed and developing countries and their political relevance. The issues discussed are the balance of payments, restrictive import franchise, and interaffiliate pricing behavior and its implications for national policy.

Perlmutter, Howard V. "Attitudinal Patterns in Joint Decision Making in Multinational Firm-Nation State Relationships." In INTERORGANIZATIONAL DECISION MAKING, edited by Matthew Tuite, et al., pp. 201-21. Chicago: Aldine, 1972.

Outlines a framework for legitimizing the use of a country's resources by the MNC. The author develops categories of attitudinal
patterns which predict the stability of MNC-nation-state relations.

Plant, C. T. H. "The Relationship between Multinational Enterprises and Social
Policy." In YEARBOOK OF WORLD AFFAIRS, 1974, edited by George W.
Keeton and Georg Schwarzenberger, pp. 174-86. London: Stevens & Sons,
1974.

Powers, Charles W., ed. PEOPLE/PROFITS: THE ETHICS OF INVESTMENT.
New York: Council on Religion and International Affairs, 1972. 214 p.

The book is in three parts, the third of which is entitled "Investor
Responsibility for the Foreign Affairs of the Multinational Enterprise"
(pages 127-96). It contains an article by Jack Behrman on social
investment issues in which he outlines the interest groups involved
in multinational business and raises some of the issues such as labor,
profit sharing, pricing, and technology transfers which can lead to
conflicts on ethical lines. Other contributions include a discussion
of Behrman's paper, a transcript of a discussion with a manager,
and a comment on corporate disclosures.

Rolfe, Sidney E. THE INTERNATIONAL CORPORATION. Paris: International
Chamber of Commerce, 1969. 202 p.

An analysis of the 1968 FORTUNE list and the extent to which the
companies included are "international" in sales, assets, employment,
and profit. Also gives an overview of the problems, costs, and
benefits associated with international corporations and discusses the
legal, economic, and political problems associated with them. The
book concludes with a chapter on the rights and responsibilities of
the MNC.

_____. "The International Corporation in Perspective." ATLANTIC COM-
MUNITY QUARTERLY 7 (Summer 1969): 255-70.

The author argues that contemporary political institutions are not
fully able to allow us to utilize the long-run benefits of the MNCs.
Therefore, political structures must evolve.

Rolfe, Sidney E., and Damm, Walter, eds. THE MULTINATIONAL CORPORA-
TION IN THE WORLD ECONOMY: DIRECT INVESTMENT IN PERSPECTIVE.
New York: Praeger, 1970. 275 p.

Six essays presented at a conference sponsored by the Committee
for Economic Cooperation which was concerned mainly with the
assessment of European and Japanese investments in the United
States. Includes a brief survey of foreign investments in the United
States and papers by Rolfe on the MNC in perspective, Damm on
economic consequences of European investments in the United States,
McLaren on antitrust and direct investment, Hellman on U. S. in-

vestments in Europe, and Powrie on investments in Canada. The conference adopted recommendations which support an internationalist view of corporate responsibility which would foster the develop- ment of a freer international capital market.

Scheer, Robert. AMERICA AFTER NIXON: THE AGE OF THE MULTINATION- ALS. New York: McGraw-Hill, 1974. 326 p.

Describes the domination of American life by a limited number of large corporations, many of which are multinational, and claims that the new American majority is not so much silent as populist and will pressure for radical changes in the organization of eco- nomic life.

Servan-Schreiber, Jean Jacques. THE AMERICAN CHALLENGE. New York: Atheneum, 1968. 210 p.

Describes the expansion of American firms in Europe and suggests what needs to be done to meet this challenge. Technological in- novation and adequate education are regarded as major factors in Europe's future development.

Smith, Robert E. "Private Power and National Sovereignty: Some Comments on the Multinational Corporation." JOURNAL OF ECONOMIC ISSUES 8 (June 1974): 417-47.

Examines the ability of national government to control the competi- tiveness of MNCs. Finds governmental power to be generally ade- quate, but cites as an exception the inability of importing nations to affect the pricing structure of their MNC suppliers.

Stephenson, Hugh. THE COMING CLASH: THE IMPACT OF MULTINATIONAL CORPORATIONS ON THE NATION STATE. 1st American ed. New York: Saturday Review Press, 1972. 186 p.

The author of this readable journalistic account takes as his thesis "that our whole framework of thought and reaction is founded in the sixteenth century concept of the sovereign nation state" and that, in order for the economic system to function properly, "large scale modern industry must increasingly be part of an interlinked and international network of production and sales."

Tugendhat, Christopher. THE MULTINATIONALS. New York: Random House, 1972. 242 p.

A popular account of the emergence of multinationals and their political implications. Describes increasing European investments in the United States as well as firms' investment decision-making processes.

Turner, Louis. INVISIBLE EMPIRES: MULTINATIONAL COMPANIES IN THE MODERN WORLD. New York: Harcourt Brace Jovanovich, 1971. 228 p.

> A general introductory account of the emergence of MNCs and their effect on U. S. and other economies including the area industrial relations. Several chapters are devoted to the political implications for developed and developing countries.

_____. POLITICS AND THE MULTINATIONAL COMPANY. Fabian Research Series, no. 279. London: Fabian, 1969. 32 p.

> A brief report, written from the perspective of Great Britain as a host country, and outlining modes of supervision and control of foreign firms.

United Nations. Department of Economic and Social Affairs. THE IMPACT OF MULTINATIONAL CORPORATIONS ON DEVELOPMENT AND ON INTERNATIONAL RELATIONS: TECHNICAL PAPERS: TAXATION (ST/ESA/11). New York: 1974. 111 p.

> Contains the following articles: "Taxation of Multinational Corporations," by Carl Shoup; "International Tax Differentials for Multinational Corporations," by Peggy Musgrave; and "State Income Taxation in the U.S.," by Charles McLure. Served as background for another United Nations document, THE IMPACT OF THE MULTINATIONAL CORPORATION (ST/ECA/6; see United Nations, chapter 14).

Vernon, Raymond. THE ECONOMIC AND POLITICAL CONSEQUENCES OF MULTINATIONAL ENTERPRISE: AN ANTHOLOGY. Boston: Division of Research, Graduate School of Business Administration, Harvard University, 1972. 236 p.

> A collection of papers published previously by Vernon on such topics as governmental policy, national sovereignty, trade, and the global economy.

_____. "The Role of U. S. Enterprise Abroad." DAEDALUS 98 (Winter 1969): 113-33.

> Outlines the effects of MNCs on advanced and developing economies and the tensions arising from the interactions between governments desiring control and enterprises organizing for profits. Suggests an internationalist form of regulation.

_____. SOVEREIGNTY AT BAY: THE MULTINATIONAL SPREAD OF U. S. ENTERPRISES. New York: Basic Books, 1971. 326 p.

> This is the author's basic introductory volume describing the results and theoretical framework of the Harvard Multinational Enterprise Project. Presents the product cycle model of foreign direct investment, short descriptions of the manufacturing industries and raw

materials industries, and three chapters on broader economic and
political issues. A final chapter outlines alternative modes of
dealing with the MNC in the future. An important standard work.

_____, ed. BIG BUSINESS AND THE STATE: CHANGING RELATIONS IN
WESTERN EUROPE. Cambridge, Mass.: Harvard University Press, 1974. 310 p.

Includes a general introduction by the editor about the relations
between enterprises and governments emerging in Europe, as well
as a series of country and industry studies by European authors.
Relevant because it shows the extent to which internationalization
of economies, enterprises, and industrial policies has occurred in
Europe. The very term "multinational enterprise" is employed in
only a few instances, although the book clearly shows how advanced the internationalization of capital in Europe has become.

Zannetos, Zenon S. THE ECONOMIC IMPACT OF THE MULTINATIONAL
ENTERPRISE ON THE HOST COUNTRY. Rev. ed. Cambridge, Mass.: Alfred
P. Sloan School of Management, Massachusetts Institute of Technology, 1973.
18 p.

Discusses the issue of technological transfer and the juxtaposition
of efficiency and equity.

Chapter 8
COUNTRIES OF ORIGIN:
POLICIES AND CONSEQUENCES

Aitkin, Thomas. FOREIGN POLICY FOR AMERICAN BUSINESS. New York: Harper, 1962. 159 p.

The author considers American business abroad a suitable tool for U.S. policy. He differentiates between business policy in developed and developing countries, and suggests that American government and business cooperate in compiling foreign statistics to make them more meaningful to the investor.

Baker, James C., and Bradford, M. Gerald. AMERICAN BANKS ABROAD: EDGE ACT COMPANIES AND MULTINATIONAL BANKING. New York: Praeger, 1974. 206 p.

Successes, shortcomings, and prospects of U.S. banks operating abroad under the Edge Act Amendment to the Federal Reserve Act of 1919. Discusses background and content of the amendment, and policies and operations under it. Also discusses reasons for growth of international banking.

Ballon, Robert J. "Japan's Investment Overseas." AUSSENWIRTSCHAFT 28 (September-December 1973): 304-29.

A descriptive essay on Japanese direct investment policies (both national and corporate) after the second World War.

Baran, Paul A., and Sweezy, Paul M. MONOPOLY CAPITAL. New York: Monthly Review Press, 1966. 402 p.

A Marxist analysis of the structure of the U.S. corporate economy and its investment policies and power plays.

Baum, Daniel J. THE BANKS OF CANADA IN THE COMMONWEALTH CARIBBEAN: ECONOMIC NATIONALISM AND MULTINATIONAL ENTERPRISES OF A MEDIUM POWER. New York: Praeger, 1974. 158 p.

Discusses the banking systems in Canada and the Caribbean, their institutional ties, and emerging nationalism in the Caribbean area.

Behrman, Jack N. DIRECT MANUFACTURING INVESTMENT, EXPORTS AND
THE BALANCE OF PAYMENTS. New York: National Foreign Trade Council,
1968. 32 p.

> A critical analysis of the U. S. Treasury Department study by Gary
> C. Hufbauer and F. Michael Adler (OVERSEAS MANUFACTURING
> INVESTMENT AND THE BALANCE OF PAYMENTS, below).

Berle, Adolf A., Jr. THE TWENTIETH CENTURY CAPITALIST REVOLUTION.
New York: Harcourt, Brace, 1954.

> In chapter 4, "The Modern Corporation in International Affairs"
> (pages 116-63), Berle claims that U. S. corporations keep informed
> about those U. S. diplomatic officials who have shown their "use-
> fulness in advancing or protecting the company interest."

Business International Corporation. THE EFFECTS OF U. S. CORPORATE FOR-
EIGN INVESTMENT 1960-1972. New York: 1974. 82 p.

> The second in a series of surveys which outlines the positive effects
> of U. S. investments in terms of the balance of payments, employ-
> ment, and investment.

Cooper, George R., Jr. "Underwriting Opportunity in the Overseas World."
JOURNAL OF INSURANCE 35 (November-December 1974): 2-7.

> Background and characteristics of a plan, presented August 21, 1974,
> which would enable private insurance companies to begin underwrit-
> ing and re-insuring political risk insurance in partnership with the
> Overseas Private Investment Corporation, the government agency
> which offers insurance and financial services to U. S. private in-
> vestors in the developing nations.

Dehner, W. Joseph, Jr. "Multinational Enterprise and Racial Non-discrimina-
tion: United States Enforcement of an International Human Right." HARVARD
INTERNATIONAL LAW JOURNAL 15 (Winter 1974): 71-125.

Eder, George J. "Expropriation: Hickenlooper and Hereafter." THE INTER-
NATIONAL LAWYER 4 (July 1970): 611-45.

> Discusses expropriation cases in Latin America and their legality.
> The author claims that the U. S. Department of State has encour-
> aged further expropriations by its reluctance to enforce the Hick-
> enlooper amendment.

Ellicott, John. "U. S. Controls on Foreign Direct Investment: The 1969 Program." LAW AND CONTEMPORARY PROBLEMS 34 (Winter 1969): 47-63.

> Strict enforcement of the constraints of the 1969 controls on foreign
> investment is discussed in terms of its success in easing the balance
> of payments problem. The author, however, thinks that these re-
> strictions should be lifted.

Frank, Richard S. "Administration Seeks Incentives to Spur Exports in Drive to Correct Huge Trade Deficit." NATIONAL JOURNAL 5 (April 21, 1973): 557-66.

> Particular emphasis on persuading major multinational corporations to export more from the United States and invest less overseas.

_____. "Improved Balance-of-Payments Prospect Prompts End to Controls on Foreign Investment." NATIONAL JOURNAL 5 (June 2, 1973): 809-15.

Guisinger, Stephen. "The Rise of the Multinational Corporation and United States Trade Policy." SOCIAL SCIENCE QUARTERLY 54 (December 1973): 552-67.

Hamada, Koichi. "Japanese Direct Investments Abroad." In JAPAN: ECONOMIC AND SOCIAL STUDIES IN DEVELOPMENT, edited by Heide Simonis and Udo Ernst Simonis, pp. 155-71. Wiesbaden: Harrassowitz, 1974.

Hancock, James H. "The Role of the American Corporation in the Economic Development of Latin America: A Study of the Conflict between the Extra-Territorial Application of United States Antitrust Laws and United States Foreign Policy." VANDERBILT LAW REVIEW 19 (June 1966): 757-810.

> Hancock states that there is a conflict between U. S. antitrust laws and U. S. policy aimed at economic growth. U. S. antitrust laws often prevent joint ventures which, by their transfer of capital, technology, and managerial talents, would foster economic growth.

Hufbauer, Gary C., and Adler, F. Michael. OVERSEAS MANUFACTURING INVESTMENT AND THE BALANCE OF PAYMENTS. Washington, D.C.: U. S. Treasury Department, 1968. 92 p.

> This well-known econometric study describes the complications involved in assessing the balance of payments when direct investment rather than trade is involved. (See also Behrman, above, and the second item by Vernon, below.)

Hughes, Helen. "Australians as Foreign Investors: Australian Investment in Singapore and Malaysian Manufacturing Industries." AUSTRALIAN ECONOMIC PAPERS, June 1967, pp. 57-76.

> In this questionnaire survey, Australian investors are shown to be very intent on maintaining control over their overseas operations.

"Japan's Direct Outward Investment." FUJI BANK BULLETIN 24 (October 1973): 199-205.

"Japan's Overseas Ventures." ORIENTAL ECONOMIST 42 (November 1974): 17-22.

Karageorgas, Dionysios. "Taxation of Foreign Firms: Discrimination and Allocative Effects." PUBLIC FINANCE QUARTERLY 1 (July 1973): 239-65.

Examines the effects of various systems of taxing foreign firms on the international movement of direct investment.

Krause, Lawrence B. "Evolution of Foreign Direct Investment: The United States and Japan." In STRONG YEN AND WEAK DOLLAR, edited by Jerome B. Cohen, pp. 149-76. New York: Japan Society, 1973.

A comparative analysis of two industrialized states.

Litvak, Isaiah A., and Maule, Christopher J. "Conflict Resolution and Extraterritoriality." JOURNAL OF CONFLICT RESOLUTION 13 (September 1969): 305-19.

Describes instances of the extraterritorial application of the laws and policies of one country to corporations resident within another country. A case study of Canadian-American relations.

_____. "Japan's Overseas Investments." PACIFIC AFFAIRS 46 (Summer 1973): 254-68.

Lupo, Leonard A. "U. S. Direct Investment Abroad in 1972." SURVEY OF CURRENT BUSINESS 53 (September 1973): 20-34.

Metzger, Stanley D. "American Trade and Investment Policy for the 1970s: The Williams Commission Report." AMERICAN JOURNAL OF INTERNATIONAL LAW 66 (July 1972): 537-59.

An analysis of the report UNITED STATES INTERNATIONAL ECONOMIC POLICY IN AN INTERDEPENDENT WORLD, see below.

Michalet, Charles Albert, and Delapierre, Michel. LA MULTINATIONALISATION DES ENTERPRISES FRANCAISES. Paris: Gauthiers-Villars, for Centre d'Etude des Techniques Economiques Modernes, 1973. 210 p.

Gives reasons for French business expansion abroad. Based on interviews with management in fifty-two enterprises. Describes strategy of expansion as well as legal and technical issues. Size is seen as a determining factor leading to multinationalization.

Miller, Arthur S. "The Multinational Corporation and the Nation State." JOURNAL OF WORLD TRADE LAW 7 (May-June 1973): 267-92.

The author is concerned with the impact of the MNC on U. S. federal structure, as well as the central political institutions, and that the executive branch will gain in power. The infrastructure of nation states is being eroded.

National Association of Manufacturers. U. S. STAKE IN WORLD TRADE AND INVESTMENT: THE ROLE OF THE MULTINATIONAL CORPORATION. Washington, D.C.: 1973. 86 p.

> Discusses the rapid growth of multinational corporations, their balance of payments effects, and the issues of employment, technology, taxes, and host-country sovereignty.

Ozawa, Terutomo. "Multinationalism--Japanese Style." COLUMBIA JOURNAL OF WORLD BUSINESS 7 (November-December 1972): 33-42.

> The factors that led to the overseas expansion of Japanese corporations differ widely from those that influenced their western counterparts.

_____. "Sociocultural Problems of Japanese Multinationalism." AKRON BUSINESS AND ECONOMIC REVIEW 5 (Spring 1974): 7-13.

> Discusses overseas investments, tourism, and employment abroad.

Polk, Judd, et al. U. S. PRODUCTION ABROAD AND THE BALANCE OF PAYMENTS. New York: National Industrial Conference Board, 1966. 200 p.

> Uses two models to analyze the relationship between the balance of payments and direct foreign investment and concludes that the latter is not responsible for the balance of payments deficit. A careful and thorough study of U. S. policy and views, and of 100 company accounts from the standpoint of their foreign exchange implications.

Reddaway, William B., et al. EFFECTS OF U. K. DIRECT INVESTMENT OVERSEAS: AN INTERIM REPORT. Cambridge: At the University Press, 1967. 196 p.

> Study of effects of British foreign investment on the balance of trade and an analysis of a fifty-two-company survey.

_____. EFFECTS OF U. K. DIRECT INVESTMENT OVERSEAS: FINAL REPORT. Cambridge: At the University Press, 1968. 211 p.

> Report on the long-term and short-term balance of payments effects of British foreign investment. The net effects are accepted as positive if the transfer of technology and managerial know-how are taken into account. Based on a company survey.

Rubin, Seymor J. PRIVATE FOREIGN INVESTMENT: LEGAL AND ECONOMIC REALITIES. Baltimore, Md.: Johns Hopkins Press, 1956. 108 p.

> A collection of lectures dealing with problems of protecting U. S. investments abroad and suggesting protection against expropriation.

Sanden, Peter, and Vahlne, Jan-Erik. "The Growth Rates of Swedish Multinational Corporations." JOURNAL OF INTERNATIONAL BUSINESS STUDIES 5 (Spring 1974): 91-105.

Scholl, Russell B. "The International Investment Position of the United States: Developments in 1972." SURVEY OF CURRENT BUSINESS 53 (August 1973): 18-23.

Snyder, Earl. "Foreign Investment Protection: A Reasoned Approach." MICHIGAN LAW REVIEW 61 (April 1963): 1087-124.

> A critique of various investment guarantee programs in industrialized and developing countries. The inefficiency of these arrangements is contrasted with a multilateral insurance program. Snyder suggests a variety of such schemes.

Stone, Lawrence M. "United States Tax Policy toward Foreign Earnings of Multinational Corporations." GEORGE WASHINGTON LAW REVIEW 42 (March 1974): 557-67.

Swansbrough, Robert H. "The American Investor's View of Latin American Economic Nationalism." INTER-AMERICAN ECONOMIC AFFAIRS 26 (Winter 1972): 61-82.

Tsurumi, Yoshi. "Japanese Multinational Firms." JOURNAL OF WORLD TRADE LAW 7 (February 1973): 74-90.

> The author uses the product cycle theory to explain Japanese foreign investments, about 80 percent of which are controlled by the ten largest firms.

U. S. Commission on International Trade and Investment Policy. UNITED STATES INTERNATIONAL ECONOMIC POLICY IN AN INTERDEPENDENT WORLD. 3 vols. July 1971. Vol. 1, 1006 p.; vol. 2, 538 p.; vol. 3, 394 p.

> Papers submitted to the Commission and published in conjunction with the Commission's Report to the President (see the first item by Vernon, below).

U. S. Congress. House. Committee on Ways and Means. MULTINATIONALS: PERSPECTIVES ON TRADE AND TAXES. 93d Cong., 1st sess., 1973. 29 p.

> Prepared in connection with hearings on the subject of foreign trade and tariffs by the Congressional Research Service.

U. S. Congress. House. Joint Economic Committee. THE EURO-DOLLAR MARKET AND ITS PUBLIC POLICY IMPLICATIONS. 91st Cong., 2d sess. 1970.

U. S. Congress. Senate. Committee on Finance. Subcommittee on International Trade. IMPLICATIONS OF MULTINATIONAL FIRMS FOR WORLD TRADE AND LABOR: REPORT, FEBRUARY 1973, ON INVESTIGATION NO. 332-69, UNDER SECTION 332 OF THE TARIFF ACT OF 1930. 92d Cong., 1st sess., 1973. 930 p.

> Official description: "Discusses the implications of the MNCs on the balance of payments of the U. S. and selected host countries, and their effects on world trade, investment, and international finance; the implications of such concerns on the technology transfer, labor, and certain aspects of the legal issues involving their operation."

_____. MULTINATIONAL CORPORATIONS. HEARINGS. 93d Cong., 1st sess., February-March 1973. 481 p.

_____. MULTINATIONAL CORPORATIONS: A COMPENDIUM OF PAPERS. 93d Cong., 1st sess., 1973. 968 p.

> A collection of papers submitted to the subcommittee by invitation. Contains a summary of Department of Commerce, labor union, and business viewpoints, and contributions by major business associations.

U. S. Congress. Senate. Committee on Foreign Relations. Subcommittee on Multinational Corporations. MULTINATIONAL CORPORATIONS AND UNITED STATES FOREIGN POLICY: HEARINGS: PTS. 1-2, MARCH 20-APRIL 2, 1973, ON THE INTERNATIONAL TELEPHONE AND TELEGRAPH COMPANY AND CHILE, 1970-71, 2 pts. 93d Cong., 1st sess., 1973. 1092 p.

> Broad examination of the role of multinational corporations as an influence on U. S. foreign policy, focusing particularly on an investigation of assertions that ITT sought to enlist the cooperation of the U. S. government in their effort to prevent Dr. Salvador Allende Gossens from taking office as President of Chile in 1970.

_____. MULTINATIONAL CORPORATIONS AND UNITED STATES FOREIGN POLICY: HEARINGS: PT. 3, JULY 18-AUGUST 1, 1973, ON OVERSEAS PRIVATE INVESTMENT CORPORATION (OPIC). 93d Cong., 1st sess., 1973. 651 p.

_____. MULTINATIONAL CORPORATIONS AND UNITED STATES FOREIGN POLICY: HEARINGS: PT. 4, JANUARY 30, 1974, ON MULTINATIONAL PETROLEUM COMPANIES AND FOREIGN POLICY. 93d Cong., 2d sess., 1974. 214 p.

_____. WESTERN INVESTMENT IN COMMUNIST ECONOMIES: A SELECTED SURVEY ON ECONOMIC INTERDEPENDENCE. By John P. Hardt et al. 93d Cong., 2d sess. Washington, D.C.: Government Printing Office, 1974. 83 p.

U. S. Congress. Senate. Committee on Labor and Public Welfare. THE MULTINATIONAL CORPORATION AND THE NATIONAL INTEREST. By Robert Gilpin. 93d Cong., 1st sess. Washington, D.C.: Government Printing Office, 1973.

> Discusses the effect of outward investment on American labor, the balance of payments, and taxation. Suggests changes in U. S. tax laws and support of technological innovativeness.

U. S. Department of Commerce. Bureau of International Commerce. Office of International Investment. THE MULTINATIONAL CORPORATION, STUDIES ON U.S. FOREIGN INVESTMENT. Vol.1. January-February 1972. 74 p.

> Includes these three studies: (1) "Policy Aspects of Foreign Investment by U.S. Multinational Corporations," a staff study; (2) "Trends in Direct Investments Abroad by U. S. Multinational Corporations, 1960-1970," a staff study; (3) "U. S. Multinational Enterprises and the U. S. Economy," by Robert Stobaugh of the Harvard Business School.

_____. THE MULTINATIONAL CORPORATION, STUDIES IN U. S. FOREIGN INVESTMENT. Vol. II. April 1973. 82 p.

> Deals primarily with the motives of American business executives for investing abroad.

_____. POLICY ASPECTS OF FOREIGN INVESTMENT BY U. S. MULTINA-TIONAL CORPORATIONS. January 1972. 86 p.

> Treats the impact of MNCs on employment, transfer of technology, response to controls, balance of payments, and political impact.

_____. TRENDS IN DIRECT INVESTMENT ABROAD BY U. S. MULTINATIONAL CORPORATIONS 1960 TO 1970. 1972. 70 p.

U. S. Department of Commerce. Office of Foreign Direct Investment. FOR-EIGN DIRECT INVESTMENT PROGRAM. 1973. 60 p.

> Describes the regulations, rules, and instructions concerning invest-ments abroad by U. S. firms.

_____. FOREIGN DIRECT INVESTMENT PROGRAM, SELECTED STATISTICS. 1974. 20 p.

_____. GENERAL BULLETIN: INTERPRETIVE EXPLANATION OF THE FOR-EIGN DIRECT INVESTMENT REGULATIONS. 1973. 77 p.

> Gives examples of how to follow and implement the Foreign Direct Investment Regulations.

U. S. Federal Reserve System. Board of Governors. MULTINATIONAL BANKS
AND MANAGEMENT OF MONETARY POLICY IN THE UNITED STATES. AD-
DRESS. 1973. 110 p.

U. S. State Department. Bureau of Intelligence and Research. DISPUTES IN-
VOLVING U. S. FOREIGN INVESTMENT: JULY 1, 1971 THROUGH JULY 1,
1973, RECS-6. February 8, 1974. 57 p.

U. S. Tariff Commission. IMPLICATIONS OF MULTINATIONAL FIRMS FOR
WORLD TRADE AND INVESTMENT AND FOR U. S. TRADE AND LABOR,
REPORT TO THE COMMITTEE ON FINANCE OF THE U. S. SENATE AND ITS
SUBCOMMITTEE ON INTERNATIONAL TRADE. 1973. 930 p.

   According to Duane Kujawa, the report is "patently biased in favor
   of multinationals," but also "the most ambitious empirical study of
   the multinational enterprise ever attempted."

Vernon, Raymond. "The Economic Consequences of U. S. Foreign Direct Investment." In REPORT TO THE PRESIDENT SUBMITTED BY THE COMMISSION
ON INTERNATIONAL TRADE AND INVESTMENT POLICY. Vol. 1, pp. 929-
52. Washington, D.C.: Government Printing Office, 1971.

   Vernon states that although it is difficult to quantify the economic
   consequences of MNCs, these corporations are making positive contributions, given the transfer of technology and other effects on the
   economies of LDCs.

_____. U. S. CONTROLS OF FOREIGN DIRECT INVESTMENTS--A REEVALU-
ATION. New York: Financial Research Foundation, 1969. 64 p.

   A discussion of the balance of payments issue and the shortcomings
   of the arguments used in the Hufbauer-Adler report (above).

_____. "U. S. Direct Investment in Canada: Consequences for the U. S.
Economy." JOURNAL OF FINANCE 28 (May 1973): 407-18.

Wert, Frank S. "A Product Cycle Model of the Balance of Payments Impact of
U. S. Based Multinationalism." JOURNAL OF INTERNATIONAL BUSINESS
STUDIES 4 (Fall 1973): 51-64.

Wheelock, Keith. "What Is the Direction of U. S. Political Risk Insurance?"
COLUMBIA JOURNAL OF WORLD BUSINESS 8 (Summer 1973): 59-67.

   Emphasis on U. S. investments in Latin America and the role of
   the Overseas Private Investment Corporation (OPIC).

Chapter 9

SPECIAL PROBLEMS OF DEVELOPMENT

GENERAL STUDIES

Adler, John H., ed. CAPITAL MOVEMENTS AND ECONOMIC DEVELOP-
MENT. New York: St. Martin's Press, 1967. 532 p.

Proceedings from a conference held by the International Economic
Association. The papers relevant here are by Rosenstein-Rodan on
the philosophy of foreign investment, Pazos on the role of the MNC
in development, Kafka on the economic effects of capital imports,
Rhomberg on MNCs and exchange rates in the LDCs, and Thomas
on the history of MNCs to 1913.

Ady, Peter H., ed. PRIVATE FOREIGN INVESTMENT AND THE DEVELOPING
WORLD. Foreword by Dudley Seers. New York: Praeger, 1971. 282 p.

The book is a collection of papers from a conference arranged by
the Society for International Development. Topics discussed in the
papers and the summary are: the effects of foreign investment on
the investing country and the host country, and the effects of taxation on overseas investment and joint ventures. The approach is
pragmatic rather than theoretical. Ady, Wells, Streeten, and
Wionczek are among the contributors.

Aharoni, Yair. "How to Market a Country." COLUMBIA JOURNAL OF
WORLD BUSINESS 1 (Spring 1966): 41-49.

The article is addressed to governments in developing countries and
states that, because risks are minimal the usual costly concessions
to investors are unnecessary. He suggests instead a complex five-
point incentive program.

Baran, Paul A. THE POLITICAL ECONOMY OF GROWTH. New York:
Monthly Review Press, 1957. 308 p.

The author, a noted Marxist scholar, gives a general account of
the causes of underdevelopment, the exploitative relationship between the rich and poor countries, and the crucial role of direct
investment in that relationship.

Bergsten, C. Fred. "Coming Investment Wars?" FOREIGN AFFAIRS 53 (October 1974): 135-52.

Blanchard, Daniel S. "The Threat to the U. S. Private Investment in Latin America." JOURNAL OF INTERNATIONAL LAW AND ECONOMICS 5 (January 1971): 221-37.

A study of expropriation policies. The author recommends joint ventures as the best safeguard.

Bronfenbrenner, Martin. "The Appeals of Confiscation in Economic Development." ECONOMIC DEVELOPMENT AND CULTURAL CHANGE 3 (1954-55): 201-18.

Three models of confiscation are used to show that confiscation is a rational strategy. Therefore, a policy of neo-isolationism is recommended.

Byres, T. J., ed. FOREIGN RESOURCES AND ECONOMIC DEVELOPMENT: A SYMPOSIUM ON THE REPORT OF THE PEARSON COMMISSION. Portland, Oreg.: International Scholarly Book Service; London: Cass, 1972. 199 p.

Responses to the report entitled "Partners in Development," prepared by the Commission on International Development under the chairmanship of Lester B. Pearson.

Cohen, Benjamin J. THE QUESTION OF IMPERIALISM: THE POLITICAL ECONOMY OF DOMINANCE AND DEPENDENCE. New York: Basic Books, 1973. 280 p.

A review of classical and modern Marxist and non-Marxist theories, and a lengthy discussion of the issues of dependence and exploitation as they relate to direct foreign investment.

Drucker, Peter F. "Multinationals and Developing Countries: Myths and Realities." FOREIGN AFFAIRS 53 (October 1974): 121-34.

Dunning, John H. "Multinational Enterprises and Trade Flows of Less Developed Countries." WORLD DEVELOPMENT 2 (February 1974): 131-38.

Duren, Albrecht. "Multinational Companies as a Political Problem." WORLD TODAY 28 (November 1972): 473-82.

Translated and revised from EUROPA-ARCHIV.

Einhorn, Jessica Pernitz. EXPROPRIATION POLITICS. Lexington, Mass.: Lexington Books, 1974. 148 p.

A study of the International Petroleum Company case in Peru and its relation to Nixon's 1972 policy statement on expropriation without compensation. Concentrates on the administrative and political issues involved on both sides.

Evans, Peter B. "National Autonomy and Economic Development: Critical Perspectives on Multinational Corporations in Poor Countries." INTERNATIONAL ORGANIZATION 25 (Summer 1971): 675-92.

An argument against the tenet that international integration is unquestionably desirable. Uses theories from a wide variety of disciplines to criticize the possible consequences of MNCs for the development process.

Falero, Frank, Jr. "Foreign Investment and the Balance of Payments: Some Negative Implications for Developing Countries." INTER-AMERICAN ECONOMIC AFFAIRS 28 (Autumn 1974): 77-85.

Farmer, Richard N. BENEVOLENT AGGRESSION: THE NECESSARY IMPACT OF THE ADVANCED NATIONS ON INDIGENOUS PEOPLES. New York: David McKay, 1972. 337 p.

The author argues that the mere size of firms and their ultrasophistication undermine economic growth through foreign investment. See especially chapters 13 and 14.

Friedmann, Wolfgang G., and Beguin, Jean-Pierre. JOINT INTERNATIONAL BUSINESS VENTURES IN DEVELOPING COUNTRIES: CASE STUDIES AND ANALYSIS OF RECENT TRENDS. With the collaboration of James Peterson and Alain Pellet. New York: Columbia University Press, 1971. 448 p.

This sequel to Friedmann and Kalmanoff's JOINT INTERNATIONAL BUSINESS VENTURES (cited in chapter 3) presents sixteen case studies of American, Canadian, and European investments in Africa, Asia, Latin America, and India. The industries covered are petroleum, iron, copper mining, food, engineering goods, chemicals, fertilizers, textiles, and office machines. There is a concluding essay about joint ventures.

Furtado, Celso. OBSTACLES TO DEVELOPMENT IN LATIN AMERICA. Garden City, N.Y.: Anchor Books, 1970. 204 p.

The book is both a general study of U. S. investment in Latin America and an analysis of economic conditions in Brazil. The author is a critic of the "underdevelopment" and "dependency" theories.

Gabriel, Peter P. "The Multinational Corporation and Economic Development." In DEVELOPMENT TODAY: A NEW LOOK AT U. S. RELATIONS WITH POOR COUNTRIES, edited by Robert E. Hunter and John E. Rielly, pp. 116-30. New York: Praeger, 1972.

The author argues against full ownership in developing countries on the grounds that it is not beneficial. He proposes instead "services" and "functions" which can be transferred and paid for individually.

Groves, Roderick T. "Expropriation in Latin America: Some Observations." INTER-AMERICAN ECONOMIC AFFAIRS 23 (Winter 1969): 47-66.

Sees the high visibility and controversial nature of certain firms as major causes of expropriations.

Helleiner, G. K. "Manufacturing for Export, Multinational Firms and Development." WORLD DEVELOPMENT 1 (July 1973): 13-21.

Hirschman, Albert O. A BIAS FOR HOPE: ESSAYS ON DEVELOPMENT AND LATIN AMERICA. New Haven: Yale University Press, 1971. 374 p.

Includes several essays on direct investment including his seminal piece on "How to Divest in Latin America and Why," which spells out the reasons for the failure of multinationals to foster economic growth in Latin America.

Johnson, Harry G. "The Multinational Corporation as an Agency of Economic Development: Some Explanatory Observations, and a reply by Albert O. Hirschman." In THE WIDENING GAP, edited by Barbara Ward, et al., pp. 324-56. New York: Columbia University Press, 1971.

Argues that the MNCs profit motive can serve the national interest of the host if only the role and function of the MNC can be clearly defined.

Katzenbach, Nicholas De B. "The Multinational Corporation and World Economic Development." AMERICAN JOURNAL OF INTERNATIONAL LAW 66 (September 1972): 14-22.

Katzenbach presided over a roundtable discussion sponsored by the American Society of International Law.

Knudsen, Harald. EXPROPRIATION OF FOREIGN PRIVATE INVESTMENTS IN LATIN AMERICA. Oslo: Universitetsforlaget, 1974. 356 p.

The author presents a sophisticated theoretical framework to explain the propensity to expropriate on the basis of national characteristics, political risk factors, and compensation constraints. Part II tests the model with empirical data from a variety of Latin American states.

Landau, Henry. "Direct Foreign Investment in Developing Countries." JOURNAL OF LAW AND ECONOMIC DEVELOPMENT 4 (Fall 1969): 182-206.

Discusses the controls and incentives for foreign direct investment in developing countries.

Loehr, William. "The Uneasy Case for Foreign Private Investment in Developing Countries." DENVER JOURNAL OF INTERNATIONAL LAW AND POLICY,
2 (Fall 1972): 179-98.

Malmgren, Harald B. TRADE AND INVESTMENT RELATIONS BETWEEN DE-
VELOPED AND DEVELOPING COUNTRIES: A REVIEW OF THE STATE OF
KNOWLEDGE. Overseas Development Council Occasional Paper no. 2, Wash-
ington, D.C.: Overseas Development Council, 1971. 54 p.

May, Ronald S. "Direct Investment in the Less-Developed Countries: British
and American Investments 1958-64." JOURNAL OF DEVELOPMENT STUDIES
4 (April 1968): 386-423.

An analysis of the variations among countries and industries regarding return on investments.

Meier, Gerald M. THE INTERNATIONAL ECONOMICS OF DEVELOPMENT:
THEORY AND POLICY. New York: Harper and Row, 1968. 338 p.

Chapter 6, "Private Foreign Investment" (pages 131-61) is an analysis
of the legal and economic problems of foreign investment in the
developing countries and their attending governmental policies.
The author argues that each case must be judged and decided on
its own merits.

_____. "Legal-Economic Problems of Private Foreign Investment in Developing
Countries." UNIVERSITY OF CHICAGO LAW REVIEW 33 (Spring 1966): 463-
93.

An analysis of host country policy effects on private investment
and of the costs and benefits of that investment to developing
countries. Host country policies, according to the author, determine the effects on distribution of income and the balance of payments. Until now, failure to circumscribe the common interest
areas of companies and countries has resulted in losses for both
sides.

Mueller, Ronald E., and Morgenstern, Richard. "Multinational Corporations
and Balance of Payments Impacts in LDCs: An Economic Analysis of Export
Pricing Behavior." KYKLOS, April 1974, pp. 304-21.

A more detailed version of this article is entitled "The Multinational
Corporation and the Underdevelopment of the Third World" (TRIME-
STRE ECONOMICO, January-April 1974). Mueller and Morgenstern
conclude that almost 75 percent of foreign-owned MNCs sell to
their own subsidiaries, and that these firms contribute less to Latin
American exports than other MNCs.

Myrdal, Gunnar. "A Contribution Towards a More Realistic Theory of Economic
Growth and Development." MONDES EN DEVELOPPEMENT 1 (1973): 23-33.

Organization for Economic and Cultural Development. INVESTING IN DEVEL-
OPING COUNTRIES: FACILITIES FOR THE PROMOTION OF FOREIGN PRIVATE
INVESTMENT IN THE DEVELOPING COUNTRIES. Rev. ed. Paris: 1972.
110 p.

> An updated version of a 1970 publication which surveys the incen-
> tive measures in the developed countries and some international
> schemes designed to encourage investments in the developing world.

Organization for Economic and Cultural Development. Executive Directorate.
Library. PRIVATE FOREIGN INVESTMENTS AND THE IMPACT IN THE DE-
VELOPING COUNTRIES. Paris: 1973. 265 p.

> Contains a special thirty-four-page annotated bibliography.

Reuber, Grant L., et al. PRIVATE FOREIGN INVESTMENT IN DEVELOPMENT.
Oxford: Clarendon Press, 1973. 371 p.

> A lucid defense of direct investment in the LDCs. A very compre-
> hensive survey of published data and monographs concerning the
> behavior of foreign firms and the consequences of foreign invest-
> ments. After a brief consideration of the negative consequences,
> the authors conclude that investments in LDCs have been beneficial
> in terms of capital, employment, and the transfer of technology.

Stamp, Maxwell. "Has Foreign Capital Still a Role to Play in Development?"
WORLD DEVELOPMENT 2 (February 1974): 123-29.

Stauffer, Robert B. NATION BUILDING IN A GLOBAL ECONOMY: THE
ROLE OF THE MULTINATIONAL CORPORATION. Sage Professional Papers in
Comparative Politics, vol. 4. Beverly Hills, Calif. and London: Sage Publi-
cations, 1973. 47 p.

> The author considers especially the effect of MNCs on the political
> economy of the third world and the unequal power relationship be-
> tween LDCs and MNCs.

Streeten, Paul. THE FRONTIERS OF DEVELOPMENT STUDIES. New York:
John Wiley and Sons, 1972. 513 p.

> A collection of twenty-seven essays published previously and col-
> lected here under four general headings: Part I deals with develop-
> ment theory and policy; part II concerns the international movement
> of capital, money, and goods; part III deals with projects and
> technology; part IV concerns the dominions. The general theme
> is a critique of neoclassical economics and the assumptions it makes
> about the positive and negative factors affecting development.
> Direct investment is an integral part of Streeten's writings on the
> subject.

_____. "The Multinational Enterprise and the Theory of Development Policy." WORLD DEVELOPMENT 1 (October 1973): 1-14.

A chapter from the forthcoming book entitled ECONOMIC ANALY-SIS AND THE MULTINATIONAL ENTERPRISE, edited by John H. Dunning.

Streeten, Paul, and Lall, Sanjaya. SUMMARY OF METHODS AND FINDINGS OF A STUDY OF PRIVATE FOREIGN MANUFACTURING INVESTMENT IN SIX LESS-DEVELOPED COUNTRIES. 3 pts. Geneva: United Nations Conference on Trade and Development (UNCTAD), 1973. 89 p.

A summary of six country studies commissioned by UNCTAD on Kenya, Jamaica, India, Iran, Columbia, and Malaysia. The study consists of three reports on the methodology employed, governmental policies, and the main findings of the country studies.

Turner, Louis. MULTINATIONAL COMPANIES AND THE THIRD WORLD. New York: Hill and Wang, 1973. 294 p.

See annotation for this item in chapter 17.

United Nations. Department of Economic and Social Affairs. FOREIGN INVESTMENT IN DEVELOPING COUNTRIES (E 4446). 1968. 61 p.

A favorable report on the contribution of foreign investment to development. Suggests policies to further this trend.

Vernon, Raymond. "The American Corporation in Underdeveloped Areas." In THE CORPORATION IN MODERN SOCIETY, edited by Edward S. Mason, pp. 236-59. New York: Atheneum, 1972.

Vernon argues for increased governmental participation which would be of benefit to the host country and not detrimental to American enterprise.

Weinberg, William R. "The Costs of Foreign Private Investment." CIVILISATIONS 21, nos. 2-3 (1971): 207-19.

Considers costs to developing countries.

Williams, Shelton L. "Direct Foreign Investment in the LDCs: A Debate Renewed and Reviewed." ROCKY MOUNTAIN SOCIAL SCIENCE JOURNAL 10 (April 1973): 71-83.

Zenoff, David B. PRIVATE ENTERPRISE IN THE DEVELOPING COUNTRIES. Englewood Cliffs, N.J.: Prentice-Hall, 1969. 282 p.

Presents thirteen case studies of business experience in LDCs.

Zink, Dolph W. THE POLITICAL RISKS FOR MULTINATIONAL ENTERPRISE IN DEVELOPING COUNTRIES, WITH A CASE STUDY OF PERU. New York: Praeger, 1973. 185 p.

> Presents a history of direct investment in LDCs and the outlook for U. S. direct investment in Peru, based on the author's own system of risk assessment.

THE RADICAL CRITIQUE

Dos Santos, Theotonio. EL NUEVO CARACTER DE LA DEPENDENCIA. Cuaderno no. 10. Santiago: Centro de Estudios Socio-Economicos, Universidad de Chile, 1968. 98 p.

> A basic statement describing dependency theory.

_____. "The Structure of Dependence." AMERICAN ECONOMIC REVIEW, PAPERS AND PROCEEDINGS 60 (May 1970): 231-36.

> A basic outline of dependency theory in English. Short but very succinct in its exposition of the domestic and international implications of dependency and inequality.

Frank, Andre Gunder. CAPITALISM AND UNDERDEVELOPMENT IN LATIN AMERICA: HISTORICAL STUDIES OF CHILE AND BRAZIL. Rev. ed. New York: Monthly Review Press, 1969. 344 p.

> Two parts of this book are of special interest: the role of direct investment in Brazil's underdevelopment, and the section entitled "Foreign Investment in Latin America," a social and economic analysis (pages 281-318).

_____. "The Development of Underdevelopment." In IMPERIALISM AND UNDERDEVELOPMENT: A READER, edited by Robert I. Rhodes, pp. 4-17. New York: Monthly Review Press, 1970.

> A condensed version of Frank's thesis concerning Latin American underdevelopment as a consequence of colonialism.

_____. LATIN AMERICA: UNDERDEVELOPMENT OR REVOLUTION: ESSAYS ON THE DEVELOPMENT OF UNDERDEVELOPMENT AND THE IMMEDIATE ENEMY. New York: Monthly Review Press, 1970. 409 p.

> Collection of Frank's essays--some new, some published previously-- on social and economic conditions in Latin America and the role of direct foreign investment.

Girvan, Norman. COPPER IN CHILE: A STUDY IN CONFLICT BETWEEN CORPORATE AND NATIONAL ECONOMY. Kingston, Jamaica: Institute of Social and Economic Research, University of the West Indies, 1972. 86 p.

A study of copper industry and trade and the role of American investments in Chile.

Hart, Judith. AID AND LIBERATION: A SOCIALIST STUDY OF AID POLICIES. London: V. Gollancz, 1973. 287 p.

The author, a former minister of Overseas Development in Great Britain, examines the role of direct foreign investment in aid policies and other topics. See especially "Aid and the Highest Stage of Capitalism" and "The Role of Private Profit."

Hymer, Stephen. "The Multinational Corporations and the Law of Uneven Development." In ECONOMICS AND WORLD ORDER FROM THE 1970'S TO THE 1990'S, edited by Jagdish N. Bhagwati, pp. 113-40. New York: Macmillan, 1972.

Taking as his point of departure the vertical integration of multinational firms, Hymer argues that developing countries will remain at the bottom of the pyramid and will be unable to change the existing division of labor between developing and industrialized nations.

Hymer, Stephen, and Resnick, S. "Interaction between the Government and the Private Sector in Underdeveloped Countries." In ECONOMIC DEVELOPMENT AND STRUCTURAL CHANGE, edited by Jan Stewart, pp. 155-80. Edinburgh: Edinburgh University Press, 1969.

The authors develop a theoretical model of government tax rates and expenditures designed to describe bargaining between firms and governments.

Ivanov, I. "International Corporations and the 'Third World'." INTERNATIONAL AFFAIRS (Moscow), August 1974, pp. 31-42.

Lazar, Arpad von. "Multinational Enterprises and Latin-American Integration: A Sociopolitical View." JOURNAL OF INTER-AMERICAN STUDIES 11 (January 1969): 111-28.

The author argues that Latin American integration as conceived and planned now would "essentially benefit the already existing large foreign international corporations." He presents a thorough discussion of political support of and opposition to the MNC.

Mueller, Ronald E. "The Multinational Corporation and the Underdevelopment of the Third World." In THE POLITICAL ECONOMY OF DEVELOPMENT AND UNDERDEVELOPMENT, edited by Charles K. Wilber, pp. 124-51. New York: Random House, 1973.

Surveys and rejects the claims made by MNCs about their contributions to development. Mueller argues that MNCs contribute to

the impoverishment of the Third World. He outlines some measures
to increase the bargaining power of the Third World countries.

Murray, Robin. "Underdevelopment, International Firms and the International
Division of Labor." In TOWARDS A NEW WORLD ECONOMY, compiled by
Society for International Development, pp. 160-247. Rotterdam: University
of Rotterdam Press, 1972.

Argues that international capitalism structures economic activity in
a way that is detrimental to developing countries. MNCs are the
most important instruments for creating and maintaining this inequality among the regions of the world.

O'Connor, James. "International Corporations and Economic Underdevelopment."
SCIENCE AND SOCIETY 34 (Spring 1970): 42-60.

The author argues that direct investment and corporate policies, as
well as their balance-of-payments effects, are detrimental to development. He does not consider regional integration to be an
adequate antidote.

Rhodes, Robert I., ed. IMPERIALISM AND UNDERDEVELOPMENT: A READER.
New York: Monthly Review Press, 1970. 416 p.

A series of critical articles describing the negative consequences
of direct foreign investment for developing economies, based on
the theory that colonialism created underdevelopment. Articles
by Magdoff on the American empire and the U. S. economy, Reno
on aluminum in the Caribbean, Frank on the consequences of imperialism for Brazil, O'Connor on the meaning of imperialism,
Arrighi on labor aristocracies in developing countries, and Schmitt
on Indonesia.

Sunkel, Oswaldo. "Big Business and 'Dependencia'." FOREIGN AFFAIRS 50
(April 1972): 517-31.

The author makes the case that U. S. MNCs do indeed act in the
interest of U. S. foreign policy and that the few economic benefits
which accrue to the developing countries are too high a price to
pay for dependence. A critique of free trade policy.

_____. "National Development Policy and External Dependence in Latin
America." JOURNAL OF DEVELOPMENT STUDIES 6 (1969-70): 23-48.

A clear and concise exposition of the "dependencia" theory and
the role that private investment plays in maintaining external dependence. The author does not reject all forms of investments,
but wishes to propose new forms of cooperation.

_____. "Transnational Capitalism and National Disintegration in Latin America."
SOCIAL AND ECONOMIC STUDIES (Kingston; special issue entitled "Dependence

and Underdevelopment in the New World and the Old," edited by Norman
Girvan), 22 (March 1973): 132-76.

> Analyzes the role of the MNC within the framework of develop-
> ment and underdevelopment, Latin American dependence, and
> marginality within the capitalist system.

_____. "Underdevelopment in Latin America: Toward the Year 2000." In
ECONOMICS AND WORLD ORDER FROM THE 1970's TO THE 1990's, edited
by Jagdish N. Bhagwati, pp. 199-231. New York: Macmillan, 1972.

> A critique of past development policies which, in the author's
> view, have produced the present state of dependence, and an out-
> line for a new policy for national development.

Wolff, Richard D. "Modern Imperialism: The View from the Metropolis."
AMERICAN ECONOMIC REVIEW 60 (May 1970): 225-30.

> The author defines imperialism as a network of controls which are
> directed by one economy--its firms and its government--over an-
> other. The methods of control employed are colonialism, MNCs,
> and foreign aid.

Chapter 10

HOST COUNTRIES AND AREAS: CASE STUDIES

AFRICA

Ahooja, Krishna. "Investment Legislation in Africa." JOURNAL OF WORLD TRADE LAW 2 (September-October 1968): 495-520.

> The author makes a case for harmonization of laws governing foreign investments in Africa. Includes a description of existing laws.

Bostock, Mark, and Harvey, Charles, eds. ECONOMIC INDEPENDENCE AND ZAMBIAN COPPER: A CASE STUDY OF FOREIGN INVESTMENT. New York: Praeger, 1972. 274 p.

> The essays cover the economic importance of the copper industry, as well as the political interest groups and labor union activities which surround the copper issue in Zambia.

Courtney, Winifred, and Davis, Jennifer. NAMBIA: UNITED STATES CORPORATE INVOLVEMENT. Published in cooperation with the Programme to Combat Racism, World Council of Churches. New York: Africa Fund, 1972. 32 p.

Ekundare, R. O. "The Political Economy of Private Investment in Nigeria." JOURNAL OF MODERN AFRICAN STUDIES 10 (May 1972): 37-56.

> The author thinks that developing host countries can, by means of correct protective policies, balance the negative consequences of direct foreign investments. Gives a survey of existing investments in Nigeria and the laws governing them.

Fordwor, K. Donkoh. "Direct Foreign Investment: A Policy for Ghana." COOPERATION CANADA, March-April 1973, pp. 20-26.

> Text in both English and French.

Humphrey, David H. "Private Foreign Investment in Malawi: A Study of the Sugar Corporation of Malawi." AFRICAN REVIEW 2, no. 3 (1972): 283-97.

Jackson, Richard A., ed. THE MULTINATIONAL CORPORATION AND SOCIAL POLICY. New York: Praeger, for the Council on Religion and International Affairs, 1974. 113 p.

A study of General Motors in South Africa.

Killick, Tony. "The Benefits of Foreign Direct Investment and Its Alternatives: An Empirical Exploration." JOURNAL OF DEVELOPMENT STUDIES 9 (January 1973): 301-16.

Using data on diamond mining activities in Sierra Leone, the author examines the benefits derived from foreign investments and compares these with a more indigenous form of production.

Killick, Tony, and During, R. W. "A Structural Approach to the Balance of Payments of a Low-Income Country." JOURNAL OF DEVELOPMENT STUDIES 5 (July 1969): 274-98.

Examines the contributions of the diamond, iron ore, and bauxite sectors to the balance of payments in Sierra Leone.

Loehr, William, and Raichur, Satish. "A Decade of United States Investment Activity in Africa: Implications for Economic Development." AFRICA TODAY 20 (Winter 1973): 45-58.

McLaughlin, Russell U. FOREIGN INVESTMENT AND DEVELOPMENT IN LIBERIA. New York: Praeger, 1966. 217 p.

A description of the contribution of foreign investment to the Liberian economy.

May, Ranald S. "Direct Overseas Investment in Nigeria, 1953-63." SCOTTISH JOURNAL OF POLITICAL ECONOMY 12 (November 1965): 243-66.

A study of British firms and their interactions with the Nigerian government, as well as the positive effects of British investment.

Mohammed, D. "Private Foreign Investment in Ethiopia (1950-1968)." JOURNAL OF ETHIOPIAN STUDIES 7 (July 1969): 53-78.

A survey description of foreign investment in Ethiopia with special emphasis on the textile and sugar industries.

Mummery, David R. THE PROTECTION OF INTERNATIONAL PRIVATE INVESTMENT: NIGERIA AND THE WORLD COMMUNITY. New York: Praeger, 1968. 220 p.

A general discussion of the problems involved in protecting foreign investment in developing countries. Gives a survey of various protective programs and their political and administrative implications.

Neers, Peter. "Selected Aspects of Tanzania's Policies on Foreign Investment." WORLD DEVELOPMENT 2 (February 1974): 139-44.

Pelissier, Raymond F. "American Private Enterprise in South Africa." CALIFORNIA MANAGEMENT REVIEW 14 (Summer 1972): 6-12.

> Some emphasis on problems resulting from South Africa's apartheid policy.

Proehl, Paul O. FOREIGN ENTERPRISE IN NIGERIA: LAWS AND POLICIES. Chapel Hill: University of North Carolina Press, 1965. 262 p.

> Mainly concerned with the "climate" for investment, the book also provides an introduction to conflicts between multinational companies' interests and national interest.

Taylor, Wayne Chatfield. THE FIRESTONE OPERATIONS IN LIBERIA. Washington, D.C.: National Planning Association, 1956. 140 p.

> Reports on a program by Firestone in Liberia by which the company helps to establish locally owned rubber plants. Two consequences of this policy, among others, are that Firestone has increased its own supply of rubber and reduced political risks, since many of the owners are members of the Liberian political elite.

United Nations. INVESTMENT LAWS AND REGULATIONS IN AFRICA. 1968. 79 p.

> Describes investment laws, regulations, and guarantees in thirty-one African countries.

United Nations. Economic Commission for Africa. THE MULTINATIONAL CORPORATION IN AFRICA (E/CN.14/INR/186). 1971. 35 p.

Vilakazi, Absolom L. "Non-Governmental Agencies and Their Role in Development in Africa: A Case Study." AFRICAN STUDIES REVIEW 13 (September 1970): 169-202.

> A case study of Zambia. The author prefers foreign investment to foreign aid, since technical and managerial skills are transferred and reinvestment is more likely than in the case of long-term foreign aid.

ASIA AND THE PACIFIC

General

Abeysinghe, A. M. Ariya. "Foreign Investment in Industry in Ceylon." INDUSTRIAL CEYLON 12 (March 1972): 51-63.

Drysdale, Peter, ed. DIRECT FOREIGN INVESTMENT IN ASIA AND THE PACIFIC. Toronto: University of Toronto Press, 1972. 360 p.

> Based on the Third Pacific Trade and Development Conference in Sydney, 1970. A series of papers of generally high quality dealing primarily with economic rather than the political issues. Contributions include Brash on Australia, H. G. Johnson on the general issues, Hymer on U. S. investments abroad, Safarian on the problems of host countries, Kindleberger on economic development, Komiya on Japan, Hamada on Japanese investments abroad, Sadli on Indonesia, Viravan on Thailand, Yang on Korea, Virata on the Philippines, Wionczek on Mexico, Perkins on the balance of payments effects in the area, and Helen Hughes on policies toward direct investment in the area.

Hughes, Helen, and Seng, You Poh, eds. FOREIGN INVESTMENT AND INDUSTRIALIZATION IN SINGAPORE. Madison: University of Wisconsin Press, 1969. 226 p.

> Eight papers showing that foreign investment is welcome and effective in Singapore.

"Japanese in Thailand: An Economic Fact of Life." BANGKOK BANK MONTHLY REVIEW 15 (September 1974): 568-78.

> Discusses Thai dependence on Japan in matters of trade and the dominant Japanese investment presence there.

Kapoor, Ashok. FOREIGN INVESTMENTS IN ASIA: A SURVEY OF PROBLEMS AND PROSPECTS IN THE 1970s. With the assistance of James E. Cotten. Princeton, N.J.: Darwin, 1972. 198 p.

> Based on interviews with American businessmen in Asian countries. The factors considered are various aspects of the investment "climate" such as governmental policies, ownership preferences, and some political problems. Includes a chapter on China.

Kim, Seung Hee. FOREIGN CAPITAL FOR ECONOMIC DEVELOPMENT: A KOREAN CASE STUDY. Foreword by Thomas M. Franck. New York: Praeger, 1970. 206 p.

> A discussion of past performance and future needs of foreign investments, as well as the role of the Korean government.

Nair, C. V. Devan. "Developing Countries in Asia and Foreign Investment." JAPAN QUARTERLY 21 (October-December 1974): 356-64.

Panglaykim, J. "Domestication of Multinational Corporations and Southeast Asia." INDONESIAN QUARTERLY 1 (January 1973): 27-37.

> Based on a conference paper.

Renouf, Alan. "Private Investments in Asian and Pacific Countries." AUSTRA-
LIAN FOREIGN AFFAIRS RECORD 45 (August 1974): 524-29.

An address which touches on some foreign policy aspects of investment.

Schreiber, Jordan C. U. S. CORPORATE INVESTMENT IN TAIWAN. New
York: Dunellen, 1970. 133 p.

A management study which investigates the financing, productline
policies, repatriation of capital, and investment decision-making
process of American firms in Taiwan. Some discussion of potential
political conflict.

Tin, Eileen Lim Poh, ed. MULTINATIONAL CORPORATIONS AND THEIR
IMPLICATIONS FOR SOUTHEAST ASIA. Singapore: Institute of Southeast
Asian Studies, 1973. 140 p.

Papers and proceedings of a seminar organized by the Institute of
Southeast Asian Studies in Singapore, December 10, 1972.

INDIA

Baranson, Jack. MANUFACTURING PROBLEMS IN INDIA: THE CUMMINS
DIESEL EXPERIENCE. Syracuse, N.Y.: Syracuse University Press, 1967. 146 p.

An examination of the technical and commercial adjustments of an
Indian affiliate. Harry G. Johnson writes in the introduction:
"Baranson shows that...the policy of development by industrialization directed at the national market and implemented by import-
substitution policies which thus far dominated both development
theory and planning practice, has been based on a mythology of
industry."

Kapoor, Astok. INTERNATIONAL BUSINESS NEGOTIATIONS: A STUDY IN
INDIA. New York: New York University Press, 1970. 361 p.

A study of a negotiation process in a developing nation which
describes the various dimensions of the investment process for firms
and countries alike. The negative outcome of the negotiation is
analyzed. Improvements for the future are suggested.

Kidron, Michael. FOREIGN INVESTMENT IN INDIA. London: Oxford University Press, 1965. 368 p.

Includes a historical review. Analyzes official Indian policies towards foreign investment in relation to such issues as the transfer
of technology, planning, and the labor market.

Kurian, K. Matthew. IMPACT OF FOREIGN CAPITAL ON INDIAN ECON-
OMY. New Delhi: People's Publishing House, 1966. 354 p.

A critical analysis of the effects of foreign investment which recommends tighter supervision and control.

Kust, Matthew J. FOREIGN ENTERPRISE IN INDIA: LAWS AND POLICIES. Chapel Hill: University of North Carolina Press, 1964. 498 p.

Describes the legal framework for investment and the protection of property, the regulations of industry, taxation, and labor in India.

Markensten, Klas. FOREIGN INVESTMENT AND DEVELOPMENT: SWEDISH COMPANIES IN INDIA. Lund: Studentlitteratur, 1972. 295 p.

Written from the perspective of Indian national objectives, this book is an outline, based on a cost-benefit analysis, of the positive and negative effects of foreign investments in India. Their positive contribution to development is questioned.

Singhal, Harish K. "Taxing for Development: Incentives Affecting Foreign Investment in India." HARVARD INTERNATIONAL LAW JOURNAL 14 (Winter 1973): 50-88.

A thorough-going analysis of the tax policies and the incentives for foreign investment in India.

Srivastava, Prem Kumar. FOREIGN COLLABORATION IN INDIAN INDUSTRY. Agra: Shiva Lal Agarwala, 1967. 256 p.

A study of joint ventures in India. Provides a listing of the firms involved, as well as a discussion of legal provisions and governmental policies.

Venu, S. "The Multinational Corporation: An Indian Balance Sheet." JOURNAL OF BUSINESS POLICY 3 (Winter 1972-73): 8-15.

JAPAN

Ballon, Robert J., and Lee, Eugene H., eds. FOREIGN INVESTMENT IN JAPAN. Tokyo and Palo Alto, Calif.: Sophia University, in cooperation with Kodansha International, 1972. 340 p.

The book contains a lengthy discussion of the impermeability of the Japanese system. In addition, it gives an overview of Japanese enterprises abroad and the management aspect of these foreign operations. Its concluding section consists of four studies of foreign enterprises which have entered the Japanese economy.

Henderson, Dan F. FOREIGN ENTERPRISE IN JAPAN: LAWS AND POLICIES. American Society of International Law, Studies in Foreign Investment and Economic Development, no. 5. Chapel Hill: University of North Carolina Press,

1973. 574 p.

A well-researched study which covers the past and present extent
of foreign investment and the political environment for it, and
gives a description of the Japanese business environment. The
second half of the book presents the legal environment for MNCs
and a lengthy account of the legal problems they face.

Okita, Saburo, and Miki, Takeo. "Treatment of Foreign Capital: A Case
Study for Japan." In CAPITAL MOVEMENTS AND ECONOMIC DEVELOPMENT,
edited by John H. Adler, pp. 139-86. With the assistance of Paul W. Kuznets.
New York: St. Martin's Press, 1967.

A survey of Japanese investment policies and business behavior.
Japanese ability to learn and adopt new technologies and take
substantial risks are seen as the major reasons for their success.

Ozaki, Robert S. THE CONTROL OF IMPORTS AND FOREIGN CAPITAL IN
JAPAN. New York: Praeger, 1972. 309 p.

A review of the legal and extra-legal restrictions on the import of
goods and capital into Japan, as well as an account of its liberalization. Includes documents.

AUSTRALIA AND NEW ZEALAND

Australia. Bureau of Census and Statistics. OVERSEAS INVESTMENT 1970-71.
1972. 59 p.

Australia. Parliament. Senate. Select Committee on Foreign Ownership and
Control of Australian Resources. REPORT NO. 1, OCTOBER 1972 (Parliamentary
Paper no. 216, 1972). 1973. 23 p.

Australia. Treasury. OVERSEAS INVESTMENT IN AUSTRALIA, May 1972
(Treasury Economic Paper, no. 1). 1972. 149 p.

Brash, Donald T. "American Investment and Australian Sovereignty." In CON-
TEMPORARY AUSTRALIA: STUDIES IN HISTORY, POLITICS, AND ECONOMICS,
edited by Richard A. Preston. Durham, N.C.: Duke University Press, 1969.
587 p.

Although the author points to economic benefits accruing from foreign investment, he feels that governmental policy to control and
steer that activity has not been effective enough.

_____. AMERICAN INVESTMENT IN AUSTRALIAN INDUSTRY. London:
Frank Cass; Cambridge, Mass.: Harvard University Press, 1966. 366 p.

The book is addressed to the question of whether Australia is maxi-
mizing the possible benefits of foreign investment. The study is

based on a 1962 survey of 200 corporations, most in manufacturing industries.

Cranston, Ross. "Foreign Investment Restrictions: Defending Economic Sovereignty in Canada and Australia." HARVARD INTERNATIONAL LAW JOURNAL 14 (Spring 1973): 345-67.

A discussion of the restrictive policies toward direct investment in Canada and Australia.

Deane, Roderick. FOREIGN INVESTMENT IN NEW ZEALAND MANUFACTURING. Wellington: Sweet and Maxwell, 1970. 540 p.

A detailed study of the positive economic consequences of foreign investment in New Zealand. The areas covered are management, employment, technology, and financial gains.

McCarthy, Gordon. THE GREAT BIG AUSTRALIAN TAKEOVER BOOK. Sydney: Angus and Robertson, 1973. 249 p.

The related issues of take-over and foreign investment and their influence on Australian life are discussed. The author suggests improvement mainly in terms of management tactics.

Parry, Thomas G. "Australia's Foreign Investment Policies: In Search of an Objective." JOURNAL OF WORLD TRADE LAW 8 (September-October 1974): 529-36.

_____. PLANT SIZE, CAPACITY UTILIZATION AND ECONOMIC EFFICIENCY: FOREIGN INVESTMENT IN THE AUSTRALIAN CHEMICAL INDUSTRY. Discussion Papers in International Business and Investment Studies, no. 8. Reading, Pa.: Department of Economics, University of Reading, 1973. 30 p.

Vernon, J., et al. REPORT OF THE COMMITTEE ON ECONOMIC ENQUIRY. The Vernon Committee Report. 2 vols. Melbourne: Wilke and Co., 1965. 1140 p.

A report commissioned by the Australian government which includes a statistical analysis of foreign direct investment there.

CANADA

Aitken, Hugh G. J. AMERICAN CAPITAL AND CANADIAN RESOURCES. Cambridge, Mass.: Harvard University Press, 1961. 217 p.

The author describes the degree of economic integration in the North American region and the U. S. interpenetration of the Canadian raw materials industry. In a final chapter he argues that the continuing trend of economic integration will not lead to political and cultural domination of Canada by the United States.

Behrman, Jack N. AN ESSAY ON SOME CRITICAL ASPECTS OF THE INTER-
NATIONAL CORPORATION. Economic Council of Canada, Special Study,
January 1970. 38 p.

A background study to the "Interim Report on Competition Policy."

Canada. FOREIGN DIRECT INVESTMENT IN CANADA. Ottawa: Information
Canada, 1971. 523 p.

This is the "Gray Report," commissioned by the Canadian government, which presents a thorough analysis of all aspects of the consequences of foreign investment in Canada. The report is also an
excellent general survey of the problems of host countries.

Carlisle, A. E. CULTURES IN COLLISION: U. S. CORPORATE POLICY AND
CANADIAN SUBSIDIARIES. Ann Arbor: Bureau of Industrial Relations, Graduate School of Business Administration, University of Michigan, 1967. 162 p.

Based on extensive interviews in Quebec and Ontario, the purpose
of the book is to identify some of the effects of cultural differences
on management and industrial relations policies in U. S.-controlled
firms in Canada.

Caves, Richard E. "Multinational Firms, Competition, and Productivity in Host-
Country Markets." ECONOMICA 41 (May 1974): 176-93.

Tests several hypotheses about the effects of foreign direct investment on domestic-owned firms competing with foreign subsidiaries
in the manufacturing sectors of Canada and Australia.

Cordell, Arthur J. THE MULTINATIONAL FIRM, FOREIGN DIRECT INVEST-
MENT AND CANADIAN SCIENCE POLICY. Science Council of Canada,
Special Study, no. 22. Ottawa: Information Canada, 1971. 95 p.

An interview study of about fifty Canadian subsidiaries and their
headquarters abroad which evaluates the possibility of an autono-
mous science policy and the extent of research activities in Canada.

Espinosa, William H. "The Canadian Foreign Investment Review Act: Red,
White and Gray." LAW AND POLICY IN INTERNATIONAL BUSINESS 5,
no. 3 (1973): 1018-41.

A report and survey of conflicting attitudes toward foreign investment in Canada.

Fayerweather, John. "Canadian Attitudes and Policy on Foreign Investment."
MSU [Michigan State University] BUSINESS TOPICS 21 (Winter 1973): 7-20.

Describes the strong trend toward less favorable views of foreign
investment in Canada.

_____. FOREIGN INVESTMENT IN CANADA: PROSPECTS FOR NATIONAL POLICY. White Plains, N.Y.: International Arts and Sciences Press; Toronto: Oxford University Press, 1973. 200 p.

> The book presents a survey of the Canadian situation concerning direct investment. It reviews the attitudes toward foreign firms, the national decision-making process, and industrial strategy. It also contains an appendix outlining the official positions of Canadian political parties concerning foreign investment.

Freeman, Susan. "Canada's Changing Posture toward Multinational Corporations: An Attempt to Harmonize Nationalism with Continued Industrial Growth." NEW YORK UNIVERSITY JOURNAL OF INTERNATIONAL LAW AND POLITICS 7 (Summer 1974): 271-315.

> Includes discussion of the Foreign Investment Review Act of 1974. Sees conflict between political autonomy and the higher standard of living offered by substantial foreign investment. Predicts that, in general, the conflict will be resolved in favor of growth and the MNCs.

Glover, George C., Jr. "Canada's Foreign Investment Review Act." BUSINESS LAWYER 29 (April 1974): 805-22.

Godfrey, Dave, and Watkins, Melville, H., eds. GORDON TO WATKINS TO YOU. Toronto: New Press, 1970. 261 p.

> Describes Canadian reactions to and attitudes about American investment, and presents a variety of solutions covering the Canadian political spectrum: creating a socialist economy, replacing American with Canadian private investment, or increasing control of American investments.

Gordon, Walter L. A CHOICE FOR CANADA: INDEPENDENCE OR COLONIAL STATUS. Toronto: McClelland and Stewart, 1966. 125 p.

> Like Kari Levitt's book (SILENT SURRENDER, below), this is an impassioned and well-argued brief against foreign investment in Canada. The author is a former minister of finance.

Hymer, Stephen. "Direct Foreign Investment and the National Economic Interest." In NATIONALISM IN CANADA, edited by Peter Russell, pp. 191-202. Toronto: McGraw-Hill, 1966.

> An application of Hymer's theory of imperfect markets and MNCs to the Canadian case. The effects of foreign investment are judged to be mainly negative ones.

Levitt, Kari. SILENT SURRENDER: THE MULTINATIONAL CORPORATION IN CANADA. New York: St. Martin's Press, 1970. 185 p.

The thesis of this book is that Canada has lost a great amount of political and economic sovereignty due to encroachment by U. S. investments. The author pleads for a "new nationalism" on the part of the Canadian government.

Leyton-Brown, David. "The Multinational Enterprise and Conflict in Canadian-American Relations." INTERNATIONAL ORGANIZATION 28 (Autumn 1974): 733-54.

Assesses the impact on the host Canadian government of the twenty-seven identifiable cases of politicized conflict that have been generated in Canada by the activities of U. S.-owned multinational enterprises from 1945 through 1971.

Litvak, Isaiah A., and Maule, Christopher J. CULTURAL SOVEREIGNTY: THE 'TIME' AND 'READER'S DIGEST' CASE IN CANADA. New York: Praeger, 1974. 140 p.

The role and posture of domestic and foreign periodical publishers in Canada. A critique of the exemptions of TIME and READER'S DIGEST under the Income Tax Act. The authors claim that undue influence has been exerted.

Litvak, Isaiah A., et al. DUAL LOYALTY: CANADIAN-U.S. BUSINESS ARRANGEMENTS. Toronto: McGraw-Hill, 1971. 242 p.

An attempt to measure U. S. awareness and sensitivity to Canada as a host nation. The study finds that Canadian social, political, and economic interests are not sufficiently protected by corporate practice or Canadian policies.

Lumsden, Ian, ed. CLOSE THE 49TH PARALLEL, ETC.: THE AMERICANIZATION OF CANADA. Toronto: University of Toronto Press, 1970. 336 p.

Essays by scholars and journalists on the dangers of American business influence in Canada. A radical critique of Canadian laissez-faire attitudes toward U. S. economic imperialism.

Marshall, Hilary S., and Montagnes, Jan. "International Publishing." In BACKGROUND PAPERS, prepared by the Ontario Royal Commission on Book Publishing, pp. 154-72. Toronto: Queen's Printers and Publisher, 1972.

A discussion of the economic and cultural advantages of international publishing with special reference to the Canadian case.

Mohr, Patrica M. ECONOMIC DEVELOPMENT STRATEGIES AND FOREIGN OWNERSHIP POLICIES OF SELECTED COUNTRIES. Mineral Bulletin, MR 123, for the Canadian Department of Energy, Mines and Resources, Mineral Resources Branch. Ottawa: 1972. 49 p.

The author contrasts Canadian development strategies and foreign ownership policies with those of Sweden, Japan, and Australia.

Murray, J. Alex, and Gerace, Mary C. "Multinational Business and Canadian Government Affairs." QUEEN'S QUARTERLY 80 (Summer 1973): 222-32.

Reuber, Grant L., and Roseman, Frank. THE TAKE-OVER OF CANADIAN FIRMS, 1945-1961: AN EMPIRICAL ANALYSIS. Economic Council of Canada, Special Study no. 10. Ottawa: Queen's Printer, 1969. 242 p.

Identifies, compares, and assesses the characteristics and factors affecting international and domestic mergers.

Rosenbluth, Gideon. "The Relationship between Foreign Control and Concentration in Canadian Industry." CANADIAN JOURNAL OF ECONOMICS 3 (February 1970): 14-38.

A statistical analysis which denies that a strong relationship exists between foreign control and concentration.

Safarian, A. E. FOREIGN OWNERSHIP OF CANADIAN INDUSTRY. Toronto: McGraw-Hill, 1966. 346 p.

Evaluates the performance of foreign and domestic firms within the framework of Canadian industrial and economic policy. The author concludes that the quality of performance is related to economic policy, rather than to individual firms' decisions.

_____. THE PERFORMANCE OF FOREIGN-OWNED FIRMS IN CANADA. Montreal: Private Planning Association of Canada; Washington, D.C.: Canadian American Committee, 1969. 123 p.

The author tests the proposition that foreign firms contribute less to the Canadian economy than domestic ones. He finds foreign firms are more efficient and differ with Canadian ones only to the extent that they rely on imports. There is also a discussion of the political relevance of the concept of economic efficiency.

_____. "Perspectives on Foreign Direct Investment from the Viewpoint of a Capital Receiving Country." JOURNAL OF FINANCE 28 (May 1973): 419-38.

An analysis of the costs and the benefits deriving from foreign investments in Canada. Claims that governmental policy and inefficiency are to blame for the negative consequences of foreign investment.

Stevenson, Gaith. "Foreign Direct Investment and the Provinces: A Study of Elite Attitudes." CANADIAN JOURNAL OF POLITICAL SCIENCE 7, no. 4 (1974): 630-47.

Thompson, A. R. "Sovereignty and Natural Resources: A Study of Canadian Petroleum Legislation." UNIVERSITY OF BRITISH COLUMBIA LAW REVIEW 4 (December 1969): 161-93.

> Canada has been able to reach agreements with large oil companies which enable continual review of and changes in present policies in light of economic changes.

Watkins, Melville H., et al. FOREIGN OWNERSHIP OF CANADIAN INDUSTRY. Report of the Task Force on the Structure of Canadian Industry. Ottawa: Privy Council Office, 1970. 427 p.

> Examines the role of multinational corporations in Canada. Recommends areas which ought to be controlled, including balance of payments and various extensions of U. S. policy into Canada. Opts for greater national independence.

Wonnacott, Paul. "United States Investment in the Canadian Economy." INTERNATIONAL JOURNAL 27 (Spring 1972): 276-86.

EUROPE

Eastern Europe

Bombelles, Joseph T. "Private Foreign Investment in Yugoslavia." CARROLL BUSINESS BULLETIN 12 (August 15, 1972): 12-18.

Burgess, Jay A. "Direct Foreign Investment in Eastern Europe: Problems and Prospects of Romania's Joint Venture Legislation." LAW AND POLICY IN INTERNATIONAL BUSINESS 6 (Fall 1974): 1059-104.

> Discusses in general terms the Romanian economic system and the new legislation allowing joint ventures with foreign firms. Sees the joint venture as mutually profitable, but emphasizes that the loose wording of the legislation leaves much to individual negotiations.

Dagon, Roger. "Cooperation Agreements and Joint Ventures with Socialist Business Associations: The Hungarian System." AMERICAN JOURNAL OF COMPARATIVE LAW 21 (Fall 1973): 752-58.

Holt, John B. "Joint Ventures in Yugoslavia: West German and American Experience." MSU [Michigan State University] BUSINESS TOPICS 21 (Spring 1973): 51-63.

Kretschmar, Robert S., Jr., and Foor, Robin. THE POTENTIAL FOR JOINT VENTURE IN EASTERN EUROPE. Foreword by Donald A. Webster and Christopher E. Stowell. New York: Praeger, 1972. 153 p.

Basically an "investment climate" study which shows past experience and future opportunities for joint ventures in Eastern Europe.

Levente, Mihail. "The Establishing of Joint Enterprises with the Participation of Capitalist Firms in the Economy of the Socialist Republic of Rumania." RE-VUE ROUMAINE DES SCIENCES SOCIALES SERIE DE SCIENCES ECONOMIQUES 16, no. 1 (1972): 57-77.

Morse, David A., and Goekjian, Samuel V. "Joint Investment Opportunities with the Socialist Republic of Romania." BUSINESS LAWYER 29 (November 1973): 133-48.

Neumann, Timothy P. "Joint Ventures in Yugoslavia: 1971 Amendments to Foreign Investment Laws." NEW YORK UNIVERSITY JOURNAL OF INTERNA-TIONAL LAW AND POLITICS 6 (Summer 1973): 271-96.

Analyzes 1971 amendments in some detail. Concludes that while amendments improve the investment climate in Yugoslavia, the problem of control in the joint venture is still a major inhibiting factor to substantial foreign investment.

Organization for Economic and Cultural Development. Committee for Invisible Transactions. FOREIGN INVESTMENT IN YUGOSLAVIA (1974). Paris: 1974. 58 p.

A quantitative survey of foreign investments and joint ventures in Yugoslavia.

Sukijasovic, Mirodrag. FOREIGN INVESTMENT IN YUGOSLAVIA. New York: Institute of International Politics and Economics and Oceana Publications, 1970. 120 p.

Presents the legal and political provisions of direct foreign invest-ment and the desire for joint ventures as the most acceptable form of investment.

_____. "Legal Aspects of Foreign Investments in Yugoslavia." LAW AND CONTEMPORARY PROBLEMS 37 (Summer 1972): 474-84.

U. S. Congress. Senate. Committee on Foreign Relations. Subcommittee on Multinational Corporations. U. S. TRADE AND INVESTMENT IN THE SOVIET UNION AND EASTERN EUROPE: THE ROLE OF MULTINATIONAL CORPORA-TIONS: A STAFF REPORT, DECEMBER 20, 1974. 93d Cong., 2d sess., 1974. 45 p.

Some emphasis on the development of Siberian natural gas projects.

The European Economic Community (EEC)

Balassa, Bela A. "American Direct Investments in the Common Market." BANCA NAZIONALE DELL LAVORO QUARTERLY REVIEW 77 (June 1966): 121-46.

The article first presents the size advantages of American firms in the EEC and then discusses the legal framework for a European Company system which could lead to European large firms capable of taking the lead in Europe. The author also suggests which aspects of American management procedures might be taken over profitably by the Europeans.

Balekjian, Wahe H. LEGAL ASPECTS OF FOREIGN INVESTMENT IN THE EUROPEAN ECONOMIC COMMUNITY. Dobbs Ferry, N.Y.: Oceana Publications, 1967. 356 p.

Both a survey of existing laws and an evaluation of the current investment climate in the EEC. The book presents legal statutes and gives a description of municipal and EEC laws.

Carbaugh, Robert J. "An Expanded EEC: Implications for the United States." INTERMOUNTAIN ECONOMIC REVIEW 4 (Spring 1973): 81-89.

Focuses on potential effects on American multinationals.

Dunning, John H. THE LOCATION OF INTERNATIONAL FIRMS IN AN ENLARGED EEC: AN EXPLANATORY PAPER, READ 28TH MARCH 1972. Manchester: Manchester Statistical Society, 1972. 45 p.

The study employs location theory to show the consequences of an enlarged customs union for British and American firms in the United Kingdom.

Edwards, Anthony D. INVESTMENT IN THE EUROPEAN ECONOMIC COMMUNITY: A STUDY OF PROBLEMS AND OPPORTUNITIES. New York: Praeger, 1964. 75 p.

The study was prepared for the Economist Intelligence Unit for those readers interested in investing in the European Common Market. A statistical survey of investment opportunities and problems in the EEC.

Everling, Ulrich. THE RIGHT OF ESTABLISHMENT IN THE COMMON MARKET. Chicago: Commerce Clearing House, 1964. 219 p.

The book is translated from German with an added chapter for the American reader on the significance for America of European laws. The book discusses the provisions of the Treaty of Rome regarding the right to do business, with special emphasis on political and legal effects and economic provisions.

Forrow, Brian D. "The Multinational Corporation in the Enlarged European Community." LAW AND CONTEMPORARY PROBLEMS 37 (Spring 1972): 306-17.

Griffin, Joseph P. "The Power of Host Countries over the Multinational: Lifting the Veil in the European Economic Community and the United States." LAW AND POLICY IN INTERNATIONAL BUSINESS 6 (Spring 1974): 375-435.

    Cases in which a host country treats the local subsidiary and foreign parent as a single entity in order to assert extraterritorial jurisdiction over the parent.

Khachaturov, An. "U. S. Capital and the Enlarged Common Market." INTERNATIONAL AFFAIRS (Moscow), August 1973, pp. 91-96.

    A Soviet view.

Krause, Lawrence B. EUROPEAN ECONOMIC INTEGRATION AND THE UNITED STATES. Washington, D.C.: Brookings Institution, 1968. 265 p.

    An analysis of the impact of the European Economic Community and the European Free Trade Area on the United States in terms of investment and trade. Concentrates on economic consequences, but pays some attention to politics.

McCreary, Edward A. THE AMERICANIZATION OF EUROPE: THE IMPACT OF AMERICANS AND AMERICAN BUSINESS ON THE UNCOMMON MARKET. Garden City, N.Y.: Doubleday, 1964. 295 p.

    Examines Europe's transformation into a consumer society and the changes in European management styles due to American influence.

McLachlan, Donald L., and Swann, Dennis. COMPETITION POLICY IN THE EUROPEAN COMMUNITY: THE RULES IN THEORY AND PRACTICE. London and New York: Oxford University Press, 1967. 482 p.

    A review of Community policy designed to promote competition. Considers the negative consequences of strict application of antitrust laws in the case of large firms.

Paliano, Guido Colonna di. "International Private Investment Problems: European Community--United States." AUSSENWIRTSCHAFT 28 (September-December 1973): 286-303.

Temple Lang, John. THE COMMON MARKET AND COMMON LAW: LEGAL ASPECTS OF FOREIGN INVESTMENT AND ECONOMIC INTEGRATION IN THE EUROPEAN COMMUNITY WITH IRELAND AS A PROTOTYPE. Chicago: University of Chicago Press, 1967. 573 p.

    An analysis of the problems raised for a capital-importing country when entering the Common Market and the effect of that entry on Community law.

Western Europe

Aglion, Raoul. "French Policy and American Investments in France." CALIFORNIA MANAGEMENT REVIEW 14 (Summer 1972): 94-102.

Blaisse, P. A. "Evolutionary Trends of European Legislative and Social Environment and Their Implications for Organization and Operation of Multi-National Companies." ECONOMIE (Netherlands) 37 (August 1973): 512-31.

Boddewyn, Jean J. WESTERN EUROPEAN POLICIES TOWARD U. S. INVESTORS. The Bulletin, nos. 93-95. New York: New York University, Graduate School of Business Administration, Institute of Finance, 1974. 96 p.

> The author compares the patterns of European policies and their future trends. He traces the development of negative attitudes toward U. S. investment despite basic legal openness. Key concerns of governments are discussed: the provision of jobs in underdeveloped regions, generation of exports, and discouragement of investment in key industries.

Boddewyn, Jean J., and Grosser, D. D. "American Direct Investment in Italy: Distribution, Profitability, and Contributions." REVIEW OF THE ECONOMIC CONDITIONS IN ITALY 36 (September 1972): 362-78.

de Marsac, Xavier Tandeau, and Rich, Robert S. "Direct Investment in France: Law and Taxes." VANDERBILT JOURNAL OF TRANSNATIONAL LAW 5 (Spring 1972): 361-76.

Deutsche Bundesbank. "Foreign Interests in Enterprises in the Federal Republic of Germany." DEUTSCHE BUNDESBANK MONTHLY REPORT 26 (November 1974): 21-31.

DIVO (Frankfurt am Main). AMERICAN SUBSIDIARIES IN THE FEDERAL REPUBLIC OF GERMANY: AN ANALYSIS AND CRITICAL EVALUATION. New York: Commerce Clearing House, 1969. 271 p.

> Contains discussions of the role of American interests and the transfer of technology. Useful statistical survey.

Dusart, Rosine. "The Impact of the French Government on American Investment in France." HARVARD INTERNATIONAL LAW JOURNAL 7 (Winter 1965): 75-112.

> Analyzes the policies and attitudes of the French government toward U. S. investments and suggests new policies.

"France: Shifting of Profits from and to Foreign Subsidiaries." EUROPEAN TAXATION 13 (August 1973): 265-71.

A discussion of Article 57 of France's general tax code, especially with respect to shifting of profits from and to French enterprises which control, or are controlled by, foreign enterprises.

Hellmann, Rainer. THE CHALLENGE TO U. S. DOMINANCE OF THE INTER-NATIONAL CORPORATIONS. New York: Dunnellen Publishing Co., 1970. 348 p.

Presents the issues for European business in terms of two alternative choices: either develop industrial giantism and economic integration or suffer American and Japanese dominance of world business.

Hu, Y. S. THE IMPACT OF U. S. INVESTMENT IN EUROPE: A CASE STUDY OF THE AUTOMOTIVE AND COMPUTER INDUSTRIES. New York: Praeger, 1973. 291 p.

A history and assessment of the present operations and consequences of foreign investment in these two industries. Christopher Layton contends in his introduction that Hu proves that "the benefits from foreign technology depend on the dynamism of the host." The author questions the assumption that foreign investment has a beneficial impact on growth and development in every case.

Issing, Otmar. "Foreign Assets and the Investment Income Balance of the Federal Republic of Germany in the Years 1950-1970." GERMAN ECONOMIC REVIEW 12, no. 1 (1974): 16-37.

Study of German balance of payments which employs a comparison with U. S. balance of payments position during the same period. Finds the German performance to have been inferior to that of the United States and faults primarily the undervaluation of the Deutschmark.

Johnstone, Allan W. UNITED STATES DIRECT INVESTMENT IN FRANCE: AN INVESTIGATION OF THE FRENCH CHARGES. Cambridge, Mass.: MIT Press, 1965. 109 p.

The author examines the claims that U. S. investment poses a threat to French economic sovereignty. Based on study of twenty-four French firms. The author finds that decentralized control would solve the problems as perceived by the French.

Lamont, Douglas F. MANAGING FOREIGN INVESTMENT IN SOUTHERN ITALY: BUSINESS IN DEVELOPING AREAS OF THE EEC. With special assistance of Robert Purtshert. Foreword by Eric N. Baklanoff. New York: Praeger, 1973. 169 p.

Treats southern Italy as a developing area and judges the performance and contribution of foreign investment to economic growth. The case is of special interest since four U. S. firms incurred great losses in the area. The study explores socio-economic con-

ditions and the state of industrial organization and their adaptation
to the influx of foreign capital.

Layton, Christopher. TRANS-ATLANTIC INVESTMENTS. The Atlantic Papers.
2d ed. Boulogne sur Seine: Atlantic Institute, 1968. 144 p.

> An empirical analysis of the validity of European arguments for and
> against American investments. Argues for European mergers to
> offset American bigness.

Organization for Economic and Cultural Development. Development Centre.
PLANNING, INCOME DISTRIBUTION, PRIVATE FOREIGN INVESTMENT:
INTERNATIONAL MEETING OF DIRECTORS OF DEVELOPMENT RESEARCH
AND TRAINING INSTITUTES, BELGRADE, YUGOSLAVIA, 28th-30th AUGUST
1972. Paris: 1974. 234 p.

Stonehill, Arthur I. FOREIGN OWNERSHIP IN NORWEGIAN ENTERPRISES.
Oslo: Central Bureau of Statistics, 1965. 213 p.

> A study of the history of foreign direct investment in Norway and
> its present status in the Norwegian economy.

Stubenitzky, Frank. AMERICAN DIRECT INVESTMENT IN THE NETHERLANDS
INDUSTRY: A SURVEY OF THE YEAR 1966. Rotterdam: Rotterdam University
Press, 1970. 191 p.

> The book tests various theories of direct investment and profit
> maximization on the basis of considerable data on magnitude and
> other characteristics of American investments in the Netherlands.
> He also discusses Dutch investments in the United States, which
> exceed American holdings in the Netherlands.

Sweeney, John. "Foreign Companies in Ireland." STUDIES (Ireland) 62 (Autumn-
Winter 1973): 273-86.

Thoman, Richard G. FOREIGN INVESTMENT AND REGIONAL DEVELOPMENT:
THE THEORY AND PRACTICE OF INVESTMENT INCENTIVES, WITH A CASE
STUDY OF BELGIUM. New York: Praeger, 1973. 148 p.

> Deals with the Belgian policy of directing foreign investment into
> the less-developed or depressed areas of the country and its eco-
> nomic success.

Torem, Charles, and Craig, William L. "Control of Foreign Investment in
France." MICHIGAN LAW REVIEW 66 (1967-68): 669-720.

> Analyzes French restrictive policies which protect French key in-
> dustries from takeover by foreign investors.

Van den Bulcke, D. THE FOREIGN COMPANIES IN BELGIAN INDUSTRY.
Ghent: Belgian Productivity Center, 1973.

The United Kingdom

Dunn, M. R. "The Impact of Multinationals." JOURNAL OF THE INSTITUTE
OF BANKERS 95 (April 1974): 73-84.

Outlines the impact of MNCs on the United Kingdom.

Dunning, John H. AMERICAN INVESTMENT IN BRITISH MANUFACTURING
INDUSTRY. London: Ruskin House, 1958. 365 p.

A historical and statistical analysis which shows the beneficial effects of American investments in the U. K.

_____. THE ROLE OF AMERICAN INVESTMENT IN THE BRITISH ECONOMY.
PEP Broadsheet 507. London, 1969. 76 p.

A cost-benefit analysis of U. S. investments and a survey of British
policy. Shows that U. S. firms are more efficient than British firms.

_____. "United States Industry in Britain." FINANCIAL TIMES (London),
1973. 105 p.

A detailed statistical survey of the performance of U. S. firms in
Britain. Deals with the consequences of British entry into the EEC.

Forsyth, David J. C. U. S. INVESTMENT IN SCOTLAND. With the assistance of Kathryn Docherty. New York: Praeger, 1972. 320 p.

A thorough-going analysis of the effects, the extent, and the nature
of and motives for U. S. and other direct foreign investment in
Scotland. Concentrates on the implications of U. S. investment
in Scotland and comes to the conclusion that the consequences,
in terms of employment, productivity, and incomes in the region,
seem to be positive enough to warrant an active policy of en-
couragement by the British government.

Hodges, Michael. MULTINATIONAL CORPORATIONS AND NATIONAL GOV-
ERNMENT: A CASE STUDY OF THE UNITED KINGDOM'S EXPERIENCE 1964-
1970. Farnborough: Saxon House, D. C. Heath, 1974. 307 p.

Examines methods used by British government to control foreign-
owned firms and government policy toward foreign investment.

McMillan, James, and Harris, Bernard. THE AMERICAN TAKE-OVER OF
BRITAIN. London: Frewin, 1968. 253 p.

Points out the efficiency of American firms in Britain, but argues

against them on political grounds. Japanese science policy is cited
as a positive example.

United Kingdom. BRITAIN'S INTERNATIONAL INVESTMENT POSITION.
HMSO Pamphlet 98. London: Central Office of Information, 1971. 67 p.

A survey of investments in Great Britain from 1962-1969.

LATIN AMERICA

General

Baer, Werner. THE DEVELOPMENT OF THE BRAZILIAN STEEL INDUSTRY.
Nashville, Tenn.: Vanderbilt University Press, 1969. 202 p.

A detailed study stressing primarily economic factors and performance criteria, but including substantial information on the role of foreign capital and technology in the development of the Brazilian steel industry.

_____. INDUSTRIALIZATION AND ECONOMIC DEVELOPMENT IN BRAZIL.
Homewood, Ill.: Irwin, 1965. 309 p.

A general analysis of factors contributing to the development of
Brazilian industry prior to 1964. Contains a well-developed presentation of the import substitution model and some discussion of
the role of foreign capital. Stresses the economic bottlenecks in
education and agriculture over the political problems associated
with foreign capital as the primary threat to continued economic
growth.

Behrman, Jack N. DECISION CRITERIA FOR FOREIGN DIRECT INVESTMENT
IN LATIN AMERICA. New York: Council of the Americas, 1974. 89 p.

Deals with definitions of MNCs and with legislation being developed
in the Americas to constrain the activities of foreign investors.

_____. "The Multinational Corporation in Latin America." In DEVELOPMENT
TODAY, edited by Robert E. Hunter and John E. Rielly, pp. 196-215. New
York: Praeger, 1972.

_____. THE ROLE OF INTERNATIONAL COMPANIES IN LATIN AMERICAN
INTEGRATION: AUTOS AND PETROCHEMICALS. Lexington, Mass.: Lexington Books, 1972. 185 p.

The author does not consider MNCs to be absolutely necessary for
economic development despite their superior efficiency. He opts
for increased use of joint ventures, but sees the necessity of creating more effective political and economic institutions to offset what

many Latin Americans consider to be undue American interference
and influence.

Bernstein, Marvin D., ed. FOREIGN INVESTMENTS IN LATIN AMERICA:
CASES AND ATTITUDES. New York: Knopf, 1966. 305 p.

A historical survey of the growth of foreign investments in Latin
America since the end of the colonial period. This highly readable book contains two sections, one a series of historical case
studies, the other a group of essays depicting different attitudes
on investment in Latin America.

Bos, Hendricus C., et al. PRIVATE FOREIGN INVESTMENT IN DEVELOPING
COUNTRIES: A QUANTITATIVE STUDY ON THE EVALUATION OF THE MACRO-
ECONOMIC EFFECTS. International Studies in Economics and Econometrics,
vol. 7. Dordrecht and Boston: Reidel, for the Development Centre, OECD,
1974. 402 p.

The book is in four parts, consisting of an analysis of the literature
on the consequences of foreign investment, the development of a
framework for a more adequate methodology, and its application to
the Philippines, Argentina, and Guatemala, among others.

Broehl, Wayne G., Jr. THE INTERNATIONAL BASIC ECONOMY CORPORA-
TION. United States Business Performance Abroad, Case Study no. 13. Washington, D.C.: National Planning Association, 1968. 314 p.

The corporation mentioned in the title was founded in 1947 by the
Rockefeller family and has been involved in service-industry development in thirty-three developing countries. Industries covered are
mutual funds, middle income housing, milk processing and distribution, supermarkets, and argicultural services. The relatively uneven performance of the corporation is seen as caused by nationalism
and resistance to American management techniques. Case studies
from Brazil and Venezuela.

Brundenius, Claes. "The Anatomy of Imperialism: The Case of the Multinational
Mining Corporation in Peru." JOURNAL OF PEACE RESEARCH 9, no. 3 (1972):
189-207.

Carl, Beverly M. "Incentives for Private Investment in Brazil." COLUMBIA
JOURNAL OF TRANSNATIONAL LAW 6 (Fall 1967): 190-257.

Reviews the laws enacted by the Brazilian government to attract
foreign investments which help the investor to maximize profits and
minimize risks.

Chen-Young, Paul L. REPORT ON PRIVATE INVESTMENT IN THE CARIBBEAN.
Prepared for the Caribbean Association of Industry and Commerce. Kingston,
Jamaica: Atlas Publishing Co., 1973. 86 p.

Council for Latin America. THE EFFECTS OF UNITED STATES AND OTHER FOREIGN INVESTMENT IN LATIN AMERICA. New York: January 1970.

Girvan, Norman. FOREIGN CAPITAL AND ECONOMIC UNDERDEVELOPMENT IN JAMAICA. Kingston, Jamaica: Unwin Brothers, for Institute of Social and Economic Research, University of the West Indies, 1971. 282 p.

> A study of the bauxite industry, the public sector, and the finan-
> cial system in Jamaica and the effects of direct foreign investment
> in the years from 1964-68. The conclusions of the study are that
> "foreign capital has been the principal single factor responsible for
> the structural change and the high rate of growth of the Jamaican
> economy since the war." Yet the form of the capital inflows and
> the behavior of foreign-owned institutions contribute to the fact
> that this growth has not been self-sustaining. "In its present forms,
> foreign capital impedes structural change in important ways."

Goodsell, Charles T. AMERICAN CORPORATIONS AND PERUVIAN POLITICS. Cambridge, Mass.: Harvard University Press, 1974. 288 p.

> A carefully researched study which traces the interactions between
> corporations and the government as well as providing economic
> analysis. Could be regarded as a "model host country study."

Gordon, Lincoln, and Grommers, Engelbert L. UNITED STATES MANUFACTUR-ING INVESTMENT IN BRAZIL: THE IMPACT OF BRAZILIAN GOVERNMENT POLICIES 1946-60. Cambridge, Mass.: Harvard University Press, 1962. 177 p.

> A study of forty-two firms and their investment decisions, perfor-
> mance, and exports in light of governmental policies and inflation
> and the labor market.

Grunwald, Joseph, and Musgrove, Philip. NATURAL RESOURCES IN LATIN AMERICAN DEVELOPMENT. Baltimore, Md.: Johns Hopkins Press, for Re-sources for the Future, 1970. 494 p.

> Discusses the present and future control over Latin American natural
> resources.

Horowitz, David. FROM YALTA TO VIETNAM: AMERICAN FOREIGN POLICY IN THE COLD WAR. Harmondsworth: Penguin Books, 1967. 465 p.

> Chapter 10 presents a study of the United Fruit Company's involve-
> ment in the overthrow of the Guatemalan government.

Ingram, G. M. EXPROPRIATION OF U. S. PROPERTY IN SOUTH AMERICA: NATIONALIZATION OF OIL AND COPPER COMPANIES IN PERU, BOLIVIA AND CHILE. New York: Praeger, 1974. 316 p.

> Discusses the causes and consequences of expropriation in both
> political and economic terms. Covers the International Petroleum

Company, the expulsion of Standard Oil and Gulf from Bolivia, the nationalization of the tin mines, and copper production in Chile.

Inter-American Development Bank. MULTINATIONAL INVESTMENT, PUBLIC AND PRIVATE, IN THE ECONOMIC DEVELOPMENT AND INTEGRATION OF LATIN AMERICA. Bogota: 1968. 381 p.

The relevant papers in this volume are: Rosenstein-Rodan on MNCs and Latin American integration, Lagos on the socio-political aspects of MNCs, Uri on MNCs and the European experience, and Cardenas on the Latin American experience with MNCs.

Lau, Stephen F. THE CHILEAN RESPONSE TO FOREIGN INVESTMENT. New York: Praeger, 1972. 118 p.

The author analyzes Chilean opinions and attitudes concerning U. S. investments and Chile's official policies towards that investment. Based on interviews made before and after Allende's ascent to power.

May, Herbert K. THE EFFECTS OF UNITED STATES AND OTHER FOREIGN INVESTMENT IN LATIN AMERICA. New York: Council of the Americas, 1971. 101 p.

The study elaborates the positive effects of such investment. An example of "apologetic" literature.

Moran, Theodore H. MULTINATIONAL CORPORATIONS AND THE POLITICS OF DEPENDENCE: THE CASE OF COPPER IN CHILE 1945-1972. Princeton, N.J.: Princeton University Press, 1974. 286 p.

An excellent case study which describes the political involvement of American copper mining companies in Chile and their mostly unsuccessful attempts to establish good relations with local unions and authorities.

Ness, Walter L., Jr. "Brazil: Local Equity Participation in Multinational Enterprises." LAW AND POLICY IN INTERNATIONAL BUSINESS 6 (Fall 1974): 1017-57.

Reviews Brazil's attempts to increase local equity voluntary participation in MNCs. Concludes Capital Markets Law and other incentives have been quite effective in opening up nationally owned family firms, but have not substantially affected MNCs. Suggests Brazilians consider other avenues to increased local control over the MNCs.

Pinelo, Alberto J. THE MULTINATIONAL CORPORATION AS A FORCE IN LATIN AMERICAN POLITICS: A CASE STUDY OF THE INTERNATIONAL PETROLEUM COMPANY IN PERU. New York: Praeger, 1973. 180 p.

The book describes the relationship between the Peruvian government, the company, and the U. S. government from 1914-68 and the impact of the company on political life in Peru. Analyzes how power is used by the company.

Reynolds, Clark W. "Development Problems of an Export Economy: The Case of Chile and Copper." In ESSAYS ON THE CHILEAN ECONOMY, edited by Markos Mamalakis and Clark W. Reynolds, pp. 203-398. Homewood, Ill.: Richard D. Irwin, 1965.

Treats the copper industry as an example of an "enclave" export sector influencing the process of growth in a country during the early stages of industralization. Special emphasis is placed on the policy implications of foreign investment for the LDCs in general.

Rogers, William D. "United States Investments in Latin America: A Critical Appraisal." VIRGINIA JOURNAL OF INTERNATIONAL LAW 11 (March 1971): 246-55.

The author first discusses the historical reasons for Latin American hostile attitudes towards U. S. investors and then suggests policies which Latin American governments should follow in order to arrive at a more satisfactory arrangement for both partners.

United Nations. PANEL ON FOREIGN INVESTMENT IN LATIN AMERICA (ST/ECA/131). 1971. 53 p.

Based on a meeting in Colombia in 1970. Treats the issue of technology transfer and makes suggestions for more favorable transfers of foreign investment.

Urquidi, Victor L., and Thorp, Rosemary, eds. LATIN AMERICA IN THE INTERNATIONAL ECONOMY. London: Macmillan, 1973. 430 p.

Considers the pattern of Latin American dependence, development problems and policy, and recent trends in Latin America's exports to industrialized countries. Analyzes the problem of external dependence and its relation to foreign investment, technology transfer, and international financial agencies. Among the authors are Sunkel, Arndt, Konig, and Ffrench-Davis.

Utley, Jon Basil. "Doing Business with Latin Nacionalists." HARVARD BUSINESS REVIEW 51 (January-February 1973): 77-86.

Vaitsos, Constantine V. "Foreign Investment Policies and Economic Development in Latin America." JOURNAL OF WORLD TRADE LAW 7 (November-December 1973): 619-65.

Describes the recent trends toward tighter control of foreign investments in Latin America. The author sees this as a positive development which will continue in the future.

Vernon, Raymond, ed. HOW LATIN AMERICA VIEWS THE U. S. INVESTOR. New York: Praeger, 1966. 117 p.

> Four essays by Wionczek, Vazquez, Jaguaribe, and the editor on investments in Latin America in general, as well as studies on Argentina, Brazil, and Mexico.

Wurfel, Seymour W. FOREIGN ENTERPRISE IN COLOMBIA: LAWS AND POLICIES. Chapel Hill: University of North Carolina Press, 1965. 578 p.

> The study describes conditions before the signing of the Andean Pact. Concentrates on the investment climate.

The Andean Common Market

"Common Treatment of Foreign Capital, Trademarks, Patents, Licensing Agreements and Royalties in the Andean Common Market." JOURNAL OF COMMON MARKET STUDIES 10 (June 1972): 339-59.

> Includes the text of a treaty entered into force June 30, 1971.

Ffrench-Davis, M. Ricardo. "Foreign Investment in Latin America: Recent Trends and Prospects." In LATIN AMERICA IN THE INTERNATIONAL ECONOMY, edited by Victor L. Urquidi and Rosemary Thorp, pp. 169-89. London: Macmillan, 1973.

> The conclusion, based on a review of the performance and effects of investment, is that the Andean group protective policies should be followed, since foreign investment does not have beneficial effects.

Furnish, Dale B. "The Andean Common Market's Common Regime for Foreign Investments." VANDERBILT JOURNAL OF TRANSNATIONAL LAW 5 (Spring 1972): 313-39.

> This is a thorough discussion of the intentions of the Andean Pact and the projected diminishing importance of foreign investment.

Lisocki, Stanley R. "The Andean Investment Code." NOTRE DAME LAWYER 49 (December 1973): 317-33.

Oliver, Covey T. "The Andean Foreign Investment Code: A New Phase in the Quest for Normative Order as to Direct Foreign Investment." AMERICAN JOURNAL OF INTERNATIONAL LAW 66 (October 1972): 763-84.

> Sees a possibility for working within the Andean Code in the same way that the more adaptable foreign investors have adjusted to "Mexicanization."

Pincus, Joseph, and Edwards, Donald E. "The Outlook for United States Foreign

Direct Investment in the Andean Pact Countries in the Seventies." JOURNAL OF INTERNATIONAL BUSINESS STUDIES 3 (Spring 1972): 69-94.

> Fairly detailed examination of the Common System. Sees the political and social benefits as outweighing the economic costs in the short run. Over the long term, however, the region will have to become competitive with other regions of the world to insure capital adequate to development needs.

Mexico

Baerresen, Donald W. THE BORDER INDUSTRALIZATION PROGRAM OF MEXICO. Lexington, Mass.: Heath Lexington Books, 1971. 133 p.

> A special case of host country incentives in a given geographic area.

Cable, Vincent. "Mexico: The Role of Foreign Investment." BANK OF LONDON AND SOUTH AMERICA REVIEW 8 (August 1974): 457-66.

Fernandez, Raul A. "The Border Industrial Program on the United States-Mexico Border." REVIEW OF RADICAL POLITICAL ECONOMICS 5 (Spring 1973): 37-52.

Gordon, Michael W. "The Contemporary Mexican Approach to Growth with Foreign Investment: Controlled but Participatory Independence." CALIFORNIA WESTERN LAW REVIEW 10 (Fall 1973): 1-46.

> Reviews recent investment legislation in Mexico.

McBride, Robert H. "Foreign Investment in Mexico: Are the Rules of the Game Being Changed?" COMERCIO EXTERIOR DE MEXICO 18 (November 1972): 5-12.

> Contains an answer by Jose Campillo Sainz entitled: "Yes, the Rules of the Game Are Being Changed."

Moore, John R., and Rollins, H. Moak. "An Analysis of Current Mexican Restrictions on Direct Foreign Investment." TEXAS INTERNATIONAL LAW FORUM 5 (Spring 1969): 245-83.

> One of the few studies which is critical of Mexico's restrictive laws regulating the flow of capital.

Schill, Charles F. "The Mexican and Andean Investment Codes: An Overview and Comparison." LAW AND POLICY IN INTERNATIONAL BUSINESS (special issue on the multinational corporation) 6 (Spring 1974): 437-83.

> Analyzes the effects of investment codes in six Latin American countries. The political implications of this new investment framework are not as rigid as the legal provisions.

Taylor, James R. "Industrialization of the Mexican Border Region." NEW
MEXICO BUSINESS 26 (March 1973): 3-9.

U. S. Information Agency. Office of Research. MEXICAN ELITE ATTITUDE
TOWARD FOREIGN INVESTMENT. May 16, 1974. 27 p.

Vilaplana, Victor A. "The Forbidden Zones in Mexico." CALIFORNIA WES-
TERN LAW REVIEW 10 (Fall 1973): 47-81.

> History and present status of the law limiting foreign investment
> into border and coastal land.

Wright, Harry K. FOREIGN ENTERPRISE IN MEXICO: LAW AND POLICIES.
American Society of International Law Studies in Foreign Investment and
Economic Development. Chapel Hill: University of North Carolina Press, 1972.
425 p.

> A review of the economic, legal, and political environment Mexico
> offers the foreign investor. A description of the role of foreign in-
> vestments in Mexican development and the restrictions on such in-
> vestment. There are topical chapters on a variety of issues of
> interest to investors.

Zanotti, John P. "Mexico's Forbidden Zones: The Presidential Decree of
April 29, 1971." LAW AND THE SOCIAL ORDER, no. 2 (1973): 455-79.

> Concerns foreign development of lands in border and coastal areas.

Zinman, Ira. "Nationalism as a Factor in Legislation Restricting Foreign Investment: Extractive Industries in Mexico." INDIANA LAW JOURNAL 45 (Summer
1970): 615-30.

UNITED STATES

Arpan, Jeffrey S., and Ricks, David A. "Foreign Direct Investments in the
U. S. and Some Attendant Research Problems." JOURNAL OF INTERNATIONAL
BUSINESS STUDIES 5 (Spring 1974): 1-7.

> Presents some preliminary findings of the most recent major research
> investigation of foreign direct investments in United States manu-
> facturing, mining, and petroleum sectors, and points out some prob-
> lems encountered in conducting research in this area.

Bleakley, Fred. "Foreign Subsidiaries in America: Is Reciprocity Getting Out
of Hand?" INSTITUTIONAL INVESTOR 6 (December 1972): 72-79ff.

Boorstin, David. "Foreign Investments in America." EDITORIAL RESEARCH
REPORTS 4 (July 26, 1974): 561-80.

Discusses the reasons for, and the extent of, foreign penetration in U. S. business. Outlines European funding of early American industrialization. Sees a slowdown of foreign investment in the U. S. caused by the global slump, the Arab nations excepted, and predicts some difficulties with the Federal Trade Commission and Congress.

Daniels, John D. RECENT FOREIGN DIRECT MANUFACTURING INVESTMENT IN THE UNITED STATES: AN INTERVIEW STUDY OF THE DECISION PROCESS. New York: Praeger, 1971. 140 p.

One of the few publications which treats the United States as host country, this interview study of forty firms considers in turn the motives for investment in the United States, firms' entry methods, and their investment policies. The findings center around factors such as market size, profitability, and stability in the United States. No single theory is found to be all-explanatory of the process.

Faith, Nicholas. THE INFILTRATORS: THE EUROPEAN BUSINESS INVASION OF AMERICA. New York: Dutton, 1972. 242 p.

A well-written and well-researched journalistic account of the establishment of European businesses in the United States.

Glazier, Kenneth M. "Canadian Investment in the United States: Putting Your Money Where Your Mouth Is." JOURNAL OF CONTEMPORARY BUSINESS 1 (Autumn 1972): 61-66.

Heller, H. Robert. "The Hawaiian Experience: Japanese Investments in Hawaii Have Increased Rapidly in the Last Few Years." COLUMBIA JOURNAL OF WORLD BUSINESS 9 (Fall 1974): 105-10.

Heller, H. Robert, and Heller, Emily E. THE ECONOMIC AND SOCIAL IMPACT OF FOREIGN INVESTMENT IN HAWAII. Honolulu: Economics Research Center, University of Hawaii, 1973. 123 p.

Develops a theoretical framework for the analysis, and then relates Hawaii's investment pattern and its implications and the attitudes toward Japanese investments in Hawaii.

Hendershot, Paul T. "Reverse Investment: A Boon for Mississippi." MISSISSIPPI'S BUSINESS 31 (April 1973): 1-8.

Klopstock, Fred H. "Foreign Banks in the United States: Scope and Growth of Operations." FEDERAL RESERVE NEW YORK 55 (June 1973): 140-54.

Krause, Lawrence B., and Damm, Kenneth W. FEDERAL TAX TREATMENT OF FOREIGN INCOME. Washington, D.C.: Brookings Institution, 1964. 145 p.

An analysis of the effects of taxation on foreign investment and the effects of foreign investment on the balance of payments and national economic growth.

Lees, Francis A. "Foreign Investment in U. S. Banks." MERGERS AND AC-QUISITIONS 8 (Fall 1973): 4-15.

Leftwich, Robert B. "Foreign Direct Investments in the United States 1962-71." SURVEY OF CURRENT BUSINESS 53 (February 1973): 29-40.

Lichtenstein, Cynthia Crawford. "Foreign Participation in United States Banking: Regulatory Myths and Realities." BOSTON COLLEGE INDUSTRIAL AND COMMERCIAL LAW REVIEW 15 (May 1974): 879-976.

Ross, D. Reid. "Direct Investment in the United States by Japanese Firms: Benefits to the U. S. of Direct Foreign Investment." AIDC [American Industrial Development Council] JOURNAL 9 (July 1974): 27-37.

U. S. Commerce Department. Bureau of International Commerce. FOREIGN DIRECT INVESTORS IN THE UNITED STATES. October 1973. 52 p.

Contains lists of foreign firms with some control and/or interest in American manufacturing and petroleum companies in the United States.

U. S. Congress. House. Committee on Foreign Affairs. Subcommittee on Foreign Economic Policy. FOREIGN INVESTMENT IN THE UNITED STATES: HEARINGS, JANUARY 29-FEBRUARY 21, 1974. 93d Cong., 2d sess., 1974. 478 p.

U. S. Congress. Senate. Committee on Banking, Housing and Urban Affairs. Subcommittee on International Finance. FOREIGN INVESTMENT IN THE UNITED STATES: HEARINGS: PT. 1, JANUARY 23 AND FEBRUARY 22, 1974. 93d Cong., 2d sess., 1974. 150 p.

U. S. Congress. Senate. Committee on Commerce. Subcommittee on Foreign Commerce and Tourism. IMPACT OF FOREIGN INVESTMENT IN THE UNITED STATES: HEARINGS, DECEMBER 27 AND 28, 1973. 93d Cong., 1st sess., 1974. 88 p.

Webley, Simon. FOREIGN DIRECT INVESTMENT IN THE UNITED STATES: OPPORTUNITIES AND IMPEDIMENTS. London: British North-American Committee, 1974. 58 p.

An analysis and survey of the kinds of investments in the United States--future short- and long-term trends.

Young, John H. "The Acquisition of United States Businesses by Foreign Investors." BUSINESS LAWYER 30 (November 1974): 111-28.

Chapter 11

CORPORATE STRATEGIES AND IDEOLOGIES

Basche, James R., Jr. INTEGRATING FOREIGN SUBSIDIARIES INTO HOST COUNTRIES. New York: Conference Board, 1970. 50 p.

> A public relations essay on how to deal with various groups and problems in host countries.

_____. U. S. BUSINESS SUPPORT FOR INTERNATIONAL PUBLIC SERVICE ACTIVITIES: PT. 2, SUPPORT FROM FOREIGN AFFILIATES--ARGENTINA. Report no. 624. New York: Conference Board, 1974. 27 p.

_____. U. S. BUSINESS SUPPORT FOR INTERNATIONAL PUBLIC SERVICE ACTIVITIES: PT. 2, SUPPORT FROM FOREIGN AFFILIATES--BRAZIL. Report no. 616. New York: Conference Board, 1974. 25 p.

_____. U. S. BUSINESS SUPPORT FOR INTERNATIONAL PUBLIC SERVICE ACTIVITIES: PT. 2, SUPPORT FROM FOREIGN AFFILIATES--COLOMBIA. Report no. 643. New York: Conference Board, 1974. 24 p.

_____. U. S. BUSINESS SUPPORT FOR INTERNATIONAL PUBLIC SERVICE ACTIVITIES: PT. 2, SUPPORT FROM FOREIGN AFFILIATES--MEXICO. Report no. 617. New York: Conference Board, 1974. 26 p.

Beresford, Martin. "And Now, le Defi Japonais." EUROPEAN BUSINESS 42 (Autumn 1974): 17-27.

> Outlines the competitive strengths and strategies of Japanese companies based on their special financial system, the unusual government/business relationship, and the ready acceptance of change by the Japanese work force. Explains why head-on opposition to Japanese corporations may not be the best response and counsels the formation of a multinational joint venture.

Boddewyn, Jean J., and Kapoor, Ashok. "The External Relations of American Multinational Enterprises." INTERNATIONAL STUDIES QUARTERLY 16 (December 1972): 433-53.

Discussion of the emergence of and need for sophisticated public relations managers to deal with governments on the local, national, regional, and global levels.

Business International Corporation. MANAGING THE MULTINATIONALS: PRE-PARING FOR TOMORROW. London: Allen and Unwin, 1971. 162 p.

Based on the deliberations of the First European Movement Symposium in Davos, 1971. The book is a very good example of corporate ideology. It describes the economic and political environment as viewed by the MNC and points to ways of dealing with the problems of legislative and labor union constraints.

_____. NATIONALISM IN LATIN AMERICA: THE CHALLENGE AND THE CORPORATE RESPONSE. Research Report 70-3. New York: 1970. 87 p.

A report which discusses the threat to the functioning of MNCs posed by the growing spirit of nationalism. Suggests some measures which foreign investors can adopt in response to the nationalists' demands. Included is a brief description of measures developed by a number of foreign firms operating in Latin America.

Duerr, Michael G. THE PROBLEMS FACING INTERNATIONAL MANAGEMENT. Report no. 634. New York: Conference Board, 1974. 41 p.

An impression of current problems facing the U. S. international business community.

Duncan, William C. U. S.-JAPAN AUTOMOBILE DIPLOMACY: A STUDY IN ECONOMIC CONFRONTATION. Cambridge, Mass.: Ballinger, 1973. 218 p.

Describes the attempt of the American automobile industry to acquire a share of the Japanese industry.

Fielding, Edward V. SOME STRATEGIC OWNERSHIP CONSIDERATIONS FOR FOREIGN INVESTORS IN THE ANDEAN PACT REGION. Working Paper 712-74. Cambridge, Mass.: Alfred P. Sloan School of Management, Massachusetts Institute of Technology, 1974. 71 p.

Frank, Richard S. "Multinationals Mobilize to Preserve Favorable Tax Status on Overseas Income." NATIONAL JOURNAL 5 (July 14, 1973): 1019-28.

Kapoor, Ashok, and Boddewyn, Jean J. INTERNATIONAL BUSINESS-GOVERN-MENT RELATIONS: U. S. CORPORATE EXPERIENCE IN ASIA AND WESTERN EUROPE. An AMA Management Briefing. New York: AMACOM (American Management Association), 1973. 86 p.

A manual which points out the importance of public relations when dealing with host governments. The topics discussed are the nature

of MNC-government relations, the growing role of governments,
using intermediaries, and planning and controlling these relations.
An interesting example of an evolving international corporate
ideology.

Keegan, Warren J., and Masuda, Shigeru. "Strategies for Investment in Japan."
COLUMBIA JOURNAL OF WORLD BUSINESS 9 (Summer 1974): 80-89.

Model, Leo. "The Politics of Private Foreign Investment." FOREIGN AFFAIRS
45 (June 1967): 639-51.

Analyzes the negative attitudes toward foreign corporations and the
reasons for these. Ways of improving relations are suggested, among
these stimulation of indigenous technological development and investments to offset growing criticism of corporate behavior and influence.

Moran, Theodore H. "Transnational Strategies of Protection and Defense by
Multinational Corporations: Spreading the Risk and Raising the Cost for Nationalization in Natural Resources." INTERNATIONAL ORGANIZATION 27 (Spring
1973): 273-87.

Rogers, William D. "A Challenge for U. S. Investment in Latin America: Some
Unconventional Suggestions." LAW AND POLICY IN INTERNATIONAL BUSI-
NESS 4, no. 3 (1972): 557-74.

Views on technology transfer, monopoly and competition, and
nationalization policies, in light of growing economic nationalism
in the area.

Sherk, Donald R. "Foreign Investment in Asia: Japan vs the U. S." COLUM-
BIA JOURNAL OF WORLD BUSINESS 9 (Fall 1974): 95-104.

Weekly, James K. "Nationalism Rampant: The Challenge to International Business Investment." BUSINESS AND SOCIETY 12 (Spring 1972): 5-12.

Chapter 12

THE IMPACT ON LABOR

American Enterprise Institute for Public Policy Research. THE BURKE-HARTKE FOREIGN TRADE AND INVESTMENT PROPOSAL. Legislative Analysis, no. 4. 93d Cong., 1st sess. Washington, D.C.: February 22, 1973. 39 p.

   A review of the issues covered by the Burke-Hartke bill.

AFL-CIO. "U. S. Multinationals--The Dimming of America, A report prepared for the AFL-CIO Maritime Trades Department Executive Board Meeting, February 15 and 16, 1973." In HEARINGS--MULTINATIONAL CORPORATIONS. Prepared by U. S. Senate Subcommittee on International Trade of the Committee on Finance. 1973. 96 p.

   Problems posed by American-based multinational conglomerates alleged to undermine labor, national economic strength, and national sovereignty.

Amsden, Alice Hoffenberg. INTERNATIONAL FIRMS AND LABOUR IN KENYA: 1945-1970. London: Cass, 1971. 181 p.

   The study consists of three sections, entitled "The Historical Setting, 1945-56," "The Intermediate Years, 1956-63," and "The Years of Independence," respectively. The study shows the effects of large foreign corporations on the character and practice of labor relations in Keyna where such enterprises have had a decisive influence. The book contains a useful bibliography.

Babson, Steve. "The Multinational Corporation and Labor." REVIEW OF RADICAL POLITICAL ECONOMICS 5 (Spring 1973): 19-33.

   Domestic effects of investment abroad of large U. S. corporations.

Baker, James C. "U. S. Multinational Business: Hartke-Burke and Other Anti-International Business Legislation." AKRON BUSINESS AND ECONOMIC REVIEW 4 (Summer 1973): 39-44.

Bates, Robert H. UNIONS, PARTIES AND POLITICAL DEVELOPMENT: A STUDY OF MINEWORKERS IN ZAMBIA. New Haven: Yale University Press, 1971. 291 p.

A study of the foreign-controlled copper industry in Zambia and the political role played by mineworkers' unions.

Blake, David H. "Corporate Structure and International Unionism." COLUMBIA JOURNAL OF WORLD BUSINESS 7 (March-April 1972): 19-26.

A discussion of those corporate traits likely to contribute to the development of cooperation among unions from different countries.

_____. "The Internationalization of Industrial Relations." JOURNAL OF INTERNATIONAL BUSINESS STUDIES 3 (1972): 17-32.

Describes union attempts to cope with the multinationals by means of different forms of international cooperation.

_____. "Trade Unions and the Challenge of Multinational Corporations." THE ANNALS, September 1972, pp. 34-45.

Discusses the diminishing power of unions with respect to the MNCs and their reactions at various national and international organizational levels.

Bussey, Ellen M. "Organized Labor and the EEC." INDUSTRIAL RELATIONS 7 (February 1968): 160-70.

Outlines the problems labor has faced since the establishment of the EEC and the freer movement of capital, as well as some of labor's new strategies.

Casserini, Karl. MULTINATIONAL COMPANIES AND COLLECTIVE BARGAINING. Report presented to the Trade Union Seminar on New Perspectives in Collective Bargaining, November 1969. Paris: Organization for Economic and Cultural Development, 1969. 64 p.

The author is an official of the International Metalworkers Federation which has been most effective in its dealings with MNCs. The need for increased internationalization of labor organizations is stressed.

Cox, Robert W. "Labor and Transnational Relations." INTERNATIONAL ORGANIZATION 25 (Summer 1971): 554-84.

Presents the possibilities of a more internationalized trade union movement as a political force and the conflicts arising between them and nation states.

Crispo, John H. G. INTERNATIONAL UNIONISM: A STUDY IN CANADIAN-

AMERICAN RELATIONS. Toronto: McGraw-Hill, 1967. 327 p.

> This study, which was financed by the Canadian-American Com-
> mittee, is an analysis of the effects of international unionism based
> on a study of the role played by international unions in Canada.
> The book is based on 400 interviews with Canadian trade union
> officials, their American counterparts, governmental officials, and
> managers. The study ends with a summary of the advantages and
> disadvantages of international unionism for Canadian workers and
> Canadian business and the country as a whole. The problem of
> dual loyalty is discussed as well.

Flanagan, Robert J., and Weber, Arnold R. BARGAINING WITHOUT BOUND-
ARIES: THE MULTINATIONAL CORPORATION AND INTERNATIONAL LABOR
RELATIONS. Chicago: University of Chicago Press, 1975. 258 p.

Forsyth, David J. C. "Foreign-Owned Firms and Labour Relations--a Regional
Perspective." BRITISH JOURNAL OF INDUSTRIAL RELATIONS 11 (March 1973):
20-28.

> Forsyth seeks to explain the difference between the strike perfor-
> mance figures for foreign-owned firms in the U. K., found by
> Gennard and Steuer (see below), and those he obtained for U. S.-
> owned firms in Scotland. Firms in Scotland were more likely to
> strike than the firms in the Gennard-Steuer sample.

Gennard, John. MULTINATIONAL CORPORATIONS AND BRITISH LABOUR:
A REVIEW OF ATTITUDES AND RESPONSES. London: British-North American
Committee, 1972. 53 p.

> A valuable booklet about the effects of multinational companies on
> the conduct of collective bargaining and the change in issues be-
> tween employers and employees, such as productivity bargaining.

Gennard, John, and Steuer, Max D. "The Industrial Relations of Foreign-
Owned Subsidiaries in the United Kingdom." BRITISH JOURNAL OF INDUS-
TRIAL RELATIONS 9 (July 1971): 143-69.

> The authors found no difference in the number of strikes among
> foreign and nationally owned firms. Includes also a more general
> description of manpower utilization and labor practices. See
> Forsyth (above) for critical reaction.

Goldenberg, Shirley B., and Bairstow, Frances B., eds. DOMINATION OR
INDEPENDENCE? THE PROBLEM OF CANADIAN AUTONOMY IN LABOUR-
MANAGEMENT RELATIONS. Montreal: McGill University, Industrial Relations
Centre, 1965. 162 p.

> Presents the relations between MNCs and trade unions in Canada
> and the threat posed for Canadian labor's independence.

Great Britain. Labour Research Department. THE MENACE OF THE MULTI-
NATIONALS. London: LRD Publishers, 1974. 31 p.

Guenter, Hans, ed. TRANSNATIONAL INDUSTRIAL RELATIONS: THE IMPACT
OF MULTINATIONAL CORPORATIONS AND ECONOMIC REGIONALISM ON
INDUSTRIAL RELATIONS. New York: St. Martin's Press, 1972. 480 p.

> The book is based on a symposium arranged by the International
> Institute for Labor Studies to examine the emergence and future
> potential of trade union response to multinationals and the conse-
> quences of regional economic organizations for industrial relations.
> The essays are almost without exception very valuable, and the
> concluding essay by the editor gives an excellent introduction to
> the subject. Nine of the sixteen articles are devoted to aspects
> of the multinational corporation. The contributors include Cox,
> Perlmutter, Nye, Roberts, and David H. Blake. Contains an an-
> notated bibliography.

Hawkins, R[obert]. G. JOB DISPLACEMENT AND THE MULTINATIONAL FIRM:
A METHODOLOGICAL REVIEW. Occasional Paper no. 3. Washington, D.C.:
Center for Multinational Studies, 1972. N.p.

> Suggests that job displacement due to foreign investment in the
> United States has been minimal compared with other factors which
> contribute to unemployment.

Heise, Paul A. "The Multinational Corporation and Industrial Relations: The
American Approach Compared with the European." INDUSTRIAL RELATIONS
(Quebec) 28, no. 1 (1973): 34-54.

Hildebrand, George H. "Problems and Policies Affecting Labor's Interests."
AMERICAN ECONOMIC REVIEW, PAPERS AND PROCEEDINGS 64 (May 1974):
283-88.

> Discusses the effects of U. S. investments on workers and unions
> in countries of origin and host countries. Contrasts the advantages
> and drawbacks.

International Confederation of Free Trade Unions. THE MULTINATIONAL CHAL-
LENGE. Brussels: 1971. 81 p.

> A critical appraisal of the labor practices of MNCs and the con-
> sequences for social welfare.

_____. "Multinational Companies in the European Communities." ECONOMIC
AND SOCIAL BULLETIN 22 (March-April 1974): 1-10.

> Statement adopted by the Executive Committee of the European
> Trade Union Confederation, Brussels, January 24-25, 1974.

International Labor Organization. "Industrial Relations in a Multinational Frame-work." INTERNATIONAL LABOUR REVIEW 107 (June 1973): 489-511.

Contrasts the issues involved in the internationalization of capital as perceived by employers and unions. Mainly a presentation of views, the paper contains little analysis.

_____. MULTINATIONAL ENTERPRISES AND SOCIAL POLICY. Studies and Reports, New Series, no. 79. Geneva: 1973. 182 p.

Based on a meeting held in Geneva in 1972. Discussions on such topics as the power to transfer, firms' ability to withstand a strike, the locus of managerial decision making, and trade unions' structural response.

Jaffe, Eugene D. "In Defense of MNC's: Implications of Burke-Hartke." MSU [Michigan State University] BUSINESS TOPICS 21 (Summer 1973): 5-14.

Jager, Elizabeth R. "The Changing World of Multinationals." AMERICAN FEDERATIONIST 31 (September 1974): 17-24.

_____. "Multinationalism and Labor: For Whose Benefit?" COLUMBIA JOURNAL OF WORLD BUSINESS 5 (January-February 1970): 54-64.

A union representative's statement of the reasons for organized labor's opposition to "runaway" shops and the "export of jobs."

Kamin, Alfred, ed. WESTERN EUROPEAN LABOR AND THE AMERICAN COR-PORATION. Washington, D.C.: Bureau of National Affairs, 1970. 573 p.

Thirty-two essays on the implications of multinational business for labor. Describes collective bargaining procedures and other aspects of industrial relations in Western Europe.

Kujawa, Duane. INTERNATIONAL LABOR RELATIONS MANAGEMENT IN THE AUTOMOTIVE INDUSTRY: A COMPARATIVE STUDY OF CHRYSLER, FORD AND GENERAL MOTORS. New York: Praeger, 1971. 297 p.

An interview study of headquarters and subsidiaries of the three companies which traces the environmental factors favoring centralization or decentralization of decision making responsibilities. The author wishes to establish a model which explains labor relations decision making structures on the basis of the company's organizational structure.

_____, ed. AMERICAN LABOR AND THE MULTINATIONAL CORPORATION. Foreword by Robert G. Hawkins. New York: Praeger, 1973. 285 p.

An anthology which presents the complete spectrum of views concerning the "export of jobs" controversy between American labor, the federal government, and the corporations.

Levinson, Charles. CAPITAL, INFLATION, AND THE MULTINATIONALS. New York: Macmillan, 1971. 229 p.

> An analysis of potential trade union response to continuing global inflation and the rise of multinational corporations. The author is secretary general of the International Federation of Chemical General Workers' Unions (ICF). He establishes a causal link between the rise of the MNC and global inflation.

———. A CONCRETE TRADE UNION RESPONSE TO THE MULTINATIONAL COMPANY. Geneva: International Federation of Chemical General Workers' Unions (IFC) Secretariat, 1974. 70 p.

> The author outlines possible ways of counteracting the tendency on the part of MNCs to export jobs to low-wage countries.

Litvak, Isaiah A. "U. S. Domination of Canadian Labor." COLUMBIA JOURNAL OF WORLD BUSINESS 7 (May-June 1972): 57-65.

Litvak, Isaiah A., and Maule, Christopher J. "The Union Response to International Corporations." INDUSTRIAL RELATIONS 11 (1972): 62-71.

> The purpose of the paper is to examine the interface between multinational corporations and unions in individual countries.

Malles, Paul. "The Multinational Corporation and Industrial Relations: The European Approach." INDUSTRIAL RELATIONS (Quebec) 26 (1971): 64-81.

> Deals mainly with the challenges and threats of the MNC as perceived by the unions.

Millen, Bruce H. THE POLITICAL ROLE OF LABOR IN DEVELOPING COUNTRIES. Washington, D.C.: Brookings Institution, 1963. 148 p.

> Presents various types of labor unions and their integration into the political system. Stresses the need for corporations to understand the political nature of unions in the LDCs.

Northrup, Herbert R., and Rowan, Richard L. "Multinational Collective Bargaining Activity: The Factual Record in Chemicals, Glass and Rubber Tires." COLUMBIA JOURNAL OF WORLD BUSINESS 9 (Spring 1974): 112-24; 9 (Summer 1974): 49-63.

> These two articles dispute ICF claims of successful bargaining with multinationals. Levinson is charged with making his name synonymous with international bargaining and international unionism without any demonstrable record of action.

Piehl, Ernst. MULTINATIONALE KONZERNE UND INTERNATIONALE GEWERKSCHAFTSBEWEGUNG IM INTERNATIONAL ORGANISIERTEN KAPITALISMUS INSBESONDERE IN WEST-EUROPA. Frankfurt am Main: Europaische

Verlagsanstalt, 1974. 343 p.

> Reviews the growth of countervailing trade union power in reaction
> to the spread of multinational corporations. The goals of MNCs
> are seen as opposed to economic democracy and the policies of
> trade unions towards this goal. Includes case studies of industrial
> relations at Ford, Philips, Dunlop-Pirelli, AKZO-ENKA, and
> Nestle.

Roberts, B. C. "Multinational Collective Bargaining: A European Prospect."
BRITISH JOURNAL OF INDUSTRIAL RELATIONS 11 (March 1973): 1-20.

> Discusses the negative attitude of MNCs towards labor unions and
> the issues which drive unions toward collective bargaining on a
> European level despite the differences among them.

Seham, Martin S. "Transnational Labor Relations: The First Steps Are Being
Taken." LAW AND POLICY IN INTERNATIONAL BUSINESS 6 (Spring 1974):
337-73.

> Article based on discussions with trade union leaders, managers,
> and ILO (International Labor Organization) officials on the inter-
> nationalization of labor. Very informative.

Shearer, John C. "The External and Internal Manpower Resources of MNC's."
COLUMBIA JOURNAL OF WORLD BUSINESS 9 (Summer 1974): 9-17.

_____. "Industrial Relations of American Corporations Abroad." In INTERNA-
TIONAL LABOR, edited by Solomon Barkin, pp. 109-31. New York: Harper
and Row, 1967.

> A comparison of industrial relations in the other developed and
> developing countries, and U. S. firms' reactions to these different
> environments.

Smith, Stephen K. "National Labour Unions vs Multinational Companies: The
Dilemma of Unequal Bargaining Power." COLUMBIA JOURNAL OF TRANSNA-
TIONAL LAW 11 (Winter 1972): 104-57.

> A well-researched study of the provisions and conditions for col-
> lective bargaining in the European six, as well as the international
> union movement and the place of organized labor in the EEC.
> Has a concluding section on suggested improvements.

Stobaugh, Robert B. "How Investment Abroad Creates Jobs at Home." HARVARD
BUSINESS REVIEW 50 (September-October 1972): 118-26.

Tudyka, Kurt P., ed. MULTINATIONAL CORPORATIONS AND LABOUR
UNIONS. Selected papers from a symposium in Nijmegen, May 17-19, 1973.
Nijmegen: Werjuitgave SUN, 1973. 325 p.

Conference papers from a meeting which brought together trade union officials and scholars from Europe and the United States. The papers cover a wide range of approaches and topics, some highly theoretical, others in the form of case studies. Relations between multinationals and the state, trade union strategies and policies in developed and developing countries, and multinationals and the working class are among the topics covered.

Tyler, Gus. "Multinationals: A Global Menace." THE ATLANTIC COMMUNITY QUARTERLY 10 (Winter 1972-73): 512-26.

The author is assistant president of the Ladies Garment Workers (ILGWU). He argues that MNCs are able to circumvent almost any form of governmental control.

Warner, Malcolm, and Turner, Louis. "Trade Unions and the Multi-national Firm." THE JOURNAL OF INDUSTRIAL RELATIONS 14 (June 1972): 143-70.

The article points out the strength of unions vis-a-vis multinationals, which the authors consider quite formidable, and suggests new forms of collective bargaining. The problems connected with an international union structure are analyzed, but the authors are optimistic about their future effectiveness.

Chapter 13

THE TECHNOLOGY FACTOR

Adams, William J. "Firm Size and Research Activity: France and the United States." QUARTERLY JOURNAL OF ECONOMICS 84 (August 1970): 386-409.

> The author finds no positive relationship between firm size and research activity and concludes that "bigness" need not be fostered by European governments to counter the technological gap between the United States and Europe.

Atlantic Institute. THE TECHNOLOGY GAP: U.S. AND EUROPE. New York: Praeger, 1970. 158 p.

> Papers on the causes and cures for the technological gap between Europe and the United States. Contributions by Kaufman, Poullier, and Knoppers.

Balasubramanyam, V. N. INTERNATIONAL TRANSFER OF TECHNOLOGY TO INDIA. New York: Praeger, 1970. 157 p.

> The author argues that no clear agreements exist as to the payments for technology and that guidelines should be worked out. For complicated technology, the MNC is still considered the best transfer vehicle, while simpler technologies could be transferred by other means.

Baranson, Jack. INDUSTRIAL TECHNOLOGIES FOR DEVELOPING ECONOMIES. New York: Praeger, 1969. 168 p.

> A series of articles on the various aspects of technology transfer, such as choosing the appropriate technology, developing the ability to use it, and the role of MNCs in the transfer.

_____. INTERNATIONAL TRANSFER OF AUTOMOTIVE TECHNOLOGY TO DEVELOPING COUNTRIES. United Nations Institute for Training and Research (UNITAR) Research Report no. 8. New York: United Nations, 1971. 101 p.

> Taking a study of Japanese relations with Taiwan as his point of departure, Baranson argues that developing countries, instead of

forming automotive industries of their own, should specialize in the
production of parts for manufacturers in developed countries. He
also suggests the kinds of adjustments the receiving country will
have to make and provides a survey of international manufacturers
of parts.

_____. "Technology Transfer through the International Firm." AMERICAN
ECONOMIC REVIEW, PAPERS AND PROCEEDINGS 60 (May 1970): 435-48.

The costs and benefits of various forms of technological transfer are
discussed, as well as the conflicts arising out of such transfers.
Host country's preference for licensing agreements and company
preferences for "package deals" are compared.

Basiuk, Victor. "Perils of the New Technology." FOREIGN POLICY 1, (Spring
1971): 51-68.

Sees the technology gap between the superpowers (the United States,
the Soviet Union, and possibly Japan) and Western Europe increasing until, by the 1980s, Western European industry will be unable
to compete, with ominous consequences for the European standard
of living and political stability. The author argues that European
industry lacks the scale necessary for advanced technology. Suggests that the United States begin cooperative programs with Western
Europe collectively instead of continuing with present bilateral
arrangements.

Chang, Y. S. THE TRANSFER OF TECHNOLOGY: ECONOMICS OF OFF-
SHORE TECHNOLOGY, THE CASE OF THE SEMICONDUCTOR INDUSTRY.
United Nations Institute for Training and Research (UNITAR) Report no. 11.
New York: United Nations, 1971. 64 p.

A study of Mexican and Taiwanese offshore plants which produce
semiconductors for American firms under conditions which are clearly
of more benefit to the individual firms involved than to the host
countries.

Cooper, C., and Sercovitch, F. THE CHANNELS AND MECHANISMS FOR
THE TRANSFER OF TECHNOLOGY FROM DEVELOPED TO DEVELOPING AREAS.
Geneva: United Nations Conference on Trade and Development (UNCTAD),
1971. 87 p.

A report in four sections covering the characteristics of technological dependence, the means of transferring technology, the impact
of that technology, and problems associated with such transfer in
terms of corporate and government policies.

Duerr, Michael G. R AND D IN THE MULTINATIONAL COMPANY. New
York: National Industrial Conference Board, 1970. 74 p.

A questionnaire survey of 160 firms which outlines the reasons for
the relative centralization of the research and development function.

Gives a review of R and D coordination attempts and the financial implications of international R and D.

Dunning, John H. "U. S. Foreign Investment and the Technological Gap." In NORTH AMERICAN AND WESTERN EUROPEAN ECONOMIC POLICIES, edited by Charles P. Kindleberger and Andrew Schonfield, pp. 364-406. New York: Macmillan, 1971.

A historical review of British transfer to the United States in the past and U. S. transfers to Europe since World War II. An analysis of the transfer according to the complexity of the technology involved and the trade patterns of the products.

Fatouros, Arghyrios A. "The Computer and the Mud Hut: Notes on Multinational Enterprise in Developing Countries." COLUMBIA JOURNAL OF TRANSNATIONAL LAW 10 (1971): 325-63.

Freeman, Christopher. "Chemical Process Plant: Innovation and the World Market." NATIONAL INSTITUTE ECONOMIC REVIEW 45 (August 1968): 29-57.

Elucidates the relationship between research, innovation, and market performance in the international chemical industry, which is dominated by American firms. The two major explanatory factors are American design innovations and the utilization of process innovations from the major oil companies. This is the third in a series of international industry and innovation studies (see also following two items).

_____. "The Plastics Industry: A Comparative Study of Research and Innovation." NATIONAL INSTITUTE ECONOMIC REVIEW 26 (November 1963): 22-62.

Explains Germany's lead on the basis of superior technology and emphasis on technological progress. The second in a series of three industry studies.

_____. "Research and Development in Electronic Capital Goods." NATIONAL INSTITUTE ECONOMIC REVIEW 34 (November 1965): 40-91.

Explains American lead in the industry on the basis of superiority of original invention and not of military spending. The first in a series of three industry studies.

Gabriel, Peter P. THE INTERNATIONAL TRANSFER OF CORPORATE SKILLS: MANAGEMENT CONTRACTS IN LESS DEVELOPED COUNTRIES. Boston: Graduate School of Business Administration, Harvard University, 1967. 230 p.

A theoretical and empirical analysis of the proposition that the traditional methods of transferring organizational and technological resources from developed to less-developed countries through private

direct investment are, for economic and political reasons, not
adequate and that the management contract "by which a foreign
private firm performs essential managerial functions for a local
enterprise in which it has no ownership interests" is an alternatve.

Gruber, William H., et al. "The R and D Factor in International Trade and
International Investment of United States Industries." THE JOURNAL OF POLIT-
ICAL ECONOMY 75 (February 1967): 20-37.

The authors confirm findings which state that industries which conduct extensive research tend to be heavily involved in world trade.
They examine innovation, scarce economies, and the role of uncertainty, and apply these to the product life cycle theory.

Haskins, Caryl P. "Science and Policy for a New Decade." FOREIGN AF-
FAIRS 49 (January 1971): 237-70.

The author reviews the positive effects of technological transfers
both to developed and developing countries.

Hufbauer, Gary C. SYNTHETIC MATERIALS AND THE THEORY OF INTERNA-
TIONAL TRADE. London: Gerald Duckworth, 1966. 165 p.

A general discussion of technology transfer and the factors determining its flow. Licensing and direct investment are treated as an
aspect of the transfer.

Jones, R. T. "Fundamentals of International Licensing Agreements and Their
Application in the European Community." INTERNATIONAL LAWYER 7 (January
1973): 78-115.

Knoppers, Antonie T. THE ROLE OF SCIENCE AND TECHNOLOGY IN ATLAN-
TIC ECONOMIC RELATIONSHIPS. Boulogne-sur-Seine: Atlantic Institute,
1967. 24 p.

An evaluation of European efforts to close the technological gap.
The author suggests that U. S. companies should receive incentives
to move their R and D facilities to Europe, thus accelerating mobility among scientists.

Layton, Christopher. EUROPEAN ADVANCED TECHNOLOGY: A PROGRAMME
FOR INTEGRATION. London: Allen and Unwin, 1969. 293 p.

A monograph on the causes of the technological gap between Europe
and the United States and suggestions for closing the gap.

Lovell, Enid Baird. NATIONALISM OR INTERDEPENDENCE. New York:
National Industrial Conference Board, 1969. 65 p.

Interview study of 122 businessmen from fifty countries. Suggests
increased use of joint ventures and local R and D facilities.

McMillan, Claude, Jr., and Gonzalez, Richard F. INTERNATIONAL ENTER-
PRISE IN A DEVELOPING ECONOMY: A STUDY OF U.S. BUSINESS IN
BRAZIL. With Leo G. Erickson. East Lansing: Bureau of Business and Eco-
nomics Research, Graduate School of Business Administration, Michigan State
University, 1964. 247 p.

   A survey of eighty-one excutives in forty-seven U. S. firms in
   Brazil which seeks to prove the thesis that "the operations of foreign firms constitute the most effective means for international
   transmission of technology and experience."

Mason, R. Hal. "The Multinational Firm and the Cost of Technology to Developing Countries." CALIFORNIA MANAGEMENT REVIEW 15 (Summer 1973):
5-13.

_____. "Some Observations on the Choice of Technology by Multinational
Firms in Developing Countries." REVIEW OF ECONOMICS AND STATISTICS
55 (August 1973): 349-55.

_____. THE TRANSFER OF TECHNOLOGY AND THE FACTOR PROPORTIONS
PROBLEM: THE PHILIPPINES AND MEXICO. United Nations Institute for Training and Research (UNITAR) Report no. 10. New York: United Nations, 1971.
109 p.

   An investigation into the charges that MNCs often knowingly transfer inappropriate technology to developing countries. The author
   finds the causes to be more general in terms of national policies
   and the price mechanism.

Mason, R. Hal, and Masson, Francis G. "Balance of Payments Costs and Conditions of Technology Transfers to Latin America." JOURNAL OF INTERNA-
TIONAL BUSINESS STUDIES 5 (Spring 1974): 73-89.

   Includes findings of interview surveys with both U. S.- and Latin
   American-based firms to determine common practices with respect
   to terms of transfers, such as market restrictions, tying of purchases,
   and pricing.

Merhav, Meir. TECHNOLOGICAL DEPENDENCE, MONOPOLY AND GROWTH.
New York: Pergamon Press, 1969. 211 p.

   A tightly reasoned book in which the basic argument is that the
   transportation of advanced technology into the LDCs produces
   stagnation rather than development since it leads to early monopo-
   lization which stunts growth. Private enterprise (e.g., MNCs) is
   not a good vehicle for development.

Morley, Samuel A., and Smith, Gordon W. MANAGERIAL DISCRETION AND
THE CHOICE OF TECHNOLOGY BY MULTINATIONAL FIRMS IN BRAZIL.
Paper no. 56. Houston: Program of Development Studies, Rice University,

1974. 38 p.

>   Adaptation of production methods of thirty-five foreign firms to a
>   low-wage economy.

National Academy of Sciences. INTERNATIONAL FIRMS AND THE R, D AND
E IN DEVELOPING COUNTRIES. Washington, D.C.: 1973. 90 p.

>   Fifteen experts in the field of technology analyze the reasons for
>   the negative record in transferring research, development, and en-
>   gineering facilities and know-how to the developing countries.
>   Various proposals are made for increasing such transfers.

Ozawa, Terutomo. "Technology Imports and Direct Foreign Investment in Japan."
JOURNAL OF WORLD TRADE LAW 7 (November-December 1973): 666-79.

Pavitt, Keith. "Technology, International Competition and Economic Growth:
Some Lessons and Perspectives." WORLD POLITICS 25 (January 1973): 183-
205.

Penrose, Edith T. "International Patenting and the Less-Developed Countries."
ECONOMIC JOURNAL 83 (September 1973): 768-86.

>   A consideration of the negative and positive aspects of the inter-
>   national patent system. The author finds that stronger controls must
>   be applied to insure that the present system does not become too
>   expensive and inhibit the transfer of technology, as has happened
>   in the past.

Pugwash Conferences on Science and World Affairs. "Draft Code of Conduct
on Transfer of Technology." WORLD DEVELOPMENT 2 (April-May 1974): 77-
82.

Quinn, John B. "Technology Transfer by Multinational Companies." HARVARD
BUSINESS REVIEW 47 (November-December 1969): 147-61.

>   Analyzes the different models of technology transfer and the choices
>   made by developing countries. Japanese licensing policies and
>   Belgian direct investment transfers are alternative possibilities.

Richman, Barry M., and Copen, Melvin R. INTERNATIONAL MANAGEMENT
AND ECONOMIC DEVELOPMENT: WITH PARTICULAR REFERENCE TO INDIA
AND OTHER DEVELOPING COUNTRIES. New York: McGraw-Hill, 1972.
681 p.

>   Based on the authors' experiences in the developing countries, this
>   study concentrates on practical problems of management, but also
>   contains an analysis of micro- and macro-economic factors impend-
>   ing upon the management transfers of MNCs in developing countries,
>   mainly India. The basic aim of the book is "to develop answers

to key questions of transferability in the fields of international business, comparative management, and economic development."

Spencer, Daniel L. TECHNOLOGY GAP IN PERSPECTIVE: STRATEGY OF INTERNATIONAL TECHNOLOGY TRANSFER. New York: Spartan Books, 1970. 187 p.

A general book on technology gaps and transfers. Contains one chapter on international business transfers and a conclusion on a varity of transfer systems.

Spencer, Daniel L., and Woroniak, Alexander, eds. THE TRANSFER OF TECH-NOLOGY TO DEVELOPING COUNTRIES. New York: Praeger, 1967. 209 p.

A more general study of technology transfers and the social and cultural aspects of such transfers for the host countries. Not directly related to transfer through the MNC.

Stobaugh, Robert B. THE INTERNATIONAL TRANSFER OF TECHNOLOGY IN THE ESTABLISHMENT OF THE PETROCHEMICAL INDUSTRY IN DEVELOPING COUNTRIES. United Nations Institute for Training and Research (UNITAR) Report no. 12. New York: United Nations, 1971. 67 p.

The author claims that the industry is no longer oligopolistic, and that local producers can buy foreign technology without becoming overly dependent. Based on 360 cases.

Subrahmanian, Kalarickal K. IMPORT OF CAPITAL AND TECHNOLOGY: A STUDY OF FOREIGN COLLABORATIONS IN INDIAN INDUSTRY. New Delhi: People's Publishing House, 1972. 248 p.

A well-argued economic analysis of the types of technology imported which contends that imported technology has been too capital-intensive and has either replaced or reduced adequate domestic technology. The costs have also been too high in terms of foreign exchange payments. Improved screening methods are suggested.

Tilton, John E. INTERNATIONAL DIFFUSION OF TECHNOLOGY: THE CASE OF SEMICONDUCTORS. Washington, D.C.: Brookings Institution, 1971. 194 p.

The nature of technological diffusion is illustrated here with this excellent case study of the semiconductor industry. The author shows that small size was most conducive to innovativeness and diffusion in American firms, while large size was most conducive in Japanese and European firms.

United Nations. Conference on Trade and Development (UNCTAD). MAJOR ISSUES ARISING FROM THE TRANSFER OF TECHNOLOGY TO DEVELOPING COUNTRIES. Geneva: 1972. 64 p.

Based on a survey of member countries, the work gives an overview of the nature of technology imported as well as the costs associated with it. Lists alternative policy improvements.

_____. POLICIES RELATING TO TECHNOLOGY IN THE COUNTRIES OF THE ANDEAN PACT: THEIR FOUNDATIONS. Prepared by Junta del Acuerdo de Cartegena (TD/107). Santiago: 1971. 36 p.

Based on a survey of 451 technology contracts in the Andean Pact countries. Examples of export restriction, expensive imports, and suggestions for reducing the costs of technology transfers.

_____. TRANSFER OF TECHNOLOGY, INCLUDING KNOW-HOW AND PATENTS: ELEMENTS OF A PROGRAM OF WORK FOR UNCTAD. Geneva: 1970. 42 p.

A brief for multilateral agreements for the transfer of technology. Gives a short introduction to the role of technology transfers within the framework of economic development.

United Nations. Department of Economic and Social Affairs. THE ACQUISI-TION OF TECHNOLOGY FROM MULTINATIONAL CORPORATIONS BY DE-VELOPING COUNTRIES (ST/ESA/12). 1974. 50 p.

The report serves as a supplement to the United Nations document, THE IMPACT OF THE MULTINATIONAL CORPORATION (ST/ECA/6; see also United Nations, chapters 7 and 14). The two major issues stressed are the kind and appropriateness of technology transferred to the LDCs and the difficulties in assessing the value or price to be paid for such technology. The report includes recommendations to improve the bargaining power of LDCs with respect to the com-panies and suggests certain international regulation of technology transfers.

United Nations. Economic Commission for Europe. GUIDE FOR USE IN DRAW-ING UP CONTRACTS RELATING TO THE INTERNATIONAL TRANSFER OF KNOWLEDGE IN THE ENGINEERING INDUSTRY. 1970. 32 p.

United Nations. Industrial Development Organization (UNIDO). GUIDELINES FOR THE ACQUISITION OF FOREIGN TECHNOLOGY IN DEVELOPING COUN-TRIES: WITH SPECIAL REFERENCE TO TECHNOLOGY LICENSE AGREEMENTS (ID/98). 1973. 55 p.

Describes the methods of transfer and government regulations of such transfer in regard to licensing agreements. Contains a bibliog-raphy.

Vaitsos, Constantine V. "Patents Revisited: Their Function in Developing Countries." JOURNAL OF DEVELOPMENT STUDIES, October 1972, pp. 71-97.

A tightly argued critical assessment of the dysfunctions of the international patent system for developing economies. The author charges that the system inhibits the transfer of adequate technology, that it supports the monopoly that MNCs have on international industrial R and D activities, and that, because of its negative effect on the terms of trade, the patent system leaves developing states in their condition of technological dependency.

Vondran, Ruprecht. "Japan's Import of Technology." In JAPAN: ECONOMIC AND SOCIAL STUDIES IN DEVELOPMENT, edited by Heide Simonis and Udo Ernst Simonis, pp. 173-87. Wiesbaden: Harrassowitz, 1974.

Wilkins, Mira. "The Role of Private Business in the International Diffusion of Technology." JOURNAL OF ECONOMIC HISTORY 34 (March 1974): 166-88.

Detailed framework for the study of international diffusion of technology. Wilkins outlines eight different methods, differentiating between geographical transfer and true absorption.

Willy, Alexander. "The Establishment of the Common Market and the Problem of Parallel Patents." ANTITRUST BULLETIN 14 (Spring 1969): 181-220.

An interesting case study of a product simultaneously patented in several EEC member states in the name of a single patentee and the resulting export problems.

Woodward, William R. "International Patents: The Road to Uniformity." COLUMBIA JOURNAL OF WORLD BUSINESS 5 (May-June 1970): 75-82.

Discusses the Patent Cooperation Treaty which is attempting to reconcile national differences while maintaining national control.

Part III

THE ROLE OF THE MULTINATIONAL
CORPORATION IN THE INTERNATIONAL SYSTEM

Chapter 14

THE MNC IN INTERNATIONAL
AND TRANSNATIONAL POLITICS

Ackerman, Frank, and Kindleberger, Charles P. "Magdoff on Imperialism: Two Views." PUBLIC POLICY 19 (Summer 1971): 525-34.

> A critique of Magdoff's basic thesis of the identical interests between U. S. foreign policy and the activities of MNCs, as presented in his AGE OF IMPERIALISM (see below).

Ajami, Fouad. "Corporate Giants: Some Global Social Costs." INTERNATIONAL STUDIES QUARTERLY 16 (December 1972): 511-29.

> The author focuses on the multinationals as oligopolists and the problems arising for consumers. He asserts that MNCs structure global taste and consumption without any governmental checks on their actions.

Angelo, Homer G. "Multinational Corporate Enterprise: Some Legal and Policy Aspects of a Modern Social-Economic Phenomenon." RECUEIL DE COURS DE L'ACADEMIE DE DROIT INTERNATIONAL 125, no. 3 (1968): 443-571.

> The author calls for sociopolitical analysis of MNCs. The topics covered are organizational structure and evolution, the international environment of MNCs, and host country policies.

Ball, George W. "Citizenship and the Multinational Corporation." SOCIAL RESEARCH 41 (Winter 1974): 657-72.

> Paper presented at the Conference on the Meaning of Citizenship, New School for Social Research, Spring 1974.

_____. "Cosmocorp: The Importance of Being Stateless." COLUMBIA JOURNAL OF WORLD BUSINESS 2 (November-December 1967): 25-30.

> The author describes those institutions which have superseded the nation state and made it into an outmoded institution. Among these he considers the multinational corporation an important innovation which will improve the prospects for world peace. A world company law is discussed.

Barnet, Richard J., and Mueller, Ronald E. GLOBAL REACH: THE POWER OF THE MULTINATIONAL CORPORATIONS. New York: Simon and Schuster, 1974. 508 p.

> A major effort to show the global consequences--political, economic, and social--of the activities of multinational corporations. Part I describes the world as viewed by the corporations; part II deals with the development issue; part III attempts to show the effects on the political system of advanced countries. The authors describe the MNC "as the most powerful human organization yet devised for colonizing the future."

Behrman, Jack N. "Multinational Enterprise: The Way to Economic Internationalism?" JOURNAL OF CANADIAN STUDIES 4 (May 1969): 12-19.

> Questions the legitimacy and the responsibility of MNCs as a legal anomaly. Questions appropriateness of relying on MNCs as instruments of international integration.

Bergsten, C. Fred, ed. THE FUTURE OF THE INTERNATIONAL ECONOMIC ORDER: AN AGENDA FOR RESEARCH. Lexington, Mass.; Toronto; and London: D. C. Heath, 1973. 357 p.

> This report to the Ford Foundation is an analysis of the dominant economic issues of the coming decade. It consists of a lengthy introduction by the editor and eight essays on a variety of issues relevant to the multinational corporation and international relations. The two most central to this bibliography are Raymond Vernon's essay on the multinational corporation and Robert O. Keohane and Joseph S. Nye, Jr.'s "World Politics and the International Economic System." Vernon's contribution is an assessment of the state of knowledge concerning MNCs in which he recommends that case studies, rather than models and theories, are needed at this time. Keohane and Nye give a valuable introduction to the theoretical, conceptual, and empirical overlap between the international political and economic systems.

Blake, David H., special ed. THE MULTINATIONAL CORPORATION. Annals of the American Academy of Political and Social Sciences, vol. 403. Philadelphia: American Academy of Political and Social Science, 1972. 247 p.

> Each of the eleven contributors was asked to examine some of the changes stimulated by the internationalization of business. The central organizing theme was the MNCs impact on (1) the industrial system, (2) the nation state, and (3) the international economic and political system.

Calleo, David P., and Rowland, Benjamin M. AMERICA AND THE WORLD POLITICAL ECONOMY: ATLANTIC DREAMS AND NATIONAL REALITIES. Bloomington: Indiana University Press, 1973. 371 p.

> This book develops a critical model of the bases of a liberal world

economic system and the role of the United States within that system. It describes the Atlantic community and its relations with the rest of the world in all its aspects, and places the MNC within that general framework of analysis. Chapter 7, entitled "The International Corporation," presents an analysis of the political implications of foreign investments.

Diebold, William, Jr. THE UNITED STATES AND THE INDUSTRIAL WORLD: AMERICAN FOREIGN ECONOMIC POLICY IN THE 1970s. New York: Praeger, for the Council on Foreign Relations, 1972. 463 p.

The author is senior research fellow for the Council on Foreign Relations. His book deals with the economic relations of the United States, Japan, Canada, and Europe. He outlines desired policies with regard to trade, exchange rates, multinational corporations, agriculture, and private investment. The study is partly a review of the past twenty-five years, which were marked by cooperation, and partly a preview of possible revived nationalism of the coming twenty-five years.

Eells, Richard S. F. GLOBAL CORPORATIONS: THE EMERGING SYSTEM OF WORLD ECONOMIC POWER. Introduction by George W. Ball. New York: Interbook, 1972. 242 p.

Juxtaposes the multinational corporation as a modern organization with outmoded political institutions and geographic boundaries. Presents a search for "congruence," i.e. a search for political boundaries which will coincide with the corporate domain in order to modernize an anachronistic international system.

Fann, K. T., and Hodges, Donald C., eds. READINGS IN U. S. IMPERIAL-ISM. Boston: P. Sargent, 1971. 397 p.

Twenty-four selections by radical critics of U. S. foreign involvements which concentrate on the economic aspects, especially in Latin America. U. S. imperialism, according to the editors, "permits economic domination within the scope of international laws, yet without...redress."

Feld, Werner J. NONGOVERNMENTAL FORCES AND WORLD POLITICS: A STUDY OF BUSINESS, LABOR, AND POLITICAL GROUPS. New York: Praeger, 1972. 284 p.

An empirical account of the growth and spread of MNCs, organized labor, and other organizations such as parties, churches, foundations, and national liberation movements. Concentrates on the issue of MNCs and treats them from three perspectives: transnational initiatives, transnational effects and consequences, and transnational business collaboration. The empirical material is superior to the theoretical framework.

_____ . "Political Aspects of Transnational Business Collaboration in the Common Market." INTERNATIONAL ORGANIZATION, Spring 1970, pp. 209-38.

A shorter version of the item listed below.

_____ . TRANSNATIONAL BUSINESS COLLABORATION AMONG COMMON MARKET COUNTRIES: ITS IMPLICATION FOR POLITICAL INTEGRATION. New York: Praeger, 1970. 137 p.

The author correlates political integration and economic integration, representing the basic functionalist view that the MNC will lead toward increased political integration. The book describes the structure and problems of foreign investment in Europe.

Galloway, Jonathan F. "Multinational Enterprises as Worldwide Interest Groups." POLITICS AND SOCIETY 2 (Fall 1971): 1-20.

Argues that a pluralist rather than a state-centric view of the international system would be more adequate to account for the operations of MNCs.

_____ . "Worldwide Corporations and International Integration: The Case of Intelsat." INTERNATIONAL ORGANIZATION 24 (Summer 1970): 503-19.

A case study in regional integration.

Galtung, Johan. "A Structural Theory of Imperialism." JOURNAL OF PEACE RESEARCH 8 (June 1971): 82-117.

A theory of international politics which accounts for the domination of the third world on the part of the industrialized states, the multinational corporations, and Western cultural organizations. This was one of the first theoretical statements to describe the MNC as an integral actor in international politics, instrumental in structuring the division of labor within and among states.

Horowitz, David, ed. THE CORPORATIONS AND THE COLD WAR. New York: Monthly Review Press, 1969. 249 p.

A collection of six essays on the economic nexus among a small number of corporation owners and their involvement with American foreign policy-making, which has become identical with their economic interests, but "whose interests run counter to what have been America's most basic ideals."

Huntington, Samuel P. "Transnational Organizations in World Politics." WORLD POLITICS 25 (April 1973): 333-68.

The author describes the symbiotic relationship between MNCs and nation states, strengthening each other and serving different integrative functions.

Hveem, Helge. "The Global Dominance System: Notes on a Theory of Global Political Economy." JOURNAL OF PEACE RESEARCH 10, no. 4 (1973): 319-40.

> The article outlines a theory of a global political economy. It presents "global dominance relationships in terms of a vertically integrated system of control and accumulation, production and distribution on a global scale."

Hymer, Stephen. "The Internationalization of Capital." JOURNAL OF ECONOMIC ISSUES 6 (March 1972): 91-111.

> In this most political of his papers, Hymer contends that the integration of world capitalism requires political power which the MNC, given its minority power base, will not be able to muster. The MNC is thus the final state of capitalism and its most prominent sign of decay. See also pages 113-24 in the same issue of JOURNAL OF ECONOMIC ISSUES for comments by R. Z. Aliber and E. Benoit.

Jalee, Pierre. IMPERIALISM IN THE SEVENTIES. Foreword by Harry Magdoff. Translated by Raymond and Margaret Sokolov. New York: Third Press, 1972. 226 p.

> A careful analysis of imperialism in its totality. Reviews Lenin and Bukharin, most important changes from agriculture to extractive, capital and commodity export, and creation of a worldwide imperialist system.

Jenkins, Robin. EXPLOITATION: THE WORLD POWER STRUCTURE AND THE INEQUALITY OF NATIONS. London: MacGibbon and Kee, 1970. 224 p.

> Three approaches to international relations are discussed. The Clausewitz-Morgenthau paradigm is considered too unrealistic; the rank order model and the Marxist model of capitalist interpenetration are considered insufficient in themselves but adequate if combined into one model. The multinational corporation becomes thus an integral part of the new approach to the study of international politics.

Kennet, Wayland, et al. SOVEREIGNTY AND MULTINATIONAL COMPANIES. London: Fabian Society, 1971. 28 p.

> Discusses the role of MNCs in the European Economic Community (EEC) economies and the international liberalization that has occurred. Proposes a method for political participation in the MNC decision-making process.

Keohane, Robert O., and Nye, Joseph S., Jr., eds. TRANSNATIONAL RELATIONS AND WORLD POLITICS. Cambridge, Mass.: Harvard University Press, 1972. 748 p.

Contains several articles on the relevance of international business activities to international studies and presents the concept of transnational politics as that most relevant to the study of nongovernmental relations across borders. Relevant articles are by Morse, Gilpin, Wells, Krause, Cox, Evans, and Vernon.

Keohane, Robert O., and Ooms, Van Doorn. "The Multinational Enterprise and the World Political Economy: A Review." INTERNATIONAL ORGANIZATION 26 (Winter 1972): 84-120.

Based on nine major books, this review outlines the motivation for foreign investments and the effect of MNCs on international welfare and national sovereignty.

Kindleberger, Charles P. AMERICAN BUSINESS ABROAD: SIX LECTURES ON DIRECT INVESTMENT. New Haven: Yale University Press, 1969. 210 p.

Describes the structure and operations of multinational corporations, the attitudes of host countries, and recommends international supervision as a control of direct foreign investments. A short analysis of investments in Europe, Japan, the Commonwealth, and the developing countries.

_____. POWER AND MONEY: THE ECONOMICS OF INTERNATIONAL POLITICS AND THE POLITICS OF INTERNATIONAL ECONOMICS. New York: Basic Books, 1970. 246 p.

A book designed to fill the conceptual gap between international economics and international politics as disciplines. A very general discussion, helpful for political scientists wishing to acquire basic concepts in international economics.

Knorr, Klaus Eugen. POWER AND WEALTH: THE POLITICAL ECONOMY OF INTERNATIONAL POWER. New York: Basic Books, 1973. 210 p.

A book which discusses the nature of power in international politics and the relative weight and impact of military and economic bases of power. Knorr emphasizes constraints on the uses of both aspects of power in the modern international system.

Kolko, Gabriel. THE ROOTS OF AMERICAN FOREIGN POLICY: AN ANALYSIS OF POWER AND PURPOSE. Boston: Beacon Press, 1969. 166 p.

Chapter 3, entitled "The United States and World Economic Power," states that the United States regulates and supports the control and organization of the world economy. MNCs are an important tool for the success of that policy.

Krosigk, Friedrich von. "Marx, Universalism and Contemporary World Business." INTERNATIONAL STUDIES QUARTERLY 16 (December 1972): 530-48.

An introduction to Marxist political thought concerning the international capital movements. An interesting account of Marx's own thoughts on international politics juxtaposed with Lenin's revision of the theory.

Lenin, Vladimir I. IMPERIALISM: THE HIGHEST STATE OF CAPITALISM: A POPULAR OUTLINE. New York: International Publishers, 1939. 128 p.

A theory which aims to explain the paradox of an international system in which economic integration and violence among states are increasing simultaneously. International competition is being replaced by cartels and international banking operations.

Litvak, Isaiah A., and Maule, Christopher J. "The Multinational Corporation: Some Economic and Political-Legal Implications." JOURNAL OF WORLD TRADE LAW 5 (November-December 1971): 631-43.

Luxemburg, Rosa, and Bukarin, Nicolai. IMPERIALISM AND THE ACCUMULATION OF CAPITAL. Edited and introduction by Kenneth J. Tarbuck. Translated by Rudolf Wichmann. London: Allen Lane, Penquin Press, 1972. 289 p.

Except for Lenin's IMPERIALISM (see above), these two authors have contributed most to the classical Marxist theory of international capital and expanded the theory to account for the resilience of the capitalist world.

Magdoff, Harry. THE AGE OF IMPERIALISM: THE ECONOMICS OF U. S. FOREIGN POLICY. New York: Monthly Review Press, 1969. 208 p.

Presents a survey of the early Marxist literature and discusses three features of the new imperialism: the roles of the United States, technology, and multinational corporations.

Malmgren, Harald B. "Managing Foreign Economic Policy." FOREIGN POLICY 6 (Spring 1972): 42-63.

Reviews the lack of overall foreign economic policy. Sees the need for departmental coordination and institutional reform, with the efforts needed in the State Department being the most fundamental and important.

Mandel, Ernest. EUROPE VS AMERICA: CONTRADICTIONS OF IMPERIALISM. New York: Monthly Review Press, 1970. 160 p.

Mandel analyzes the competition between the United States and the Common Market and traces the movement toward international concentration and interpenetration of capital. Outlines a socialist policy to combat modern international imperialism.

Metzger, Stanley D. "Private Foreign Investment and International Organizations." INTERNATIONAL ORGANIZATION 22 (Winter 1968): 288-309.

A discussion of the relationship between private foreign investment and such international organizations as the International Trade Organization (ITO), the OECD, the United Nations, and the International Bank of Reconstruction and Development (IBRD). Sees the practical approach to the participation of foreign capital in the development of the LDCs as becoming more important and the ideological approach less so. Expresses some concern, however, over unilateral and doctrinaire attempts by the United States to protect American investments beyond the normal limits of international law.

Miller, Arthur S. "The Global Corporation and American Constitutionalism: Some Political Consequences of Economic Power." THE JOURNAL OF INTERNATIONAL LAW AND ECONOMICS 6 (1972): 235-46.

A plea for corporations to establish an equitable and just international order. The corporation is treated as "a political order" whose legitimacy should be accepted since the "nation state is obsolescent."

Modelski, George. "The Corporation in World Society." In YEARBOOK OF WORLD AFFAIRS 1968, edited by George W. Keeton and Georg Schwarzenberger, vol. 22, pp. 64-79. New York: Praeger, 1968.

The author argues that corporations can contribute to global society if they respond to global interests and needs before acting in their own pure business interests. The problems which host nations face in the present situation are discussed.

_____. "Multinational Business: A Global Perspective." INTERNATIONAL STUDIES QUARTERLY 16 (December 1972): 407-32.

Describes the global distribution of MNCs, analyzes the relationship between MNCs and war, and projects a world ruled by corporate giants.

_____, ed. "Multinational Corporations and World Order." INTERNATIONAL STUDIES QUARTERLY 16 (December 1972): special issue.

Contains seven articles on a variety of issues such as elite attitudes, the global social costs of MNCs, the military industrial linkages of U. S. MNCs, and a survey of classical Marxist theories concerning world business. Articles by Modelski, Boddewyn and Kapoor, Barnes, Fayerweather, Galloway, Ajami, and Krosigk are listed separately in this bibliography.

Moran, Theodore H. "Foreign Expansion as an 'Institutional Necessity' of U. S. Corporate Capitalism: The Search for a Radical Model." WORLD POLITICS 25 (April 1973): 369-86.

The models suggested and examined are based on the theory of sur-
plus capital and on the theory of declining profit opportunities in
the industrialized economies.

Nearing, Scott, and Freeman, Joseph. DOLLAR DIPLOMACY: A STUDY IN
AMERICAN IMPERIALISM. 1925. Reprint. New York: Monthly Review Press,
1966. 353 p.

A Marxist classic which describes "the growth of U. S. economic
interests abroad, and the diplomatic and military support accorded
them by the Federal Government." The book covers the period
from 1870 to 1920, tracing the expansion of American economic
interests abroad.

Nye, Joseph S., Jr. "Multinational Corporations in World Politics." FOREIGN
AFFAIRS 53 (October 1974): 153-75.

Discusses three roles of the MNC in world politics: (1) direct involvement in politics (the ITT case in Chile), (2) as a tool of one
government against another (U. S. extraterritorial control), and
(3) by creating issues to which other actors, such as states, must
react (intracorporate trade). The strains on the international system
and possible cooperative solutions are discussed.

Nye, Joseph S., Jr., and Keohane, Robert O.   "Transnational Relations and
World Politics: An Introduction." In TRANSNATIONAL RELATIONS AND
WORLD POLITICS, edited by Robert O. Keohane and Joseph S. Nye, Jr.,
pp. 329-49. Cambridge, Mass.: Harvard University Press, 1972.

Sets out the framework for the study of nongovernmental transnational relations which structure world politics in a new way, ques-
tioning the state centric view. The MNC is one of these new,
important actors.

_____. "Transnational Relations and World Politics: A Conclusion." In TRANS-
NATIONAL RELATIONS AND WORLD POLITICS, edited by Robert O. Keohane
and Joseph S. Nye, Jr., pp. 721-48. Cambridge, Mass.: Harvard University
Press, 1972.

Sets out a framework for research on the interrelationship between
governmental and nongovernmental international, transnational, and
national actors, and classifies them according to their degree of
central control.

Osterberg, David, and Ajami, Fouad. "The Multinational Corporation: Expanding the Frontiers of World Politics." JOURNAL OF CONFLICT RESOLUTION
15 (December 1971): 457-70.

An attempt to integrate the MNC into the study of world politics,
tying them into Rosenau's framework of "linkage politics."

Perlmutter, Howard V. "Emerging East-West Ventures: The Transideological Enterprise." COLUMBIA JOURNAL OF WORLD BUSINESS 4 (September-October 1969): 39-50.

> Using his own conceptual scheme and the literature on East-West divergence, the author assesses the possibilities for superseding ideology in favor of universal business practice and exchange.

_____. "Super-Giant Firms in the Future." WHARTON QUARTERLY 3 (Winter 1968): 8-14.

> An updated version of the view that economic interpenetration-- in this case through the vehicle of the multinational corporation-- will make war impossible or at least highly unlikely in the future.

Perroux, Francois. "Multinational Investments and the Analysis of Development and Integration Poles." ECONOMIES ET SOCIETES 7 (May-June 1973): 831-68.

Said, Abdul A., and Simmons, Luiz R., eds. THE NEW SOVEREIGNS: MULTI-NATIONAL CORPORATIONS AS WORLD POWERS. Englewood Cliffs, N.J.: Prentice-Hall, 1975. 186 p.

> Contains twelve essays (by Said and Simmons, Martyn, Mueller, Horowitz, Perlmutter, and others) on the "structural, functional, and developmental dimensions" of MNCs. The introduction by the editors challenges the view of the all-powerful, malevolent MNC.

See, Harold F., and Weston, Burns H., eds. "The Global Corporation: Agent of Change--a Symposium." JOURNAL OF INTERNATIONAL LAW AND ECONOMICS 6 (January 1972): special issue, 211-15.

> Papers by Behrman, Miller, and Vagts (listed separately in this bibliography), all concerning MNCs.

Staley, Eugene. WAR AND THE PRIVATE INVESTOR: A STUDY IN THE RE-LATIONS OF INTERNATIONAL POLITICS AND INTERNATIONAL PRIVATE INVESTMENT. Garden City, N.Y.: Doubleday, 1935. Reprint. New York: Howard Fertig, 1967. 526 p.

> A classic text in which the author discusses the following questions: "What are the various services which private investments abroad perform in the interest of governmental policy?" "What are the various services which governments may perform in the interest of its citizens' private investments abroad?" "What is the role of private international investment in the origin and development of international political friction and war?"

Strange, Susan. "International Economics and International Relations: A Case of Mutual Neglect." INTERNATIONAL AFFAIRS 46 (April 1970): 304-15.

The author argues that the two fields should pay more attention to each other. The importance of direct foreign investment for international politics is stressed, although the author doubts that the MNC will undermine the state as a basic unit of international politics.

United Nations. Department of Economic and Social Affairs. THE IMPACT OF MULTINATIONAL CORPORATIONS ON DEVELOPMENT AND ON INTERNATIONAL RELATIONS (ST/ESA/6). 1974. 162 p.

This is the final document to which the study MULTINATIONAL CORPORATIONS IN WORLD DEVELOPMENT (below) served as background information. The focus of this study is on international machinery and action. It is divided into three parts: (1) a general analysis of the role and impact of MNCs, (2) specific issues such as ownership, technology, employment, transfer pricing, information, and others, and (3) comments by individual members from the group. (See also United Nations, chapters 7 and 13.)

———. MULTINATIONAL CORPORATIONS IN WORLD DEVELOPMENT (ST/ECA/190). 1973. 195 p.

Contains a summary of existing research on MNCs, points out their contribution to growth and the need for controls. A code of conduct written and enforced by the United Nations is deemed feasible. Includes a chapter on the differential consequences of MNCs for developed and developing countries.

———. SUMMARY OF THE HEARINGS BEFORE THE GROUP OF EMINENT PERSONS TO STUDY THE IMPACT OF MULTINATIONAL CORPORATIONS ON DEVELOPMENT AND INTERNATIONAL RELATIONS (ST/ESA/15). 1974. 455 p.

Summaries of the oral and written statements presented for the report in the entry above. Hearings were held in New York and Geneva in 1973.

Vernon, Raymond. MULTINATIONAL ENTERPRISES AND NATIONAL SECURITY. Adelphi Papers, no. 74. London: International Institute for Strategic Studies, 1971. 34 p.

Vernon projects increasing independence for MNCs from the foreign policies of their countries of origin and decreasing interest in controlling the foreign policies of their home countries.

———. "Rogue Elephant in the Forest: An Appraisal of Transatlantic Relations." FOREIGN AFFAIRS 51 (April 1973): 573-87.

The author argues forcefully that U. S. preeminence will continue, as it is based mainly on technological superiority and leadership.

Wells, Louis T., Jr. "The Multinational Business Enterprise: What Kind of International Organization?" INTERNATIONAL ORGANIZATION 25 (Summer 1971): 447–64.

Presents the classification of organizational structures of MNCs (also used in his work with Stopford, cited in chapter 3) and their evolution. Some attempt is made to describe the MNC as a transnational actor.

Chapter 15

THE MNC IN THE INTERNATIONAL ECONOMY

Backman, Jules, and Block, Ernst. MULTINATIONAL CORPORATIONS, TRADE AND THE DOLLAR IN THE SEVENTIES. Foreword by Harold S. Geneen. New York: New York University Press, 1974. 108 p.

> A series of essays which describe the problems faced by multinationals in the present international economic system. Among the authors are Kindleberger, Vernon, and the editors.

Bain, Joe S., ed. ESSAYS ON ECONOMIC DEVELOPMENT. Berkeley: Institute of Business and Economic Research, University of California, 1970. 90 p.

> The book consists of four essays, delivered as the Rayer lectures at Berkeley, dealing with foreign investment and its impact on trade and welfare, as well as the current status of and prospects for Western investments.

Balassa, Bela A. TRADE LIBERALIZATION AMONG INDUSTRIAL COUNTRIES: OBJECTIVES AND ALTERNATIVES. New York: McGraw-Hill, for the Council on Foreign Relations, 1967. 251 p.

> Not strictly on the topic of multinational corporations, this book is an excellent description of policies which lead toward the creation of an environment favorable to the development of the MNC.

Balogh, Thomas. UNEQUAL PARTNERS. 2 vols. London: Basil Blackwell, 1963. 253 p., 296 p.

> Volume I presents the author's theoretical framework; volume II is a historical account of Balogh's contention that "the theory of international trade as it has developed over the years, and as still practised, has contributed to inequality and instability rather than to policies which stimulate a balanced growth of the communities based on decentralized decision making."

Barratt-Brown, Michael. THE ECONOMICS OF IMPERIALISM. London: Penguin, 1974. 380 p.

The author describes MNCs, which he calls "transnational companies," as an integral part and cornerstone of the new imperialism.

Behrman, Jack N. "Sharing International Production through the Multinational Enterprise and Sectoral Integration." LAW AND POLICY IN INTERNATIONAL BUSINESS 4, no. 1 (1972): 1-36.

Brau, Edward H. "Climate for Development: The Fund's Influence." FINANCE AND DEVELOPMENT 9 (September 1972): 40-45.

Discusses the role of the International Monetary Fund in economic development.

Brookings Institution. RESHAPING THE INTERNATIONAL ECONOMIC ORDER: A TRIPARTITE REPORT BY TWELVE ECONOMISTS FROM NORTH AMERICA, THE EUROPEAN ECONOMIC COMMUNITY, AND JAPAN. Washington, D.C.: 1972. 23 p.

"The report...suggests how the principle of greater interdependence and joint management could be applied to monetary policy, trade, investment, development assistance, and the monetary aspects of mutual defense arrangements."

Cannelos, Peter C., and Silbert, Horst S. "Concentration in the Common Market." COMMON MARKET LAW REVIEW 7, no. 5 (1970): 5-35.

Discusses the legal and economic bases for EEC merger policy which lead to the development of European multinational companies.

Caves, Richard E. INTERNATIONAL TRADE, INTERNATIONAL INVESTMENT AND IMPERFECT MARKETS. Special Papers in International Economics, no. 10. Princeton, N.J.: International Finance Section, Department of Economics, Princeton University, 1974. 38 p.

Cooper, Richard N. THE ECONOMICS OF INTERDEPENDENCE: ECONOMIC POLICY IN THE ATLANTIC COMMUNITY. New York: McGraw-Hill, for the Council on Foreign Relations, 1968. 316 p.

Devotes some space to U. S. direct investment, although the central topic of the book is international economic interdependence and a more effective payments system.

_____, ed. A REORDERED WORLD: EMERGING INTERNATIONAL ECONOMIC PROBLEMS. Washington, D.C.: Potomac Associates, 1973. 260 p.

A collection of articles first published in FOREIGN POLICY dealing with economics and foreign policy, monetary policy, relations with developing nations, and the allocation of the world's resources. Many of the entries are relevant to the role of MNCs in the global economic system.

Duprez, Colette, and Kirschen, Etienne S. MEGISTOS: A WORLD INCOME AND TRADE MODEL FOR 1975. New York: American Elsevier Publication, 1970. 668 p.

The book reviews traditional trade and income models and analyzes the world economy as it was in 1960 according to the Megistos model. The model divides the world into three zones--the capitalist, the communist, and the underdeveloped. These are then presented in terms of economic growth and foreign aid, and trade and capital flows. It concludes with a projection of the effects on the flow of commodities and investments throughout the world.

The Economist. THE FUTURE OF INTERNATIONAL BUSINESS. Special Supplement, January 22, 1972. 55 p.

_____. THE YEAR OF BARRIERS: AN INTERNATIONAL BANKING SURVEY. Special survey on international banking, January 27, 1973. SI-86.

Emergency Committee for American Trade. THE ROLE OF THE MULTINATIONAL CORPORATION (MNC) IN THE UNITED STATES AND WORLD ECONOMIES. 2 vols. Washington, D.C., 1972. 92 p., 132 p.

Volume I contains information about the operations of American multinationals during the 1960s: domestic and foreign investments and sales, domestic and foreign employment, contribution to balance of trade, technology transfer. Foreign direct investment in the United States. Volume II, subtitled INDIVIDUAL INDUSTRY ANALYSIS, presents detailed data about seventy-four U. S. corporations: investment activity, domestic and foreign sales, employment, contribution to U. S. balance of payments, technology transfer. The industries covered are food, paper, metal products, electrical machinery, auto, and aircraft.

Emmanuel, Arghiri. UNEQUAL EXCHANGE: A STUDY IN THE IMPERIALISM OF TRADE. With additional comments by Charles Bettelheim. Translated by Brian Pearce. New York: Monthly Review Press, 1972. 453 p.

The book is relevant to the topic of direct investment, although it deals mainly with international trade, because it recommends the creation of a "cordon sanitaire" around the developing countries to allow them to develop their own internal economies. Emmanuel argues that Marx's economic forecasts are being realized on a global scale and presents a theory of international trade based on the Marxian theory of labor value.

Goodman, Elliot R. "The Impact of the Multinational Enterprise upon the Atlantic Community." ATLANTIC COMMUNITY QUARTERLY 10 (Fall 1972): 357-67.

The author claims that MNCs have a far greater effect on international finance than does trade.

129

Hamada, Koichi. "Economic Growth and Longterm International Capital Movements." YALE ECONOMIC ESSAYS 6 (Spring 1966): 49-96.

> A mathematical model which combines growth theory and international capital movement theory. Applied and tested with a study of the United States and Canada.

Hymer, Stephen. "The Efficiency (Contradictions) of Multinational Corporations." AMERICAN ECONOMIC REVIEW 60 (May 1970): 440-48.

> Hymer's much discussed article which questions the assumptions that foreign investment is usually more efficient than domestic investment. The MNC will result in an uneven distribution of resources and power and will create great social and political problems.

Kojima, Kiyoshi. "A Macroeconomic Approach to Foreign Direct Investment." HITOTSUBASHI JOURNAL OF ECONOMICS 14 (June 1973): 1-21.

> The author compares the types, goals, and consequences of Japanese and American direct investment. Japanese are "trade-oriented" and will improve the industrial structure for all parties involved, while American investments are "anti-trade oriented" and will result in all the ills associated with U. S. MNCs: export of jobs, balance-of-payments difficulties, and protectionist policies.

_____. "International Impact of Foreign Direct Investment: A Japanese vs. an American Type." ORIENTAL ECONOMIST 41 (December 1973): 28-39.

> A shorter version of the article above.

Krause, Lawrence B. "The International Economic System and the Multinational Corporation." ATLANTIC COMMUNITY QUARTERLY 10 (Winter 1972-73): 497-511.

> The effects of the MNC on the system are identified as diffusion of technology and stress on the international monetary system.

_____. "Private International Finance." INTERNATIONAL ORGANIZATION 25 (Summer 1971): 523-40.

> Discusses the ability of private financial markets to infringe upon governmental policies, and the resultant international monetary crisis.

Krause, Walter. "The Implications of UNCTAD III for Multinational Enterprise." JOURNAL OF INTERAMERICAN STUDIES AND WORLD AFFAIRS 15 (February 1973): 46-59.

Machlup, Fritz, et al., eds. INTERNATIONAL MOBILITY AND MOVEMENT OF CAPITAL. New York: National Bureau of Economic Research, 1972. 708 p.

Two of the papers relate directly to foreign investment: Stevens on "Capital Mobility and the International Firm," and Severn on "Investment and Financial Behavior of American Direct Investors in Manufacturing." The rest of the book gives important theoretical clarifications of such issues as the effects of taxation and the measurement of capital flows.

Marcus, Mildred Rendl. "Developing Economic Growth in the World." SOCIAL STUDIES 64 (March 1973): 120-26.

Sweezy, Paul M., and Magdoff, Harry. THE DYNAMICS OF U. S. CAPITALISM. New York: Monthly Review Press, 1972. 237 p.

A collection of previously published essays on monopoly power, the international expansion of corporations, the theory of capitalistic growth, and direct foreign investment.

_____. "Notes on the Multinational Corporation." MONTHLY REVIEW 21 (October-November 1969): 1-7, 1-13.

A Marxist reaction to the growing literature and interest in the field. The authors argue that all capital has a national base and that the name "multinational," therefore, covers up Western imperialistic capitalist expansion.

Uri, Pierre, ed. TRADE AND INVESTMENT POLICIES FOR THE SEVENTIES: NEW CHALLENGES FOR THE ATLANTIC AREA AND JAPAN. Foreword by Sir Eric Roll. New York: Praeger, with the Atlantic Institute, 1971. 286 p.

Collection of seven papers which discuss the future of international trade and investment, trade policies of the EEC, the United States and the Soviet bloc in the 1970s, Japanese trade and investment policies, and the role of MNCs in this decade.

U. S. Congress. Joint Economic Committee. A FOREIGN ECONOMIC POLICY FOR THE 1970s: HEARINGS. PART VI: THE MULTINATIONAL CORPORATION AND INTERNATIONAL INVESTMENT. 91st Cong., 2d sess., 1970. Pp. 745-958.

An investigation of the effects of American corporations on the balance of payments and on technological innovation and productivity. Includes discussion of certain aspects of international labor reactions, and short statements by various American and European experts, including Kindleberger, Dunning, Rolfe, Stobaugh, Servan-Schreiber, Hymer, Rubin, and Watkins.

U. S. Congress. Senate. Committee on Finance. Subcommittee on International Trade. THE MULTINATIONAL CORPORATION AND THE WORLD ECONOMY (staff study). 93d Cong., 1st sess., February 1973. 48 p.

Whitman, Marina von Neumann. GOVERNMENT RISK-SHARING IN FOREIGN INVESTMENT. Princeton, N.J.: Princeton University Press, 1965. 358 p.

Describes and analyzes the International Finance Corporation, the World Bank, the Export Import Bank, the Inter-American Development ment Bank, the Investment Guarantee Program, and the Agency for International Development. Written mainly for foreign investors.

Chapter 16

THE INTERNATIONAL LEGAL SYSTEM

APPLICATION OF DOMESTIC LAWS

Becker, Loftus E. "Effect of the Common Market Antitrust Laws on American Companies." ANTITRUST BULLETIN 8 (January-February 1963): 3-79.

Behrman, Jack N. "Assessing the Foreign Investment Controls." LAW AND CONTEMPORARY PROBLEMS 34 (Winter 1969): 84-94.

> Argues that the Office of Foreign Direct Investment controls placed on foreign investment by American firms may be worsening the balance of payments deficit they are intended to remedy.

Blake, Harlan M., and Rahl, James A., eds. BUSINESS REGULATIONS IN THE COMMON MARKET NATIONS. 4 vols. New York: McGraw-Hill, 1969.

> Volume 1 covers the Benelux countries; volume 2, France and Italy; volume 3, West Germany; volume 4 the Common Market and American antitrust. The first three volumes were edited by Blake, the fourth by Rahl. The set is a handbook for businessmen as well as scholars. The first three volumes cover the institutional and economic facts of the six countries and provide information about the national laws which concern restraints of trade and monopoly. In addition, there are sections in each volume which treat the basic laws concerning economic regulations. Volume 4 is a treatment of European and American laws concerning antitrust matters and an examination of possible conflicts and international attempts to avoid such conflicts of laws.

Brewster, Kingman, Jr. ANTITRUST AND AMERICAN BUSINESS ABROAD. New York: McGraw-Hill, 1958. 509 p.

> Based partly on discussions with executives and partly on case studies, the book is concerned with how, and to what extent, the United States should try to enforce antitrust laws outside the country. It provides a thorough analysis of American antitrust laws and their effect on American relations with other countries.

Cattan, Henry. THE LAW OF OIL CONCESSIONS IN THE MIDDLE EAST AND NORTH AFRICA. Dobbs Ferry, N.Y.: Oceana Publications, for the Parker School of Foreign and Comparative Law, 1967. 214 p.

> A historical account of the law of oil concessions and an analysis of possible alternatives to such laws in view of the law applicable to state contracts and legal systems.

Commission of the European Communities. MULTINATIONAL UNDERTAKINGS AND COMMUNITY REGULATIONS. Unrevised translation. Brussels, 1973.

> Gives an overview of the evolving legal structure and arrangements within the Common Market.

Delupis, Ingrid. FINANCE AND PROTECTION OF INVESTMENT IN DEVELOP-ING COUNTRIES. New York: Wiley, 1973. 183 p.

> Designed as a practical guide for businessmen, this book was written by an international law professor and reviews governmental policies of potential host countries and the various investment incentives in such countries. It also covers possible areas of conflicts of interest, such as investment guarantees, nationalization, insurance arrange-ments, and joint ventures.

Donovan, Peter. "Antitrust Considerations in the Organization and Operations of American Business Abroad." BOSTON COLLEGE INDUSTRIAL AND COM-MERCIAL LAW REVIEW 9 (Winter 1968): 239-353.

> A thorough discussion of how extraterritorial issues, capital invest-ments, and overseas business establishment impinge on U. S. anti-trust laws.

_____. "The Legality of Acquisitions and Mergers Involving American and Foreign Corporations under the U. S. Antitrust Laws." SOUTHERN CALIFORNIA LAW REVIEW 39 (1966): 526-65; 40 (1967): 39-125.

> Discussion of the Sherman and Clayton Acts and their relevance for direct investment.

"Expropriation and the Act of State Doctrine: The Supreme Court Reassesses Sabbatino: First National City Bank v. Banco Nacional de Cuba (U. S. 1972)." LAW AND POLICY IN INTERNATIONAL BUSINESS 5, no. 1 (1973): 292-318.

> A reinterpretation of the court's 1964 decision regarding American investments abroad in the case mentioned in the title.

Falk, Richard. "Complexity of Sabbatino." AMERICAN JOURNAL OF INTER-NATIONAL LAW 58 (October 1964): 935-51.

> In its decision in the Sabbatino case (1964), the Supreme Court reaffirmed the Act of State Doctrine, but reinterpreted several occasions on which it might not hold. The Sabbatino case more

clearly delimits the role a domestic court can play in international disputes.

Friedmann, Wolfgang G., and Pugh, Richard C., eds. LEGAL ASPECTS OF FOREIGN INVESTMENT. Boston: Little, Brown, 1959. 812 p.

The principles and methods of protecting foreign investment in forty countries are presented by experts from those countries. In their conclusion, the editors give a comparative analysis of the material presented. Alternative forms of organization are discussed at length.

Fugate, Wilbur L. "Antitrust Aspects of Transatlantic Investment." LAW AND CONTEMPORARY PROBLEMS 34 (Winter 1969): 135-45.

Discusses the applications of American antitrust laws to United States firms operating abroad and the possible conflicts accompanying such applications.

Fulda, Carl H., and Schwartz, Warren F. REGULATIONS OF INTERNATIONAL TRADE AND INVESTMENT, CASES AND MATERIALS. University Casebook Series. Minneola, N.Y.: Foundation Press, 1970. 796 p.

Divided into two major sections--international trade in goods and commodities, and direct investment--the book covers various regulatory and legal aspects of these topics. Two issues are used to organize the work: the tension created between the principle of a free market, and governmental restrictions on trade, and the efforts of governments or institutions to regulate transactions in order to achieve certain objectives.

Goldstein, E. Ernest. AMERICAN ENTERPRISE AND SCANDINAVIAN ANTI-TRUST LAW. Austin: University of Texas Press, 1963. 391 p.

Comparative case studies of the variety of legislative devices employed to control restraints of competition and contrasting methods of approach to antitrust problems in Denmark, Sweden, and Norway. The author provides no conclusions and concentrates instead on presenting facts and case studies of American companies operating in all three countries.

Griffin, Joseph P. "The Power of Host Countries over the Multinational: Lifting the Veil in the European Economic Community and the United States." LAW AND POLITICS IN INTERNATIONAL BUSINESS 6 (Spring 1974): 375-436.

The article demonstrates "that a host country may, if it chooses, assert substantial extraterritorial control, both adjudicatively and legislatively, over the foreign parent within the limits of customary international law."

Joelson, Mark. "International Antitrust: A Look at Recent Developments." WILLIAM AND MARY LAW REVIEW 12 (Spring 1971): 565-79.

Discusses legal innovations in the United States and the European Economic Community, especially regarding patents and technology.

Lancaster, William, Jr. "The Foreign Direct Investment Regulations: A Look at Ad Hoc Rule Making." VIRGINIA LAW REVIEW 55 (1969): 83-137.

Addressed to the balance of payments problems in 1968-69 within the framework of U. S. direct investment regulations.

Lederer, William. "Long-Arm Application of the Sherman Anti-Trust Act to Industry in the Central American Common Market." UNIVERSITY OF FLORIDA LAW REVIEW 22 (1969-70): 235-60.

Discusses the relationship between the Central American Common Market (CACM) and the joint-venture implications of the Sherman Act, which creates uncertainties on the part of investors and thus prevents them from entering joint venture agreements.

Leleux, P. "Corporation Law in the U. S. and in the EEC: Some Comments on the Present Situation and Future Prospects." COMMON MARKET LAW RE-VIEW 5 (September 1967): 133-76.

Compares the consequences of the U. S. federal structure and the EEC political structure for acquisitions and mergers. Contrasts the more integrated U. S. structure with the nonunified capital market in Europe.

Lillich, Richard B. THE PROTECTION OF FOREIGN INVESTMENT: SIX PRO-CEDURAL STUDIES. Syracuse, N.Y.: Syracuse University Press, 1965. 222 p.

A study of various procedures used to protect foreign business, such as sovereign immunity, acts of state, and investment guarantee programs.

Mazaroff, Stanley. "An Evaluation of the Sabbatino Amendment as a Legislative Guardian of American Private Investment Abroad." GEORGE WASHINGTON LAW REVIEW 37 (May 1969): 788-815.

An analysis of the difficulties involved in implementing the Sabbatino Amendment.

Nehemkis, Peter. "Expropriation Has a Silver Lining." CALIFORNIA MANAGE-MENT REVIEW 17 (Fall 1974): 15-22.

Examines the possibilities of negotiating liquidation to the benefit of the American investor and the appropriating state.

Nwogugu, E. I. THE LEGAL PROBLEMS OF FOREIGN INVESTMENT IN DE-VELOPING COUNTRIES. Dobbs Ferry, N.Y.: Oceana Publications, 1965. 320 p.

The author concentrates his study on the legal problems involved in investing in developing countries and goes on to discuss various ways of guaranteeing those investments and recouping incurred losses.

Pfeifer, Michael G. "The Legal Framework for American Direct Investment in Eastern Europe: Rumania, Hungary and Yugoslavia." CORNELL INTERNATIONAL LAW JOURNAL 7 (May 1974): 187-203.

Rehbinder, Eckard. "The Foreign Direct Investment Regulations: A European Legal Point of View." LAW AND CONTEMPORARY PROBLEMS 34 (Winter 1969): 95-117.

A discussion of German and French laws in conflict with U. S. legal restrictions on direct foreign investment.

Rodley, Nigel S. "Corporate Nationality and the Diplomatic Protection of Multinational Enterprises: The Barcelona Traction Case." INDIANA LAW JOURNAL 47 (Fall 1971): 70-86.

Rollins, Cynthia. "The Extraterritorial Application of American Antitrust Law and the Export Expansion Act of 1971." NEW YORK UNIVERSITY JOURNAL OF INTERNATIONAL LAW AND POLITICS 5 (Winter 1972): 531-54.

Discusses the difficulties involved in the extension of American antitrust laws to international corporations, from both theoretical and practical points of view. Sees the need for international regulation of international antitrust, but also sees great difficulties in overcoming the sovereignty of individual states.

Rubin, Seymor J. "Multinational Enterprise and National Sovereignty: A Sceptic's Analysis." LAW AND POLICY IN INTERNATIONAL BUSINESS 3 (1971): 1-41.

The author interprets reactions against American MNCs as a reaction against foreigners rather than the extraterritorial threat of domination. Discusses legal means of reducing these fears. Outlines an international corporate law.

Stein, Eric. HARMONIZATION OF EUROPEAN COMPANY LAWS: NATIONAL REFORM AND TRANSNATIONAL COORDINATION. Indianapolis: Bobbs Merril, 1971. 558 p.

A description of the legal movement toward a system which facilitates European mergers and the Europeanization of capital.

Sturm, P. M., et al. BRANCHES AND SUBSIDIARIES IN THE EUROPEAN COMMON MARKET: LEGAL AND TAX ASPECTS. London: Dluwer, Harrap, 1973. 199 p.

Discusses the effects of company law, tax law, and other legal restrictions on the establishment of subsidiaries and branches.

INTERNATIONAL LAW

American Arbitration Association. NEW STRATEGIES FOR PEACEFUL RESOLU-
TION OF INTERNATIONAL BUSINESS DISPUTES. Dobbs Ferry, N.Y.: Oceana
Publications, 1972. 252 p.

> Describes the accession of the United States to the United Nations
> Regulation for Resolution of International Business Disputes. The
> book contains the rules to be followed in case of a dispute within
> the United States. The U.N. rules are very similar to those de-
> veloped by the International Chamber of Commerce for the settle-
> ment of disputes in other countries.

Athey, Ronald. "Foreign Investment Disputes: Access of Private Individuals to
International Tribunals." CANADIAN YEARBOOK OF INTERNATIONAL LAW
5 (1967): 229-40.

Cummins, Richard. "Protection of Foreign Investments: A Role for the International Court of Justice." NEW YORK UNIVERSITY LAW REVIEW, November
1963, pp. 918-47.

> Gives a short review of present means of protecting foreign invest-
> ments and outlines a proposal for individual direct rather than in-
> direct representation before the International Court.

Doman, Nicholas. "New Developments in the Field of Nationalization." NEW
YORK UNIVERSITY JOURNAL OF INTERNATIONAL LAW AND POLITICS 3
(Winter 1970): 306-22.

> Investments by socialist states in other states cannot be classified
> as "private" direct investment. The international legal issues are
> discussed.

Domke, Martin. "Arbitration between Government Bodies and Foreign Private
Firms." ARBITRATION JOURNAL 17 (1962): 129-44.

> A review of alternative proposals for arbitration agencies suggested
> by international organizations and associations.

Katzarov, Konstantin. THE THEORY OF NATIONALIZATION. With assistance
of A. W. Bradley for English edition. Preface by William A. Robson. Rev. ed.
The Hague: M. Nijhoff, 1964. 392 p.

> A comprehensive study of nationalization with examples from a
> variety of countries.

Kronfol, Zouhair A. PROTECTION OF FOREIGN INVESTMENT: A STUDY

IN INTERNATIONAL LAW. Leiden: A. W. Sijthoff, 1972. 176 p.

A study of the guarantees given directly or indirectly by states to foreign investors and the problems this raises for international law with respect to the settlement of disputes, etc.

Lalive, Jean-Flavien. "Contracts between a State or a State Agency and a Foreign Company." INTERNATIONAL AND COMPARATIVE LAW QUARTERLY 13 (July 1964): 987-1021.

Discusses the inequality between the partners involved in such contracts and suggests that transnational rather than international law applies.

Landwehrmann, Friedrich. "Legislative Development of International Corporate Taxation in Germany: Lessons for and from the United States." HARVARD INTERNATIONAL LAW JOURNAL 15 (Spring 1974): 238-97.

Notes a convergent trend in changes in international tax law in the two countries. They differ in regard to the treatment of income from the LDCs.

Schwarzenberger, Georg. FOREIGN INVESTMENTS AND INTERNATIONAL LAW. New York: Praeger, 1969. 237 p.

A comprehensive text which gives a historical overview of the development of international law in the area of foreign investment, as well as an international perspective on the legal policies of the IBRD (International Bank for Reconstruction and Development) and OECD (Organization for Economic and Cultural Development) and several major countries. The book concludes with a comparative study of current legal practices.

Steiner, Henry J., and Vagts, Detlev F. TRANSNATIONAL LEGAL PROBLEMS. Mineola, N.Y.: Foundation Press, 1968. 1280 p.

This is a series of cases, accompanied by some analysis of transnational legal problems. Among these are a number which deal with MNC-related issues.

Vagts, Detlev F. "The Global Corporation and International Law." JOURNAL OF INTERNATIONAL LAW AND ECONOMICS 6, no. 2 (1972): 247-62.

Reviews the "haphazard melange" of national rules, conventions, and tacit understandings which comprise the state of the law governing the global corporation. Discusses the possibilities for several means of control: deconcentration, restructuring, chartering as global corporations, establishing an international regulatory agency. Sees the first step as establishing an information-gathering agency with the authority to gain information from global corporations.

. "The Multinational Enterprise: A New Challenge for Transnational Law." HARVARD LAW REVIEW 83 (January 1970): 739-92.

The article presents a comprehensive review of the weaknesses of present national and transnational law to deal with issues and conflicts arising from the operations of MNCs. Conflicts must now be resolved by bargaining, rather than by legal means.

Weston, Burns H. "International Law and the Deprivation of Foreign Wealth: A Framework for Future Inquiry." VIRGINIA LAW REVIEW, October 1968, pp. 1069-1134; November 1968, pp. 1265-1354.

Written in the analytical mode of the Yale School of International Law, the article describes the process of deprivation and the possible reactions of the actors involved (states, firms, and individuals). The article gives an insight into the contextual complexities involved in each individual decision, but does not enable one to predict any specific outcome.

INTERNATIONAL CONTROL MECHANISMS

Furnish, Dale B. "A Transnational Approach to Restrictive Business Practices." INTERNATIONAL LAWYER 4 (January 1970): 317-51.

The author reviews the history of attempts to control restrictive business practices.

Goldberg, Paul M., and Kindleberger, Charles P. "Toward a GATT for Investment: A Proposal for Supervision of the International Corporation." LAW AND POLICY IN INTERNATIONAL BUSINESS 2 (Summer 1970): 295-325.

A much-quoted article on the possibilities of establishing a permanent international regulatory agency. The topics covered are taxation, antitrust, balance of payments, exports, and security.

Keohane, Robert O., and Ooms, Van Doorn. "The Multinational Firm and International Regulation." INTERNATIONAL ORGANIZATION 29 (Winter 1975): 169-212.

A comprehensive discussion of international control mechanisms and their institutional vehicles such as the OECD, covering both the formal and informal arrangements of control and regulation. The article discusses the effects of direct investment which determine the attitude toward regulation, as well as international measures to promote investment, international strategies to deal with investment, and speculations about the future.

Nehemkis, Peter. "Supranational Control of the International Corporation: A Dissenting View." CALIFORNIA WESTERN LAW REVIEW 10 (Winter 1974): 286-324.

Argues against international regulation of multinationals on the following grounds: (1) nation states are adequately powerful vs. MNCs and are satisfactorily defending their interests, (2) developing nations are too nationalistic to accept the international structures necessary for international controls, and (3) effects of MNCs have been generally beneficial to developing countries--ITT in Chile excepted.

Rubin, Seymour J. "Developments in the Law and Institutions of International Economic Relations: The Multinational Enterprise at Bay." AMERICAN JOURNAL OF INTERNATIONAL LAW 68 (July 1974): 475-88.

Focuses on the restraints on multinational enterprise.

Wallace, Don, Jr., ed. INTERNATIONAL CONTROL OF INVESTMENTS: THE DUSSELDORF CONFERENCE ON MULTINATIONAL CORPORATIONS. With assistance of Helga Ruof-Koch. New York: Praeger, 1974. 281 p.

An inquiry into the desirability and feasibility of an international organization that would affect the multinational operations of multinational corporations. Problems of developed and developing countries as well as organizational problems are discussed by a number of international authorities, among them Behrman, Rubin, Kindleberger, Hellman, Prebisch, Gordon, and Martyn.

Chapter 17

THE SCOPE OF INTERNATIONAL
INDUSTRY AND THE CONTROL OF RESOURCES

INDUSTRY STUDIES

Alexandersson, Gunnar, and Norstrom, Goran. WORLD SHIPPING: AN ECO-
NOMIC GEOGRAPHY OF PORTS AND SEABORNE TRADE. New York: Wiley;
Stockholm: Almquist and Wiksell, 1963. 507 p.

> A comprehensive survey of the global shipping industry and its re-
> lation to trade and port traffic.

Brown, Martin S., and Butler, John. THE PRODUCTION, MARKETING AND
CONSUMPTION OF COPPER AND ALUMINIUM. New York: Praeger, 1968.
216 p.

> Part II of this study deals with the marketing of copper and alumin-
> ium, stockpiling, pricing, substitution, and the problems associated
> with these factors.

Bryden, John M. TOURISM AND DEVELOPMENT: A CASE STUDY OF THE
COMMONWELATH CARIBBEAN. Cambridge: At the University Press, 1973.
236 p.

> A study of foreign investment in international tourism. Shows that
> the characteristics of the international hotel industry do not contrib-
> ute to development. A case study of the British West Indies.

Dahl, Frederick R. "International Operations of U. S. Banks: Growth and
Public Policy Implications." LAW AND CONTEMPORARY PROBLEMS 32 (Winter
1967): 100-130.

> A study of the international operations of major American banks
> and the difficulties in supervising the system. The article gives a
> survey of the existing global distribution of U. S. banks, as well
> as the structure of the international banking system.

Gaedeke, Ralph M. "Selected U. S. Multinational Service Firms in Perspective." JOURNAL OF INTERNATIONAL BUSINESS STUDIES 4 (Spring 1973): 61-66.

> Considers advertising, consulting, and law firms.

Girvan, Norman. "Making the Rules of the Game: Country-Company Agreements in the Bauxite Industry." SOCIAL AND ECONOMIC STUDIES (Kingston) 20 (December 1971): 378-419.

> The author aims to show that company-country agreements are institutionalized so as to benefit the former. This is seen as part of a wider strategy to control their political environment.

Grant, C. H. "Political Sequel to Alcan Nationalization in Guyana--the International Aspects." SOCIAL AND ECONOMIC STUDIES (Kingston) 22 (June 1973): 249-71.

> Nationalization of the Domerara Bauxite Company (Demba), a subsidiary of Aluminium Company of Canada (Alcan), in 1971 is considered in light of the political situation in Guyana and international pressures.

Gray, H. Peter. INTERNATIONAL TRAVEL--INTERNATIONAL TRADE. Lexington, Mass.: D. C. Heath, 1970. 264 p.

> Describes the international expansion of hotels and motels as well as retail and wholesale firms across national frontiers. A good economic analysis exhibiting some awareness of political consequences.

Guback, Thomas H. THE INTERNATIONAL FILM INDUSTRY: WESTERN EUROPE AND AMERICA SINCE 1945. Bloomington: Indiana University Press, 1969. 244 p.

> The book is a case study of an internationalized industry. Its thesis is that oligopoly and growth have developed at the expense of filming as an art. The author describes the loss of diversity and cultural pluralism.

Harman, Alvin J. THE INTERNATIONAL COMPUTER INDUSTRY: INNOVATION AND COMPARATIVE ADVANTAGE. Cambridge, Mass.: Harvard University Press, 1971. 181 p.

> The book's thesis is that any country with technological superiority in any area will gain comparative advantage over less innovative countries.

Hochmuth, Milton S. ORGANIZING THE TRANSNATIONAL: THE EXPERIENCE WITH TRANSNATIONAL ENTERPRISE IN ADVANCED TECHNOLOGY. Foreword by Christopher Layton. Leiden: Sijthoff, 1974. 211 p.

> A general account of transferring highly advanced technology in developed regions.

Horst, Thomas. AT HOME ABROAD: A STUDY OF THE DOMESTIC AND FOREIGN OPERATIONS OF THE AMERICAN FOOD PROCESSING INDUSTRY. Cambridge, Mass.: Ballinger, 1974. 158 p.

> Gives the acquisition of marketing advantage as the major determinant of "going multinational" in an otherwise uncharacteristic multinational industry.

International Bank for Reconstruction and Development. International Development Association. MANUFACTURE OF HEAVY ELECTRICAL EQUIPMENT IN DEVELOPING COUNTRIES. Report no. EC-161. Prepared by Ayhan Cilingiroglu. 2d ed. Washington, D.C.: 1969. 133 p.

> The main focus of the study is on the comparison of prices and costs in developing countries with those in the international market. The role of the corporations and governments and their policies is closely analyzed. The study evaluates corporate contributions to development as positive ones.

Knudsen, Olav. THE POLITICS OF INTERNATIONAL SHIPPING: CONFLICT AND INTERACTION IN A TRANSNATIONAL ISSUE-AREA, 1946-1968. Lexington, Mass.: Lexington Books, 1973. 221 p.

> An empirical study of the international shipping industry.

Konig, Wolfgang. "Financial Institutions in Latin American Development." In LATIN AMERICA IN THE INTERNATIONAL ECONOMY, edited by Victor L. Urquidi and Rosemary Thorp, pp. 116-63. London: Macmillan, 1973.

> Deals with the IMF (International Monetary Fund), IBRD (International Bank for Reconstruction and Development), IFC (International Finance Corporation), IDA (International Development Agency), and IDB (International Development Bank) as mechanisms for multilateral collaboration.

Lee, Wayne J., ed. THE INTERNATIONAL COMPUTER INDUSTRY. Washington, D.C.: Applied Library Resources, 1971. 299 p.

Lees, Francis A. INTERNATIONAL BANKING AND FINANCE. New York: Wiley, 1974. 419 p.

> A study of the international activities of American, British, Swiss, German, and Japanese banks, their options and strategies. The issues discussed are loans, money transfers, investment banking, and merchant banking.

Moore, John R., and Padovano, Frank A. U. S. INVESTMENT IN LATIN AMERICAN FOOD PROCESSING. New York: Praeger, 1967. 208 p.

> The study is based largely on interviews with businessmen and public officials in eleven Latin American countries. It outlines

the extent of U. S. involvement in food processing and discusses the incentives and barriers to foreign investors.

Moore, Russell M. "The Role of International Firms in Latin American Automobile Industry." JOURNAL OF INTERNATIONAL BUSINESS STUDIES 3 (Spring 1972): 51-67.

Moran, Theodore H. "New Deal or Raw Deal in Raw Materials." FOREIGN POLICY 5 (Winter 1971-72): 119-34.

An analysis of the problems encountered by a government wishing to nationalize a highly vertically integrated multinational which has tight control over the market. The controls and the dominance of the global market by an oligopoly in any of the extractive industries might be an equally threatening alternative.

Pillai, K. G. J. THE AIR NET: THE CASE AGAINST THE WORLD AVIATION CARTEL. New York: Grossman, 1969. 212 p.

A critique of the International Air Transport Association and its monopoly pricing. The author claims that the absence of governmental control, despite governmental ownership and subsidies, is largely to blame for the high passenger and freight fares.

Robinson, Stuart W., Jr. MULTINATIONAL BANKING: A STUDY OF CERTAIN LEGAL AND FINANCIAL ASPECTS OF THE POSTWAR OPERATIONS OF U. S. BRANCH BANKS IN WESTERN EUROPE. Leiden: Sijthoff, 1972. 316 p.

An analysis of the establishment and organizational structures of private financial institutions and the transfer of purchasing power across national borders.

Strazheim, Malcolm. THE INTERNATIONAL AIRLINE INDUSTRY. Washington, D.C.: Brookings Institution, 1969. 297 p.

A book about the economics and politics of pricing in the airlines industry, and the connections between the industry and international tourism.

Sundstrom, G. O. Zacharias. PUBLIC INTERNATIONAL UTILITY CORPORATIONS: CASE STUDIES OF PUBLIC INTERNATIONAL INSTITUTIONS IN CORPORATE FORM. Introduction by Wolfgang G. Friedmann. Leiden: Sijthoff, 1972. 140 p.

Thayer, Fredrick C. "International Air Transport: A Microcosm in Need of New Approaches, A Review." INTERNATIONAL ORGANIZATION 25, no. 4 (1971): 875-98.

Turner, Louis. MULTINATIONAL COMPANIES AND THE THIRD WORLD. New York: Hill and Wang, 1973. 294 p.

The book describes the political and economic impact of MNCs on developing economies. It contains special chapters on the negative effects of international tourism and the emerging international division of labor.

Vaughn, Charles L. "International Franchising." CORNELL HOTEL AND RESTAURANT ADMINISTRATION QUARTERLY 14 (February 1974): 103-10.

An account of franchising by American firms.

Weinstein, Arnold K. "The International Expansion of U. S. Multinational Advertising Agencies." MSU [Michigan State University] BUSINESS TOPICS 22 (Summer 1974): 29-35.

Reports on a study of the entry motivations and entry and ownership strategies used by U. S. multinational advertising agencies to effect their overseas expansions. Sees some motivations as offensive and some defensive.

Wells, Alan F. PICTURE TUBE IMPERIALISM? THE IMPACT OF U. S. TELEVISION ON LATIN AMERICA. Maryknoll, N.Y.: Orbis Books, 1972. 197 p.

A study in cultural imperialism and the natural dominance of large American TV producers. Discusses the role of U. S. investments in Latin American broadcasting and television.

Wortzel, Laurence. SCIENTISTS AND SALESMEN: THE MULTINATIONAL SPREAD OF THE U. S. PHARMACEUTICAL INDUSTRY. New York: Basic Books, forthcoming.

THE CASE OF PETROLEUM

Adelman, Morris A. THE WORLD PETROLEUM MARKET, 1946-1969. Baltimore, Md.: Johns Hopkins University Press, for Resources for the Future, 1972. 438 p.

Both an industry study and a natural resources study, the book is divided into three parts: part I deals with production costs and the structure of the market; part II concerns market price and is an attempt to assess the "real price of crude oil"; part III contains a summary and conclusions. The author is more interested in economic questions than in political or strategic ones.

_____. "Is the Oil Shortage Real?" FOREIGN POLICY 9 (Winter 1972-73): 69-107.

The author argues that there is "absolutely no basis to fear an acute oil scarcity over the next 15 years." U. S. policies make possible the high prices charged consumer countries by the major multinational companies.

          . " 'World Oil' and the Theory of Industrial Organization." In INDUS-
TRIAL ORGANIZATION AND ECONOMIC DEVELOPMENT, edited by Jesse W.
Markham and Gustav F. Papanek, pp. 136-53. Boston: Houghton Mifflin,
1970.

Barrows, Gordon H. THE INTERNATIONAL PETROLEUM INDUSTRY. 2 vols.
New York: International Petroleum Institute, 1965, 1967. 285 p., 371 p.

Volume 1 describes the oil and gas industry on a global level, in
Europe, and in the Middle East. Volume 2 covers the Americas,
Africa, and the Far East.

Chase Manhattan Bank. CAPITAL INVESTMENTS OF THE WORLD PETROLEUM
INDUSTRY. New York. Annual.

An annual survey of the worldwide capital investments in the
petroleum industry, prepared by the Energy Division of the Chase
Manhattan Bank.

Evan, Harry Z. "The Multinational Oil Company and the Nation State."
JOURNAL OF WORLD TRADE LAW 4 (September-October 1970): 666-85.

An analysis of the industry in terms of the major actors involved:
the major companies, the producing countries, the parent company
countries, and the consuming countries.

Hartshorn, J. E. OIL COMPANIES AND GOVERNMENTS: AN ACCOUNT
OF THE INTERNATIONAL OIL INDUSTRY IN ITS POLITICAL ENVIRONMENT.
London: Faber and Faber, 1967. 410 p.

A considerably revised edition of a book which first appeared in
1962. Describes the behavior of the international oil industry and
its interaction with various national governments.

Issawi, Charles P., and Yeganeh, Mohammed. THE ECONOMICS OF MIDDLE
EASTERN OIL. New York: Praeger, 1962. 230 p.

The book concentrates on the period 1948-60, a period of major
growth, and the interdependence between producers, transit countries, and consumers.

Jacoby, Neil H. MULTINATIONAL OIL: A STUDY IN INDUSTRIAL DYNAMICS.
New York: Macmillan, 1974. 323 p.

Focuses on the competition in and performance of the international
oil industry. Also treats the roles of consumers, governments, and
enterprises.

Klebanoff, Shoshana. MIDDLE EAST OIL AND U. S. FOREIGN POLICY: WITH SPECIAL REFERENCE TO THE U. S. ENERGY CRISIS. New York: Praeger, 1974. 288 p.

Examines the role of the multinational oil companies in shaping U. S. foreign policy.

Levy, Walter J. "World Oil Cooperation or International Chaos." FOREIGN AFFAIRS 52 (July 1974): 690-713.

McKie, James W. "The Political Economy of World Petroleum." AMERICAN ECONOMIC REVIEW 64 (May 1974): 51-57.

Mikdashi, Zuhayr M. THE COMMUNITY OF OIL EXPORTING COUNTRIES: A STUDY IN GOVERNMENTAL COOPERATION. Ithaca, N.Y.: Cornell University Press, 1972. 239 p.

Describes the genesis of OPEC since 1960. Concludes that the early problems stemmed from the fact that OPEC remained confined to its original objectives. Describes the transfer of control from the oil companies to governments, the conflicting interests and ideologies involved in the cooperative attempt. Includes a chapter on the terms of trade between producing and consuming countries.

Mikesell, Raymond F., et al. FOREIGN INVESTMENT IN THE PETROLEUM AND MINERAL INDUSTRIES: CASE STUDIES OF INVESTOR-HOST COUNTRY RELATIONS. Baltimore, Md.: Johns Hopkins University Press, for Resources for the Future, 1970. 459 p.

A very comprehensive volume with four general chapters and ten case studies. According to the authors, there are "two major interests of this book, namely (a) how can the extractive industries make a larger contribution to the economic welfare of the developing countries? and (b) how can the resources produced by the developing countries make a larger contribution to world welfare?"

Murphy, E. E., Jr. "Oil Operations in Latin America: The Scope for Private Enterprises." INTERNATIONAL LAWYER 2 (April 1968): 455-98.

Nash, Gerald D. UNITED STATES OIL POLICY, 1890-1964: BUSINESS AND GOVERNMENT IN TWENTIETH CENTURY AMERICA. Pittsburgh: University of Pittsburgh Press, 1968. 286 p.

The study analyses and describes the growth of cooperation as a prime characteristic of public policy in the petroleum industry.

National Council of Churches. Corporate Information Center. GULF OIL-- PORTUGUESE ALLY IN ANGOLA. New York: December 1972. 26 p.

Issued in cooperation with a project on U. S. investments in Southern Africa.

Pearson, Scott R. PETROLEUM AND THE NIGERIAN ECONOMY. Stanford, Calif.: Stanford University Press, 1970. 235 p.

Places the Nigerian petroleum industry into the context of the international oil industry and the special problems of foreign investment in a developing country. Pearson considers the economic contributions as so substantial that they offset any political costs.

Penrose, Edith T. THE GROWTH OF FIRMS, MIDDLE EAST OIL AND OTHER ESSAYS. London: Frank Cass, 1971. 336 p.

Section II (pages 139-244), entitled "Multinational Firms in the International Petroleum Industry," contains seven of the author's articles concerned generally with the impact of multinational corporations on their Middle Eastern hosts. Included are historical and structural analyses of the industry pre- and post-OPEC.

_____. THE LARGE INTERNATIONAL FIRM IN DEVELOPING COUNTRIES: THE INTERNATIONAL PETROLEUM INDUSTRY. London: George Allen and Unwin, 1968. 311 p.

Describes the history of expansion of large firms in the oil industry, discusses governmental attitudes, and suggests international controls. The multinationality of these firms is analyzed at length.

Rouhani, Fuad. A HISTORY OF OPEC. New York: Praeger, 1971. 281 p.

The author was the first Secretary General of OPEC from 1961-64. He suggests that an alliance between OPEC countries and companies against the interests of consumers in lower prices might be feasible in the future.

Schatzl, Ludwig H. PETROLEUM IN NIGERIA. Ibadan: Oxford University Press, 1969. 257 p.

A detailed account of the history and present state of the role of Nigerian petroleum in the Nigerian economy and the role of the international petroleum corporations in determining the course of development in the industry.

Schurr, Sam H., and Homan, Paul T., et al. MIDDLE EASTERN OIL AND THE WESTERN WORLD: PROBLEMS AND PROSPECTS. New York: American Elsevier Publishing, 1971. 206 p.

The book measures the interdependence between oil importing and exporting countries and the economic importance of oil to the exporting countries. The central problems discussed are the possibility of supply interruptions and the relationship between the oil companies and the producing countries.

Stocking, George W. MIDDLE EAST OIL: A STUDY IN POLITICAL AND

ECONOMIC CONTROVERSY. Nashville, Tenn.: Vanderbilt University Press, 1970. 485 p.

Tanzer, Michael. THE POLITICAL ECONOMY OF INTERNATIONAL OIL AND THE UNDERDEVELOPED COUNTRIES. Boston: Beacon Press, 1969. 435 p.

> The relationship between the oil companies and the oil exporting and importing developing countries is described from both political and economic perspectives. In a case study of India, the special problems of importing countries are described. The author ends with a program for solidarity and independence for the oil importing developing countries.

Tugendhat, Christopher. OIL, THE BIGGEST BUSINESS. New York: Putnam, 1968. 318 p.

> An account of the international oil industry which covers the United States, Venezuela, and the Middle East from 1859-1960. The book emphasizes the political relationships of these countries and the oil companies, and presents quantitative data up to the year 1966.

COMPANY STUDIES

Barnes, Robert. "International Oil Companies Confront Governments: A Half-Century of Experience." INTERNATIONAL STUDIES QUARTERLY 16 (December 1972): 454-71.

> An article analyzing the corporate reactions of two major oil firms (Standard Oil and Dutch Shell) when confronting negative national policies, such as expropriation. Covers a fifty-year period.

Donner, Fredrick G. THE WORLD-WIDE INDUSTRIAL ENTERPRISE: ITS CHALLENGE AND PROMISE. New York: McGraw-Hill, 1967. 121 p.

> Written by the chairman of the board of General Motors, the book outlines the international expansion of the company. Changes in shareholders' geographical distribution are suggested.

Haden-Guest, Anthony. DOWN THE PROGRAMMED RABBIT HOLE: TRAVELS THROUGH MUSAK, HILTON, COCA-COLA, WALT DISNEY AND OTHER WORLD EMPIRES. London: Hart-Davis, McGibbon, 1972. 310 p.

> A series of case studies of American big business at home and abroad.

May, Stacy, and Plaza, Galo. THE UNITED FRUIT COMPANY IN LATIN AMERICA. Washington, D.C.: National Planning Association, 1958. 263 p.

> A carefully researched case study of the development of the United

Fruit Company, its spectacular growth, and its contribution to local development.

Neufeld, Edward P. A GLOBAL CORPORATION: A HISTORY OF THE INTER-NATIONAL DEVELOPMENT OF MASSEY-FERGUSON LIMITED. Toronto: University of Toronto Press, 1969. 427 p.

A descriptive and analytical history of the organizational growth and international expansion of Massey Ferguson.

Rodgers, William H. THINK: A BIBLIOGRAPHY OF THE WATSONS AND IBM. New York: Stein and Day, 1969. 320 p.

A popular account of one of the largest and most successful multi-national companies.

Sampson, Anthony. THE SOVEREIGN STATE OF ITT. New York: Stein and Day, 1973. 288 p.

A popular account of the historical development and present structure of a multinational conglomerate. Discusses the firm's political activities and its corporate ideology.

Wilkins, Mira, and Hill, Frank E. AMERICAN BUSINESS ABROAD: FORD ON SIX CONTINENTS. Introduction by Allan Nevins. Detroit, Mich.: Wayne State University Press, 1964. 541 p.

A history of the international expansion of the Ford Motor Company and the successive shifts in managerial thinking.

Wilson, Charles H. UNILEVER 1945-1965: CHALLENGE AND RESPONSE IN THE POST-WAR INDUSTRIAL REVOLUTION. London: Cassell, 1968. 290 p.

The book is an updating and extension of Wilson's earlier work on the history of Unilever from the 1850s. The author traces the history as one of increasing centralization as a response to competition.

Chapter 18

BIBLIOGRAPHIES

Chin Kim. "A Lawyer's Guide to Overseas Trading and Investment: Sources in English, Annotated Bibliography." JOURNAL OF INTERNATIONAL LAW AND ECONOMICS 7 (December 1972): 115-66.

Daniels, Lorna M., comp. BUSINESS REFERENCE SOURCES: AN ANNOTATED GUIDE FOR HARVARD BUSINESS SCHOOL STUDENTS. Cambridge, Mass.: Baker Library, Harvard University, 1971. 108 p.

Lall, Sanjaya. FOREIGN PRIVATE MANUFACTURING INVESTMENT AND MULTINATIONAL CORPORATIONS: AN ANNOTATED BIBLIOGRAPHY. New York: Praeger, 1975. 196 p.

Lindfors, Grace V., ed. BIBLIOGRAPHY: CASES AND OTHER MATERIALS FOR THE TEACHING OF MULTINATIONAL BUSINESS. Boston: School of Business Administration, Harvard University, 1964. 366 p.

Mostecky, Vaclav. DOING BUSINESS ABROAD: A SELECTED AND ANNO-TATED BIBLIOGRAPHY OF BOOKS AND PAMPHLETS IN ENGLISH. Cambridge, Mass.: Library, School of Law, Harvard University, 1962. 88 p.

Organization for Economic and Cultural Development. Executive Directorate. Library. PRIVATE FOREIGN INVESTMENTS AND THEIR IMPACT IN DEVELOP-ING COUNTRIES. Special Annotated Bibliography 34. Paris: 1973. 265 p.

Stewart, Charles F., and Simmons, George B. A BIBLIOGRAPHY OF INTER-NATIONAL BUSINESS. New York: Columbia University Press, 1964. 603 p.

United Nations. Secretariat. MULTINATIONAL CORPORATIONS: A SELECT BIBLIOGRAPHY. August 27, 1973. 22 p.

Chapter 19

PERIODICALS

ATLANTIC COMMUNITY QUARTERLY. Washington, D.C.: Atlantic Council of the United States, 1963- . Quarterly.

COLUMBIA JOURNAL OF TRANSNATIONAL LAW. New York: Columbia University, School of Law, 1961- . 3/year.

COLUMBIA JOURNAL OF WORLD BUSINESS. New York: Columbia Graduate School of Business, 1965- . Quarterly.

FOREIGN AFFAIRS. New York: Council on Foreign Relations, 1922- . Quarterly.

FOREIGN POLICY. New York: National Affairs, 1970- . Quarterly.

HARVARD BUSINESS REVIEW. Boston: Graduate School of Business Administration, Harvard University, 1922- . Bimonthly.

INTERNATIONAL ORGANIZATION. Madison: University of Wisconsin Press, 1947- . Quarterly.

INTERNATIONAL STUDIES QUARTERLY. Beverly Hills, Calif.: Sage Publications, 1957- . Quarterly.

JOURNAL OF INTERNATIONAL BUSINESS STUDIES. Atlanta: Georgia State University, Institute of International Business, 1970- . Semiannual.

JOURNAL OF INTERNATIONAL LAW AND ECONOMICS. Washington, D.C.: George Washington University, National Law Center, 1966- . 3/year.

JOURNAL OF WORLD TRADE LAW. Middlesex, Eng.: Vincent Press, 1967- . Bimonthly.

Periodicals

LAW AND POLICY IN INTERNATIONAL BUSINESS. Washington, D.C.: Georgetown University Law Center, 1969– . 4/year.

MONTHLY REVIEW. New York: Monthly Review, 1949– . Monthly.

WORLD DEVELOPMENT. Oxford, Eng.: Pergamon Press, 1931– . Monthly.

WORLD POLITICS. Princeton, N.J.: Princeton University Press, 1948– . Quarterly.

Chapter 20
RECOMMENDED LIBRARY LIST

1. Barnet, Richard J., and Mueller, Ronald E. GLOBAL REACH: THE POWER OF THE MULTINATIONAL CORPORATIONS. New York: Simon and Schuster, 1974. 508 p.

2. Behrman, Jack N. U.S. INTERNATIONAL BUSINESS AND GOVERNMENTS. New York: McGraw-Hill, 1971. 244 p.

3. FOREIGN DIRECT INVESTMENT IN CANADA. Published by the government of Canada (The "Gray Report"). Ottawa: Information Canada, 1971. 573 p.

4. Dunning, John H., ed. THE MULTINATIONAL ENTERPRISE. London: George Allen and Unwin, 1971. 368 p.

5. Fann, K. T., and Hodges, Donald C., eds. READINGS IN U.S. IMPERIALISM. Boston: P. Sargent, 1971. 397 p.

6. Gunter, Hans, ed. TRANSNATIONAL INDUSTRIAL RELATIONS: THE IMPACT OF MULTINATIONAL CORPORATIONS AND ECONOMIC REGIONALISM ON INDUSTRIAL RELATIONS. New York: St. Martin's Press, 1972. 480 p.

7. Keohane, Robert O., and Nye, Joseph S., Jr. TRANSNATIONAL RELATIONS AND WORLD POLITICS. Cambridge, Mass.: Harvard University Press, 1972. 748 p.

8. Kindleberger, Charles P., ed. THE INTERNATIONAL CORPORATION: A SYMPOSIUM. Cambridge, Mass.: MIT Press, 1970. 415 p.

9. Vernon, Raymond. SOVEREIGNTY AT BAY, THE MULTINATIONAL SPREAD OF U.S. ENTERPRISES. New York: Basic Books, 1971. 326 p.

10. Wilkins, Mira. THE MATURING OF MULTINATIONAL ENTERPRISE: AMERICAN BUSINESS ABROAD FROM 1914 TO 1970. Cambridge, Mass.: Harvard University Press, 1974. 590 p.

INDEXES

Author Index

Title Index

Subject Index

AUTHOR INDEX

Included in this index are all authors, editors, compilers, contributors, and translators whose works are cited in this bibliography. This index is alphabetized letter by letter.

Author Index

Author Index

Author Index

Lambeth, Helen S. 31
Lamont, Douglas F. 80
Lancaster, William, Jr. 136
Landau, Henry 54
Landwehrmann, Friedrich 139
Lau, Stephen F. 86
Layton, Christopher 80, 81, 108, 144
Lazar, Arpad von 59
Lea, Sperry 8, 34
Lederer, William 136
Lee, Eugene H. 68
Lee, Wayne J. 145
Lees, Francis A. 92, 145
Leftwich, Robert B. 24, 92
Leleux, P. 136
Lenin, Vladimir I. 121
Leonard, A.J.W.S. 26
Levente, Mihail 76
Levinson, Charles 102
Levitt, Kari 72
Levy, Walter J. 149
Leyton-Brown, David 73
Lichtenstein, Cynthia Crawford 92
Lillich, Richard B. 136
Lindenberg, Marc 20, 24
Lindfors, Grace V. 153
Lisocki, Stanley R. 88
Litvak, Isaiah A. 34, 44, 73, 102, 121
Lloyd, Bruce 20
Loehr, William 55, 64
Lovell, Enid Baird 28, 108
Lumsden, Ian 73
Lundgren, N. 26
Lupo, Leonard A. 5, 6, 44
Luxemburg, Rosa 121

M

McBride, Robert H. 89
McCarthy, Gordon 70
McCreary, Edward A. 78
MacDougall, G.D.A. 2
Machlup, Fritz 130
McKay, John P. 2
MacKenzie, Fayette A. 3
McKie, James W. 149
McLachlan, Donald L. 78
McLaren, Richard 36

McLaughlin, Russell U. 64
McLure, Charles 38
McMillan, Claude, Jr. 109
McMillan, James 82
Magdoff, Harry xxi, 60, 115, 119 121, 131
Mahfouz, Rashwan 24
Maley, Leo C., Jr. 5
Malles, Paul 102
Malmgren, Harald B. 55, 121
Mamalakis, Markos 87
Mandel, Ernest xxi, 121
Manser, William A.P. 24, 26
Marcus, Mildred Rendl 131
Markensten, Klas 68
Markham, Jesse W. 148
Marshall, Hilary S. 73
Martyn, Howe 34, 124, 141
Mason, Edward S. 35, 57
Mason, R. Hal 35, 109
Masson, Francis G. 109
Masuda, Shigeru 95
Mauer, Laurence J. 20, 21
Maule, Christopher J. 34, 44, 73, 102, 121
May, Herbert K. 86
May, Ronald S. 55, 64
May, Stacy 151
Mazaroff, Stanley 136
Mazzolini, Renato 15
Meier, Gerald M. 55
Mellors, John 24
Merhav, Meir 109
Metzger, Stanley D. 44, 122
Michael, Walther P. 6
Michalet, Charles Albert 44
Mikdashi, Zuhayr M. 149
Mikesell, Raymond F. 35, 149
Miki, Takeo 69
Millen, Bruce H. 102
Miller, Arthur S. 44, 122, 124
Model, Leo 95
Modelski, George 122
Mohammed, D. 64
Mohr, Patricia M. 73
Montagnes, Jan 73
Moore, Jack 35
Moore, John R. 89, 145
Moore, Russell M. 146
Moran, Theodore H. 86, 95, 122, 146

Author Index

Prebisch, Raul 141
Preston, Richard A. 69
Priel, Victor Z. 20
Proehl, Paul O. 65
Pugh, Richard C. 135
Pugwash Conferences on Science and
  World Affairs 110
Purtshert, Robert 80

Q

Quinn, John B. 110

R

Ragazzi, Giorgio 20
Rahl, James A. 133
Raichur, Satish 64
Reddaway, William B. 45
Rehbinder, Eckard 137
Reilly, John E. 53
Remmers, H. Lee 11
Reno, Philip 60
Renouf, Alan 67
Resnick, S. 59
Reuber, Grant L. xxv, 56, 74
Reynolds, Clark W. 87
Rhodes, Robert I. 58, 60
Rhomberg, Rudolf R. 51
Rich, Robert S. 79
Richman, Barry M. 110
Ricks, David A. 25, 90
Rielly, John E. 83
Roach, John M. 6, 13
Robbins, Sidney M. 25
Roberts, B.C. 100, 103
Robertson, David 8
Robinson, Richard D. 9, 10, 20
Robinson, Stuart W., Jr. 146
Robock, Stephan H. xv, 11
Rodgers, William H. 152
Rodley, Nigel S. 137
Rogers, William D. 87, 95
Roig, Barto 13
Rolfe, Sidney E. 11, 26, 36, 131
Roll, Sir Eric 131
Rollins, Cynthia 137
Rollins, H. Moak 89
Rometsch, S. 26
Roseman, Frank 74

Rosenbluth, Gideon 74
Rosenstein-Rodan, Paul 51, 86
Ross, D. Reid 92
Rouf-Koch, Helga 141
Rouhani, Fuad 150
Rowan, Richard L. 102
Rowland, Benjamin M. xxii, 116
Rowthorn, Robert 6, 9
Rubin, Seymour J. xxiv, 10, 45,
  131, 137, 141
Russell, Peter 72
Rutenberg, David P. 15

S

Sachdev, J.C. 21
Sadli, Mohammad 66
Safarian, A.E. 66, 74
Said, Abdul A. xviii, xxiv, 124
Sainz, Jose Campillo 89
Sampson, Anthony 152
Sanden, Peter 46
Scaperlanda, Anthony E. 21, 25
Schatzl, Ludwig H. 150
Scheer, Robert 37
Scheffer, C.F. 26
Schill, Charles F. 89
Schoellhammer, Hans 11
Scholl, Russell B. 46
Schonfield, Andrew 107
Schreiber, Jordan C. 67
Schurr, Sam H. 150
Schwartz, Warren F. 135
Schwarzenberger, Georg 36, 122,
  139
Schydlowsky, D.M. 25
See, Harold F. 124
Seers, Dudley 51
Seham, Martin S. 103
Seng, You Poh 66
Sercovitch, F. 106
Servan-Schreiber, Jean Jacques 30,
  37, 131
Sethi, S. Prakash 11, 21
Severn, Alan K. 131
Shapiro, Eli 9
Shearer, John C. 103
Sherk, Donald R. 95
Sheth, Jagdish N. 11
Shoup, Carl 38

Author Index

TITLE INDEX

This index is alphabetized letter by letter and in some cases titles have been shortened. Titles of books and congressional hearings and reports cited in the text have been indexed. Journals, titles of articles, and chapter titles are not included.

Title Index

Title Index

Title Index

177

N

O

Title Index

Title Index

SUBJECT INDEX

This index is alphabetized letter by letter and numbers refer to page numbers. Underlined numbers refer to major entries on a topic.

Subject Index

Arab countries 91
Argentina 34, 84, 93
Asia 4, 53, 65-67, 94, 95
Australia 17, 30, 34, 43, 66,
   69-70, 71, 73-74
Belgium 81, 82
Brazil 58, 83, 84, 85, 86, 93
Canada 3, 17, 18, 30, 34,
   36-37, 41, 49, 53, 70-75,
   157
Caribbean area 41, 84
Ethiopia 64
Europe 1, 3, 17, 30, 36, 37,
   53, 79-82, 91, 94-95, 120,
   146
Europe, Eastern 75-76
European Economic Community
   countries 21, 77-78
France 1, 44, 79, 81
Germany 17, 75, 79
Ghana 63
Great Britain 1, 3, 8, 15, 18,
   21, 24, 32, 38, 45, 64,
   82-83
Guatemala 84, 85
Hungary 75
India 15, 34, 53, 57, 67-68
Indonesia 60, 66
Iran 57
Ireland 78, 81
Italy 79, 80-81
Jamaica 57, 85
Japan 4, 17, 34, 36-37, 41,
   43, 44, 45, 46, 66, 68-69,
   73-74, 91, 94, 95, 120,
   130
Kenya 57, 97
Korea 66
Latin America 4, 14, 43, 49,
   53, 54, 55, 59, 60-61,
   83-88, 94, 95, 145-46,149,
   151-52
Liberia 64, 65
Malawi 63
Malaysia 20, 57
Mexico 66, 89-90, 93
Morocco 20
Netherlands 81
New Zealand 70
Nigeria 63, 64, 65, 150

Norway 34, 81
Pakistan 15
Peru 58, 84, 85, 86-87
Philippine Islands 66, 84
Romania 75, 76
Russia 1, 2, 76
Scotland 82
Sierra Leone 64
Singapore 66
South Africa 34, 64, 65, 149
Southeast Asia 66, 67
Spain 34
Sweden 46, 73-74
Taiwan 67
Tanzania 65
Thailand 66
Tunisia 20, 34
underdeveloped countries 8, 10,
   14, 17, 20, 21, 31, 32, 49,
   51-61, 120, 122, 125, 128,
   147, 150
U.S. 1, 2, 3, 4, 5-6, 8, 9,
   17, 18, 21, 24, 30, 35, 36,
   37, 41, 42, 43, 44, 45, 46,
   47, 48, 49, 52, 53, 54, 57,
   58, 60, 64, 65, 66, 69, 70,
   71, 72, 73, 75, 77, 78, 79,
   80, 81, 82, 83-84, 85, 86,
   87, 88, 89, 90-92, 93, 94,
   95, 97, 122, 129, 130-31,
   146, 149
Venezuela 84
western countries 47
Yugoslavia 34, 75, 76
Zambia 63, 65, 98
cost of 57
direct 17-22, 30, 32, 34, 36,
   38-39, 42, 43, 44, 45, 48,
   49, 51-52, 54, 55, 56, 57,
   58, 60, 63, 64, 66, 70, 71,
   72, 74, 75, 76, 79, 81, 83,
   89, 90, 91, 92, 107-8, 110,
   120, 124-25, 128, 129, 130,
   131, 135, 136, 137, 138,
   140, 157
efficiency of 130
future of 130
historical evolution of 1-4
negotiation in 67
philosophy of 51

Subject Index

M

MNC. See Multinational corporations
Macroeconomics 24, 84, 110, 130
Malawi, foreign investment in 63
Malaysia, foreign investment in 20, 57
Management, international 18, 20, 24,
   corporate organization and 13
   research in 11
   sale of skills in 9
   transfer of skill in 43, 65, 78, 107-8, 110-11
   See also Executives, international; Public relations, international
Manufacturing 38-39
   development of multinational structures in 2
   foreign investment in 42
      in Australia 69-70
      in Brazil 85
      in France 2
      by Great Britain 3, 21
      in Great Britain 82
      in India 67
      by Japan 4
      by the U.S. 85, 130-31
      in the U.S. 90
   See also Industry; Multinational corporations; Production, international
Marketing, international 8, 18, 19, 24
   in the copper and aluminum industries 143
   investments in French 2
   public relations function in 28
   See also Distribution of goods; Prices and price policy; Sales, international
Market size
   capital availability and 29
   direct foreign investment and 17, 21, 91
Marxist economic theories 41, 51, 52, 119, 121, 122, 123, 129, 131
Massey Ferguson Ltd. 152

Mergers and consolidations 15, 35, 74, 81, 128, 136, 137.
   See also Divestitures of foreign subsidiaries
Metal industries and trade, foreign investment in 129
Mexico, foreign investment in 66, 89-90
   by the U.S. 93
Microeconomics 110
Military policy
   linkages to multinational corporations 122, 123
   relationship to aid and investment policies 33
   See also Foreign policy
Milk processing 84
Mineral industries, foreign investment in 90, 149
Monetary policy
   in international economics 128, 130
   U.S. 49
Money, international flow of 56.
   See also Capital; Deutschmark; Foreign exchange rates; Inflation
Monopoly 10, 32, 41, 95, 109, 131, 133. See also Cartels, Oligopoly; Sherman Anti-trust Act; Trusts and anti-trust law
Morocco, foreign investment in 20
Motel industry. See Hotel industry, international
Motion picture industry. See Film industry, international
Motivation 10, 27
Multinational corporations xi-xxv
   bibliographies concerning 153
      of periodicals 155-56
      recommended reading 157-58
   concentration of production in 7
   decision-making in 13, 15, 20-21, 23, 37, 101, 127
   definition of 7, 10, 83
   directories of American 5
   distribution and growth of 5-12
   economic growth and development and 51-61, 64, 65, 66, 67,

Subject Index

Socialist countries
  imperialism and 121
  investments of 138
Society and industry. See Industry
  and society
Society for International Develop-
    ment 51
South Africa, foreign investment in
    34
  by the U.S. 64, 65, 149
South America
  nationalization of industry in 85-
    86
  petroleum industry in 4
  See also Latin America
Southeast Asia, foreign investments
    in 66, 67
Sovereignty 120, 137, 157. See
  also Act of state doctrine
Soviet bloc nations. See Europe,
  Eastern
Spain, foreign investment in 34
Standard of living and foreign invest-
    ment 72
Standard Oil Co. 85-86, 151
Steel industry and trade, investment
    in Brazil's 83. See also
    Iron industry and trade
Stockpiling 143
Strikes and lockouts 99, 101. See
    also Collective bargaining,
    international; Industrial re-
    lations, international; Trade
    unions
Sugar Corporation of Malawi 63
Sugar industry and trade, foreign in-
    vestment in 64
Supermarkets 84. See also Retail
    trade, international
Sweden
  economic laws of 135
  foreign investment by 46
  foreign investment in 73-74

T

Taiwan
  American investment in 67
  technology transfer in 105-6
Tanzania, foreign investment in 65

Tariff. See Trade regulation
Taxation, international 23, 24, 25,
    31, 34, 35, 38, 44, 45, 46,
    48, 51, 59, 68, 73, 79-80,
    91-92, 94, 131
  law of 137-38, 139, 140
Technology 1-2, 17, 21, 37, 45, 69,
    105-13, 121, 125, 131, 144
  contractual agreements concerning
    112
  costs of 109, 111, 112
  dependence upon 30
  development of indigenous 95
  firm size and 105
  legal aspects 135-36
  sale of 9
  in the steel industry 83
  transfer of 8, 11, 35, 36, 39,
    43, 45, 47, 48, 49, 56,
    65, 67, 79, 87, 95, 105,
    106, 107, 108, 109, 110,
    111, 112, 113, 129, 144
  See also Industrial research
Television, impact of 147
Textile industry and trade, foreign
    investment in 53, 64
Thailand, foreign investment in 66
Third world. See Underdeveloped
    countries
Tin mines and mining, foreign invest-
    ment in Chilean 85-86
Tourism, international 45, 143, 144,
    146, 147
Trademarks in international economics
    35, 88. See also Patents in
    international economics
Trade regulation 32, 34, 35, 69,
    135, 140. See also Com-
    merce; Customs unions; Eco-
    nomic policy, national; Free
    trade and protection; Gen-
    eral Agreement on Tariff and
    Trade
Trade unions 94, 100, 101, 102,
    103, 104
  in Canada 99
  in Chile 86
  internationalization of 98-99, 103
  political role of 98, 102
  in Zambia 63, 98

Subject Index

See also Collective bargaining,
  international; Industrial relations, international; Labor
  in the international market;
  Strikes and lockouts
Transfer pricing 10, 24, 33, 125
Travel. See Tourism
Treaty of Rome 77
Trusts and anti-trust law 3, 14, 30,
  31, 34, 36, 78, 133, 134,
  135, 137, 140. See also
  Cartels; Monopoly; Oligopoly; Restraint of trade; Sherman Anti-trust Act
Tunisia, foreign investment in 20, 34

U

UNCTAD III 130
Underdeveloped countries
  domination by industrialized states
  117
  economic laws and 136-37, 139
  foreign investment in 8, 10, 14,
    20, 31, 49, 51-61, 120,
    122, 125, 128, 147,
    150
    by Great Britain 32
    by the U.S. 17, 21, 54, 57
  role of trade unions in 102
  technology transfer and 105-6,
    107, 109, 110, 111, 112
Unemployment. See Employment and
  foreign investment; Job ex-
  portation
Unilever Ltd. 152
Union of Soviet Socialist Republics.
  See Russia
United Fruit Co. 85, 151-52
United Kingdom. See Great Britain;
  Ireland; Scotland
United Nations 122
United Nations Regulation for Reso-
  lution of International Busi-
  ness disputes 138
United States
  competition with the EEC 121
  corporate mergers in the 35
  economic laws and 133, 134,
    135, 136, 137

economic policy of the 131, 149
economy of the 60
exports from 43
foreign investment by the 1, 3,
  4, 5-6, 9, 17, 18, 24, 30,
  35, 41, 42, 44, 45, 46, 47,
  48, 49, 53, 93, 97, 122,
  130-31
  in Africa 64
  in Andean Pact countries 88-
    89, 94
  in Argentina 88, 93
  in Asia 4, 66, 94, 95
  in Australia 17, 69, 71
  in Brazil 85, 88, 93
  in Canada 49, 70, 71, 72, 73,
    75
  in Chile 58-59, 85, 86
  in Colombia 93
  in Europe 3, 17, 30, 36, 37,
    79, 80, 81, 94-95, 146
  in European Economic Commu-
    nity countries 21, 77, 78
  in France 2, 79, 80
  in Germany 17, 79
  in Great Britain 1-2, 3, 8, 82
  in India 5, 34, 53, 57, 67-68
  in Italy 79
  in Japan 17, 94
  in Latin America 4, 43, 49,
    52, 53, 83-84, 85, 86, 87,
    88, 95
  in Liberia 65
  in Mexico 89
  in the Netherlands 81
  in Peru 52-53, 58, 85-86,
    86-87
  in Russia 2
  in Scotland 82
  in South Africa 64, 65, 149
  in underdeveloped countries 17,
    21, 54, 57, 60
  in Yugoslavia 75
foreign investments in the 36, 37,
  90-92, 129
role in international economic relations 128, 129, 130
technology transfer and 105, 106,
  107, 108, 109
transnational politics and 4, 43,